BREAKFAST

AltaMira Studies in Food and Gastronomy

General Editor: Ken Albala, Professor of History, University of the Pacific (kalbala@pacific.edu)
AltaMira Executive Editor: Wendi Schnaufer (wschnaufer@rowman.com)

Food Studies is a vibrant and thriving field encompassing not only cooking and eating habits but issues such as health, sustainability, food safety, and animal rights. Scholars in disciplines as diverse as history, anthropology, sociology, literature, and the arts focus on food. The mission of **AltaMira Studies in Food and Gastronomy** is to publish the best in food scholarship, harnessing the energy, ideas, and creativity of a wide array of food writers today. This broad line of food-related titles will range from food history, interdisciplinary food studies monographs, general interest series, and popular trade titles to textbooks for students and budding chefs, scholarly cookbooks, and reference works.

Appetites and Aspirations in Vietnam: Food and Drink in the Long Nineteenth Century, by Erica J. Peters

Three World Cuisines: Italian, Mexican, Chinese, by Ken Albala

Food and Social Media: You Are What You Tweet, by Signe Rousseau

Food and the Novel in Nineteenth-Century America, by Mark McWilliams

Man Bites Dog: Hot Dog Culture in America, by Bruce Kraig and Patty Carroll

New Orleans: A Food Biography, by Elizabeth M. Williams (Big City Food Biographies series)

A Year in Food and Beer: Recipes and Beer Pairings for Every Season, by Emily Baime and Darin Michaels

Breakfast: A History, by Heather Arndt Anderson (The Meals series)

BREAKFAST

A HISTORY

Heather Arndt Anderson

ALTAMIRA
PRESS

A division of
ROWMAN & LITTLEFIELD PUBLISHERS, INC.
Lanham • New York • Toronto • Plymouth, UK

Published by AltaMira Press
A division of Rowman & Littlefield Publishers, Inc.
A wholly owned subsidiary of The Rowman & Littlefield Publishing Group, Inc.
4501 Forbes Boulevard, Suite 200, Lanham, Maryland 20706
www.rowman.com

10 Thornbury Road, Plymouth PL6 7PP, United Kingdom

British Library Cataloguing in Publication Information Available

Library of Congress Cataloging-in-Publication Data

Arndt Anderson, Heather, 1976-
  Breakfast : a history / Heather Arndt Anderson.
     pages cm. — (AltaMira studies in food and gastronomy (The meals series))
  Includes bibliographical references and index.
  ISBN 978-0-7591-2163-8 (cloth : alk. paper) — ISBN 978-0-7591-2165-2 (ebook)
1. Breakfasts—History. 2. Food habits—History. I. Title.
  GT2850.A755 2013
  394.1'252—dc23
                                                                    2013008495

♾™ The paper used in this publication meets the minimum requirements of
American National Standard for Information Sciences—Permanence of Paper
for Printed Library Materials, ANSI/NISO Z39.48-1992.

Printed in the United States of America

CONTENTS

SERIES FOREWORD

Custom becomes second nature, and this is especially true of meals. We expect to eat them at a certain time and place, and we have a set of scripted foods considered appropriate for each. Bacon, eggs, and toast are breakfast; sandwiches are lunch; meat, potatoes, and vegetables are dinner, followed by dessert. Breakfast for dinner is so much fun precisely because it is out of the ordinary and transgressive. But meal patterns were not always this way. In the Middle Ages people ate two meals, the larger in the morning. Today the idea of a heavy meal with meat and wine at 11:00 a.m. strikes us as strange and decidedly unpleasant. Likewise when abroad, the food that people eat, at what seems to us the wrong time of day, can be shocking. Again, our customs have become so ingrained that we assume they are natural, correct, and biologically sound.

The Meals series will demonstrate exactly the opposite. Not only have meal times changed, but the menu as well, both through history and around the globe. Only a simple bowl of soup with a crust of bread for supper? That is where the name comes from. Our dinner, coming from *disner* in Old French, *disjejunare* in Latin, actually means to break fast and was eaten in the morning. Each meal also has its own unique characteristics that evolve over time. We will see the invention of the picnic and barbecue, the gradual adoption of lunch as a new midday meal, and even certain meals practiced as hallowed institutions in some places but scarcely at all elsewhere, such as tea—the meal, not the drink. Often food items suddenly appear in a meal as quintessential, such as cold breakfast cereal, the invention of men like Kellogg and Post. Or they disappear, like oysters for breakfast. Sometimes an entire meal springs from nowhere under unique social conditions, like brunch.

Of course, the decay of the family meal is a topic that deeply concerns us, as people catch a quick bite at their desk or on the go, or eat with their eyes glued to the television set. If eating is one of the greatest pleasures in life, one has to wonder what it says about us when we wolf down a meal in a few minutes flat or when no one talks at the dinner table. Still, mealtime traditions persist for special occasions. They are the time we remind ourselves of who we are and where we come from, when grandma's special lasagna comes to the table for a Sunday dinner, or a Passover Seder is set exactly the same way it has been for thousands of years. We treasure these food rituals precisely because they keep us rooted in a rapidly changing world.

The Meals series examines the meal as both a historical construct and a global phenomenon. A single meal in each volume is anatomized, its social and cultural meaning brought into sharp focus, and the customs and manners of various people are explained in context. Each volume also looks closely at the foods we commonly include and why. In the end I hope you will never take your mealtime customs for granted again.

Ken Albala
University of the Pacific

ACKNOWLEDGMENTS

To my dear husband Scott and little son Zephyr, thank you for giving me an opportunity to put my boring environmental consulting career on the back burner so that I would have time for this.

To my editors Ken Albala and Wendi Schnaufer, I appreciate all of your sensible feedback and cheerleading, and I have learned so much through this process.

Thank you to my writing group, who tirelessly workshopped every page: Dana Cuellar, Art Edwards, Sarah Gilbert, Laurel Hermanson, David Lindenbaum, Rebecca Kelley, Mark Russell, and Michael Zeiss. I could not have done this without your invaluable, diverse input, and I am a better writer because of you.

Big thanks to the Multnomah County Library, for allowing me to flood your online interlibrary loan system with requests for obscure 19th-century housekeepers' guides and war-era magazine articles, I owe you my gratitude. You are worth every tax dollar.

Speaking of tax dollars, thank you, U.S. School Breakfast Program, for ensuring I had a (free) hot morning meal every school day.

INTRODUCTION

Whether a bowlful of cloying, artificially fruit-flavored O's with milk, or a stinking pile of fermented soybeans on steamed rice, breakfast fuels hungry brains. As the old adage says, breakfast is the most important meal of the day. It is the meal that makes the champion. Breakfast literally "breaks the fast" of nighttime slumber, filling one's raging belly and providing the stamina to face the day. From the development of agriculture and the use of stone grinding tools in the Neolithic to the hardboiled eggs and Malt-O-Meal in today's kitchens, much of what is eaten for breakfast has changed curiously little. Human attitudes toward breakfast have, however, changed plenty.

One of the major influences on the morning meal was, unsurprisingly, religion. After Ancient Roman and Classical Hellenic written accounts of breakfast as a matter-of-fact beginning to one's day, overzealous moralists of the Middle Ages and Early Modern periods of Europe stigmatized the morning meal, hitching it to the Seven Deadly Sins. This association of breakfast to gluttony likely picked up steam with the influential 13th-century Dominican priest Thomas Aquinas. In his *Summa Theologica* (1265–1274), he outlines six delightful methods for committing gluttony, one of which may be attributed to breakfast: *praepropere*—eating too soon. While allowances were granted to children, the elderly, the infirm, and to laborers, regular people either did not eat breakfast or did not talk about it. Meanwhile, the times of the other two meals—dinner and supper—were being shuffled around and pushed later.

Toward the middle of the 15th century, breakfast had begun to reclaim its rightful place in the morning, with the help of advocates like Francis I of France declaring it proper "to rise at 5, dine at 9, sup at 5, and couch at 9."[1] As the meals followed suit, eating breakfast came back into fashion. There were still grouchy detractors and general busybodies, who insisted that eating in the morning was unhealthy, but by the late 16th century, Queen Elizabeth, an early riser, included a hearty breakfast of ale and oat cakes as part of Her Royal Morning Regimen. Associating breakfast with the routines of wholesome and pragmatic morning people helped to move the meal back into the public favor.

In the 17th century, the Golden Age of Dutch painting coincided with—perhaps was inspired by—the golden age of breakfast. The morning meal inspired an entire subgenre of art—the Dutch still lifes known as "breakfast paintings"—during the same period when Dutch art was among the most acclaimed in the world. The 17th century was a fantastic era of discovery for much of European culture, leading us to the next important factor in breakfast's stellar ascent: trade.

Tea, coffee, and chocolate all arrived to Europe from their respective, exotic locales, and astonishingly, each beverage came at nearly the same time. Europe was delirious with joy. Chocolate had caused such an ecstatic uproar among Europe's social elite that the Catholic Church began to feel the pressure to change the rules; in 1662, Cardinal Francis Maria Brancaccio declared that "*Liquidum non frangit jejunum*," meaning "liquid does not break the fast."[2] Chocolate lovers and other members of newly caffeine-addicted society rejoiced.

The 18th-century English and the colonists in the infant America were breakfasting on ponderous amounts of food. It was not unusual to see recommended for breakfast—by *doctors*, no less—oatmeal porridge to start, then some fish, next a poached or lightly boiled egg with a little broiled ham or bacon, a slice of buttered bread (or dry toast, if one is watching one's figure), a dollop or two of marmalade or a nice fruit compote, all washed down with tea, coffee, or cocoa. This was intended for the average businessman who was too busy for a substantial lunch.

The third, and perhaps greatest, influence on breakfast was technology. The Industrial Revolution between 1750 and 1850 (and subsequent triumph of the middle class) had a wide-sweeping effect on breakfast. In the United States, train transport suddenly meant that smoked salmon from Oregon and citrus fruits from Florida could be on the breakfast table in New York. Electricity in American and English homes meant that many morning tasks were expedited. New wealth meant that luxurious breakfast foods like sage-infused pork sausages, pancakes with butter and honey, and coffee with cream and sugar were a common sight, along with the abundant servants champing at the bit to prepare them. New homes were built with an entire room devoted to morning dining, allowing the breakfast parlor to become one more way to showcase one's recently gained riches.

By the end of the 19th century, breakfast cereal had been invented and the fourth major factor affecting breakfast—convenience—manifested itself. Household electricity became fairly widespread, allowing breakfast to be prepared in a fraction of the time, and with fastidious consistency. Time is of the matutinal essence, and although it was the health fanaticism of the Clean Living movement that spawned the development of breakfast cereals, it was their convenience that had the most obvious impact on their widespread adoption. Housewives (those who could not afford household staff) were completely enamored of a food they could simply pour into a bowl. The rationing of meat and eggs during World Wars I and II further cemented cereal's placement as the center of a complete breakfast.

Breakfast is the first meal of the day and, sometimes, the last meal of one's life. During World War II, a soldier heading into a particularly dangerous combat zone was served a "battle breakfast" of steak and eggs. Twenty years later, the same breakfast was served to astronauts heading off to launch; though the heavy meal was designed to stay digestion until the astronaut could accommodate his bowels in a more convenient location, bacon-wrapped filet mignon and fried eggs were a fitting meal for a man who may not be returning. A death row inmate is offered steak and eggs as his last meal if no other request is specified, but some, like notorious English serial killer Charles Peace, choose breakfast as a last meal entirely of their own volition.

After World War II, breakfast cereals became nearly singularly marketed toward children, and the sugar content skyrocketed. Pop Tarts, Tang, and chocolate-flavored Carnation Instant Breakfast were invented. Conversely, crunchy health foods were coming back into vogue with the rise of back-to-land hippies; granola came out of the Clean Living movement's 19th-century shadow and into the warm, California sunshine, and soy- and turkey-based bacons were invented for those watching their cholesterol. Regardless, bacon and eggs are here to stay.

HISTORY AND
SOCIAL CONTEXT

Throughout history, most people partook of a simple breakfast. This was as much to stimulate the stomach for the rest of the day's meals as it was to provide nourishment to begin the day's labor. Even today, most of the world begins the day with naught more than a warm liquid (tea, coffee, soup) and a grain (porridge, toast, cereal). Throughout history, though, breakfast was not always so simple.

ETYMOLOGY

Before its elevation in status to the meal of utmost necessity, the term "breakfast" was rife with befuddlement and confusion. Until relatively recently, lunch was the first meal of the day, but it was called dinner. The English word "breakfast," derived from the French *disdéjeuner* (via late-Latin *disieiunare*; translating to "un-fast," or break the fast) was contracted in Romance languages to *disnare* or Old French *disner* in the 11th century, and eventually found its way to the English word dinner.[1] This shift in word use apparently came with the 13th-century shift of the main meal of the day (dinner) from midday to evening—dinner's present-day timeslot. This is not to be confused with 13th-century "supper," defined as "the last meal of the day."

The modern French word *déjeuner* means lunch, and other early words for breakfast, including the Spanish *almuerzo* (from the Latin *admordere*, meaning "to bite"), eventually shifted in meaning toward lunch as well. The present-day French phrase for breakfast, *petit déjeuner*, relegates the meal to a "small lunch." To confuse matters further, the modern Italian word for breakfast, *colazione*, is derived from the Latin word that initially meant "a light supper": *collationem* (now means "to bring together"; collation). *Colazione* may be further distinguished between *prima colazione* ("first breakfast") and *seconda colazione* ("second breakfast," or lunch). However, lunch is more commonly referred to as *pranzo*, which can mean either lunch or dinner.

It was not until the 15th century that "breakfast" came into use in written English to describe a morning meal, but it is unclear why it took so long to catch on. Either people did not eat it—and the startling dearth of written records would suggest this—or breakfast was obscured by the written accounts of the midday meals and evening feasts that were deemed more important—by those keeping the records, at least.

PREHISTORY

"It would be hard to overestimate grains . . . in the life of our species," wrote preeminent food scientist Harold McGee in his 1984 tome *On Food and Cooking*.[2] People have been eating foods typically associated with breakfast since the Paleolithic period, when humans first began to use stone querns to grind grains.[3] Twelve thousand years ago, rice (*Oryza sativa*) was domesticated in the Yangtze River Valley of China; across Asia today, cereals still make up roughly 70–80 percent of total caloric intake.[4] A rice porridge called *congee* has been eaten in China for thousands of years, though the original version of congee was likely made from broomcorn millet (*Panicum miliaceum*), one of the Chinese Five Cereals.[5] Mentions of millet congee are recorded by China's mythic Yellow Emperor, Qin Shi Huangdi, during his reign in the 2700s BCE.

Starting in the Fertile Crescent around 10,000 years ago, the domestication of the eight so-called founder crops, of which three are cereals—emmer wheat (*Triticum dicoccum*), einkorn wheat (*Triticum boeoticum*), and barley (*Hordeum vulgare*)—revolutionized humankind by introducing us to the sedentary lifestyle that allowed the luxury of leisure time.[6] (Four of the other founder crops, though not cereals, are legumes that eventually found their way into breakfast porridges.) Rather than following food around (it would also be hard to overestimate meat in the life of the human species), early humans suddenly had time for sophisticated tool development and social organization. Much of what defines humanity—the capacity for complex language, intellectual reasoning, and artistic expression—may not have developed so fully had we remained nomadic hunter-gatherers. The domestication of grain was the major driving force in human cultural evolution.

The domestication of grain also culminated in the intricacies of the modern market system. Maize was a primary component of the socioeconomic development of pre-Hispanic Mesoamerica.[7] Although the earliest maize fossils date back to around 5000 BCE, pollen and starch analysis indicates that maize domestication may have taken place even earlier—as early as 5800 BCE. The domestication of maize has been cited as a factor in the development of sophisticated Mesoamerican societies. Accordingly, maize has been central to Aztec, Tolmec, and Maya mythologies.

By 3000 BCE, alphabet systems and the use of arithmetic were invented as a means of logging grain transactions. Another important consequence of the domestication of cereals was the development of controlled fermentation. The fermentation of barley into beer dates back in Neolithic Europe to as early as 3000 BCE, although the history of beer dates as far as 6000 BCE in the Middle East.[8] The earliest records of Mesopotamian writing in 4000 BCE contain references to beer.[9] As water was typically of dubious quality, beer would go on to become the preferred breakfast beverage during the Middle Ages.

Rye (*Secale cereale*) and oats (*Avena Sativa*) were cultivated in Europe starting in the early Neolithic in Anatolia before spreading to the rest of Europe in the Iron and Bronze Ages, and brown rye breads still dominate the northern and

Timucua Indians planting maize, 1591. Courtesy of the Library of Congress.

eastern European baking landscape.[10] Oat porridge has been found in northern Europe in the stomach contents of 5000-year-old Neolithic bog bodies—perfectly preserved to tanned leather by the low pH of the sphagnum.[11] Since it is widely speculated that bog bodies were victims of either human sacrifice or execution as punishment for crime, it may be presumed that these hapless victims were of lower socioeconomic status, and for whom humble porridges were a daily staple.

CLASSICAL ANTIQUITY

Ample written record supports the notion that Ancient Romans had a three-meals-a-day (plus an afternoon snack) routine similar to that of today's United States and Europe, though the times for these meals shifted around plenty, depending on who was doing the telling. The Roman breakfast known as *jentaculum* (or *ientaculum*) was always consumed in the morning, however, and usually comprised everyday staples like bread, cheese, olives, salad, nuts, dried grapes, and cold meat left over from the night before.[12]

Depending on their resources, Romans may have included milk, eggs, and *mulsum* with their morning meal. *Mulsum* was a mixture of wine and honey; to add aromatic spices including cassia (*Cassia fistulosa*; a cinnamon relative), myrrh (*Myrrhis odorata*), nard (*Nardostachys jadamansi*; a ginseng relative), costum (*Chrysanthemum balsamita*), saffron (*Crocus sativus*), or pepper (*Piper nigrum*) turned *mulsum* to *Conditum Paradoxum*, which was often served at celebrations, but sometimes enjoyed with breakfast.[13] If the wine was flavored, *jentaculum* was sometimes called *silatum* after the word *selis* (the old Latin name of *Seseli* spp.), an umbelliferous herb also known as moon carrot, which was used to enhance the breakfast wine.[14] According to 1st-century Latin poet Martial, *jentaculum* may also have included pastry or other freshly baked goods (rather than simply leftovers) provided by bakers at daybreak, as in the passage, "*Surgite: jam vendit peuris jentacula pistor . . . sonant undique lucis aves*" ("Get up; the baker is already selling the boys breakfast, as the birdsong and light surround us").[15]

Farro was also commonly eaten in a porridge dish called *pulmentum* (meaning "pottage"), particularly by the lower classes and slaves. In actuality, *pulmentum* is named for the porridge (*puls*) that is, not unlike African *fufu*, merely the vehicle for delivering the real dish—salted meats and/or fish, olives, oil, and vinegar—to the mouth. What exactly defines farro is somewhat nebulous; Pliny the Elder identified millet as the primary grain of *puls*,[16] but the founder crops emmer wheat and einkorn wheat as well as the ancient grain spelt are all called *farro* in Italy today (from Pliny's *farrago*; fodder for cattle, and from which "forage" is apparently derived). There is no evidence that it was strictly breakfast fare; on the contrary, it appears that may have been altogether distinct from breakfast. Plautus mentions *puls* as a food for young children too young for *jentaculum,* perhaps before they were able to feed themselves or have at least grown enough teeth for chewing regular food.[17]

Martial mentioned that *jentaculum* was eaten at 3:00 or 4:00 in the morning, and 16th-century scholar Claudius Saumaise contradicted that it was typically eaten at 9:00 or 10:00 a.m., but it seems unlikely that any fixed time was truly assigned for this meal.[18] More than any hard, written rules, it was likelier the relocation of the other two, larger meals to later in the day that had the largest effect on breakfast's morning timeslot. The two meals were *prandium*—equal to today's *pranzo,* which was lunch, taken at around 11:00 a.m. or noon—and *caesna,* or *cena* (or somewhat less accurately *coena*),[19] which was supper, taken at around 3:00 or 4:00 p.m. An afternoon snack, *merenda,* eaten between lunch (actually dinner) and supper, was later added once supper was moved from mid-afternoon to later in the evening. This shuffling of mealtimes was a trend that would continue for centuries.

In Roman playwright Plautus's comedy *Curculio* (3rd century BCE), the character Phædromus gathers wine and provisions including olives and capers for a pre-dawn "early breakfast" for Planesium, with whom he is desperately in love. The reason Phædromus is providing for his mistress such an odd choice of entertainment is probably that Planesium's pimp, the Procurer, was not likely to interfere, as he was staying the night in the Temple of Æsculapius. Serving an early breakfast to his love, it seemed, would provide Phædromus with an opportunity for a clandestine sojourn.

In Greek literature fifty years earlier, Homer makes numerous mentions of *ariston,* a meal taken not long after sunrise. Breakfast preparation seems to have been a necessary, if not comforting, part of the morning ritual for most people at the time. *The Iliad* notes this meal with regard to a labor-weary woodsman, eager for this light repast to start his day, preparing it even as he is aching with exhaustion. Here, the hunger for breakfast (and willingness to spend energy preparing it, despite utter weariness) is used as a metaphor for the steely determination needed to overpower one's foes.

The opening prose of the 16th book of *The Odyssey* (*The Discovery of Odysseus*) mentions breakfast as the meal being prepared "[in dawn's] thin light, paying little heed to the barnyard din," suggesting it was customary to eat in the morning before attending to one's chores.[20] In this scene, swineherd Eumaeus is busily mixing water and wine in a bowl, which he accidentally drops in joyful amazement as his young master Telemachus arrives home safely after a long absence. After fetching Telemachus a suitable chair for the breakfast table, Eumaeus lays out a platter of cold meat left over from the previous night's supper; this would likely have been all the breakfast a normal day would require, but in celebration of his master's return, the breakfast wine is instead mixed with honey (in similar fashion to the Roman *mulsum*, no doubt), and baskets heaped with freshly baked bread are additionally presented.

Eventually, *ariston* was moved to around noon, and a new morning meal was introduced. In the post-Homeric classical period of Greece, a meal called *akratisma* was typically consumed immediately after rising in the morning, replacing the now-lunchtime meal *ariston*.[21] This quick nibble consisted of little more than bread dipped in undiluted wine, or *akratis*, for which the meal was named, different from the watered-down wine of Homer's time. Again, this was merely a morning morsel to boost energy levels for the day's chores.

MEDIEVAL AND EARLY MODERN EUROPE

Written records of most social and cultural exploits dropped off precipitously in the centuries between the fall of the Roman Empire and the early Middle Ages (Late Antiquity; between the second and eighth centuries), earning this time period the dubious moniker the Dark Ages. Of the records that do exist, many written accounts seem to go to great lengths to admonish eating in the morning.

During medieval times, the monarchy and their entourage could squander entire days around a table, sometimes to the exclusion of all other business. When one considers the gross amount of time that the social elite spent languishing over meals, it begins to make some sense that the morning meal may be the first to be eliminated.

As with most basic human pleasures, gluttony and other indulgences of the flesh were frowned upon during the Middle Ages and fasting was *de rigeur*. Proper medieval moralists did not need any more sustenance than was provided in the day's two meals—a light, midday dinner and a more substantial supper for the evening meal; hence, breakfast was considered crass and boorish by the Catholic Church.[22] The indulgent reresoper ("rear supper") of the late evening, a snack associated with copious amounts of wine, was similarly shunned by most decent folk; it seems plausible that at least some of the impetus for breakfast's censure was due to the amount of ale and wine typically imbibed at the meal. It was presumed that if one ate breakfast, it was because one had other lusty appetites as well.

Conversely, eating breakfast meant that one was poor, and needed precious calories to get to the business of peasantry—a marginally more tolerable reason to eat breakfast. Morning feeding was accepted for low-status farmers and laborers who truly needed the energy to make it through the first few hours of toiling, as well as those too weak to make it to the large, midday dinner—children, the elderly, and the infirm, who were allowed to supplement their meals with porridges.[23] Whatever the reason for eating it, breakfast was generally treated with a fair amount of derision.

In 13th-century England, breakfast (when eaten) consisted of little more than a sustaining hunk of rye bread, a bit of cheese, and some ale consumed by regular working stiffs, but by the 15th century even the nobility indulged in a bit of bread, ale, and meat in the hours between waking and dinner, though this was not necessarily considered a proper meal. In Europe, many people had a posset of warm custard mixed with ale or wine upon waking. This was enjoyed while still in the bedchamber, just as modern Parisians take a café au lait with a bit of croissant before getting on with the day, hours before *déjeuner*.[24]

Over the centuries, the earlier of the acceptable meals—dinner—was pushed later and later. Tenth-century Normans ate a midmorning meal (not yet called dinner) at around 9:00 a.m.[25] A few hundred years later, by the time of the Tudor period (mid-15th century), people were eating dinner at around 11:00 a.m., further lengthening the time between waking and the first meal. Frances I of France, perhaps in light of this ever-widening gap between mealtimes, stuck to the maxim "rise at 5, dine at 9, sup at 5, couch at 9."[26]

Though the hour of meals shifted many times throughout the generations, it was generally agreed that meals should nonetheless happen at specific times; anything less than timely was chaotic and savage, so said Sir John Harington, in 1624: "I would not that you should observe a certaine houre, either for dinners or suppers, lest that daily custome should be altered into nature; and after this inter-mission of this custome of nature hurt may follow."[27]

Travelers were also apparently granted license to eat breakfast while they were away from home. In March of 1255, six tuns of wine were delivered to Henry III at the cathedral at St. Albans for his breakfast while away on pilgrimage.[28] When one considers that a tun is equivalent to approximately 252 gallons of wine, this is astonishing. It seems, then, that if a king was on religious pilgrimage (as he frequently was), not only was the ban on breakfast completely lifted, but supplies were adjusted—often quite zealously, as demonstrated by Henry III's 1,500 gallons of wine—to compensate for the unpredictable quality at the cook shops or market stalls that would be encountered along the way. If the king were to sin by eating breakfast, he may as well enjoy good tipple while he was at it.

The justification for laborers to eat breakfast came in opposition to the widely held belief that one should never exercise on a full stomach; to do so, it was feared, would result in food entering the bloodstream before it could become sufficiently "concocted." In fact, 17th-century Strasburg physician Melchior Sebizius warned that without the heat of labor to stimulate digestion and the elimination of wastes through the sweat and breath, the superfluities left in the body would fester into scabies or ulcers.[29]

Regular men were usually too embarrassed to admit that they ate breakfast, being a meal associated with children, invalids, the elderly, and the working poor. However, the first record of a businessman recording "Expensys in brekfast" occurred in an account log of the court of Edward IV in 1463.[30] His financial needs must have helped him overcome his embarrassment. By the early 1600s, recorded expenses for breakfast became customary and more detailed, logging the price, foods eaten, and to whom the invoice should be paid.

Another interesting consideration is that by the 1500s, physicians across Europe consistently warned healthy adults against eating breakfast. It was considered insalubrious to eat before fully digesting the prior meal, lest the "pure" become somatically integrated with the "impure."[31] A brisk morning constitutional was prescribed to get the blood pumping, to produce the body heat needed to facilitate digestion, and perhaps to encourage the other morning constitutional. Perhaps the 16th-century introduction of caffeinated beverages into the European diet was part of the consideration to allow breakfast; coffee and tea famously aid the body in "evacuation of superfluities." Perhaps this is why coffee and tea were consumed in the morning in the first place.

English author Thomas Wingfield believed breakfast to be necessary among the British, writing in 1551 that although the 2nd-century Roman physiologist Galen never ate breakfast, that "in this Realme" it was necessary.[32] Though Wingfield was among the first 16th-century authors to come out in favor of breakfast, he nonetheless echoed the medieval sentiment by suggesting that only babies and the infirm should require a morning meal. Going against convention, Manchester schoolmaster Thomas Cogan wrote in 1589 that it was not only fine to eat breakfast, but that it was unhealthy to miss it, insisting that "[t]o suffer hunger long filleth the stomack with ill humors." Cogan was among the notable few to identify the need for even healthy, robust people to eat breakfast, rather than reserving it for the very young, the very old, and the choleric, as Wingfield had.

Another author from the British Isles, Thomas Moffett, explains that Scottish people need something wholesome first thing in the morning; if they lack access to fresh, clean air, then a healthful breakfast should be a suitable facsimile.[33] This had been construed to mean that anyone living in a filthy city should eat breakfast regularly. In a recurring theme of circumstantial allowance, Moffett goes on to explain that children, choleric people, and laborers should also keep something in their stomachs.

Breakfast was also eaten to stave off the cold. Welsh writer Sir William Vaughan instructed eating hot, buttered bread with cinnamon and sugar and caudles of oatmeal with butter and raisins.[34] A caudle was somewhat like a cross between a thin gruel and eggnog, made by combining a starch—in Vaughan's case oats, but sometimes wheat or breadcrumbs—with honey, raisins, eggs, and wine or ale, and sometimes seasoned with ginger or saffron. A breakfast so hearty surely should have provided enough warmth to Vaughan's colonists in Newfoundland. Perhaps they paid him no heed: the colony failed.

At least some members of the nobility completely ignored the banter and had breakfast anyway, eating what they liked, when they liked. Queen Elizabeth I, an exceedingly civilized monarch with nothing but disdain for inebriated revelry, was known to be an early riser. During a visit with her cousin Mary of Scots, she arranged a meeting with Mary's ambassador Sir James Melvil for 8:00 a.m. When he arrived, he found her strolling about the garden, having already tended to her devotions, her other civil affairs, and her breakfast, which consisted of "manchet [a loaf of white bread], ale, beer, wine and a good pottage [stew], like a farmer's, made of mutton or beef with 'real bones.'"[35]

In a different entry in her personal journal, Queen Bess makes pragmatic notes about a less spectacular breakfast: "10 May 1451. Six o'clock. Breakfasted. The buttock of beef rather too much boiled, and the ale a little the stalest. Memorandum: to tell the cook about the first fault, and to mend the second myself by tapping a fresh barrel directly." [36] That even the judicious queen partook of ale, beer, *and* wine at breakfast leads one to question just how much consumption it took to make a medieval inebriate.

By the 15th century, it appears that many members of the upper crust either were permitted to eat breakfast or paid no mind to the instructions otherwise. Accounts of what certain earls and duchesses were having for breakfast begin to trickle in at around this time and sometimes even go into great detail about the amount of food being consumed. Following Elizabeth's example, it would seem that those virtuous early risers were at last granted clearance to eat before dinner, as in this substantial breakfast of one earl and his countess: two loaves of bread, a quart of beer, a quart of wine, two pieces of salt fish, six baconed herrings, four white herrings, or a dish of sprats.[37] As described in his 1911 *Good Cheer: The Romance of Food and Feasting*, English historian Frederick Hackwood does not name the earl and countess; it is possible they were William Paston (2nd Earl of Yarmouth) and his wife Margaret of Norfolk. The *Paston*

Letters document the correspondence between the gentry Pastons in the years between 1422 and 1509, chronicling many historical affairs, as well as a very similar daily breakfast supplied by Margaret to her family: "a machet a quarte of beer a dyshe of butter a pece of saltfisch a dyshe of sproitts or white herrying."[38]

In the mid-17th century, Queen Henrietta Maria (wife of King Charles I of England) also enjoyed a pottage every morning, hers consisting of herbed meat broth thickened with toast. Her chancellor and personal chef Kenelm Digby goes into great detail on the recipe, which is included in his posthumously published cookbook, *The Closet of the Eminently Learned Sir Kenelme Digbie Knight Opened*. He goes on to recommend finishing the breakfast with two poached eggs and a bit of bacon, an idea he may have borrowed from physician Tobias Venner.[39]

Even as breakfast foods begin to resemble the modern version of the meal, the same caveats persisted. Though Tobias Venner recommends a sensible breakfast of "a couple of poached eggs, sprinkled with vinegar, seasoned with black pepper and salt, served with bread-and-butter and completed with a draught of claret (wine)" in his medical text *Via Recta ad Vitam Longam*, he goes on to somewhat contradictorily suggest that it is not necessary for the 25- to 60-year-old demographic or for students and sedentary people.[40] Once again, breakfast is relegated to a meal for children and the elderly.

By the 17th century, with the likes of diarist Samuel Pepys providing discursive accounts of his breakfasts, eating in the morning had more or less lost its stigma. In the newly settled America, colonists seem to have left old hang-ups behind in the Old World; that, or they were too busy trying to survive to quibble about the moral dilemma of skipping breakfast. By the middle of the 18th century, England and America alike were basking in the glow of breakfast's budding golden age; matutinal feasts of mutton chops, bacon, eggs, corn cakes, and muffins—even pie—were favorites of American Founding Fathers Benjamin Franklin and Thomas Jefferson, and commonplace among the upper classes. Franklin's only complaint was that his coworkers drank too much beer in the morning.

Breakfast was so adored in the middle of the 18th century that rooms devoted exclusively to the morning meal were built into new homes. Instead of taking a light repast in one's bedchambers, the breakfast room was a place to enjoy a sip of tea or coffee while languishing over a newspaper and a sweet roll, a place to host guests for casual dining, or where gentlemen could make merry over coffee and spirited political discourse. Breakfast parties afforded young people an opportunity to meet and mingle without a chaperone's vigilant supervision.

As the breakfast debate began to wind down in Europe, in Arabia, Sufis of Yemen had been busy experimenting with roasting Ethiopian coffee beans.[41]

Though the story of Ethiopian sheepherder Kaldi claims that coffee had been in use since the 9th century, the transformation of the bitter green seeds into an inky, aromatic brew through roasting was a revelation that would not occur until the late 15th century.[42] Coffee as it is known today quickly spread throughout the Middle East and soon it had reached Persia and Turkey. Then the roasting techniques made it back to northern Africa, and eventually spread to India, then Italy, Indonesia, the rest of Europe, and the Americas by the mid-17th century.[43] Soon, trendy coffee houses began popping up in Venice, Paris, Oxford, and Boston.

The earliest written records of the Chinese using tea as a beverage date back to the 10th century BCE. Though the Portuguese expansion in the 16th century introduced tea to Europe, new evidence suggests it has been used since the Paleolithic.[44] When Charles II of England married Portuguese tea drinker Catherine of Braganza in 1662, such became the frenzy for tea among the fashionable wealthy that the consumption of tea exploded, eventually exceeding that of alcohol, at least among the affluent.[45] A few years later, it became available in Massachusetts in the United States and became a favorite of colonists.

Most credit for the invention of so-called English Breakfast tea goes to one Scottish tea master called Drysdale, who purportedly developed the blend of Ceylon, Keemun, and Assam leaves to market as "Breakfast Tea" in the late 1800s. But according to the *Journal of Commerce*, it had already been invented and named English Breakfast by an English-born apothecary in 1843, in New York.[46] Tea went suddenly from being an afternoon affair to an official breakfast beverage. By the 19th century, tea was widely consumed by all social tiers.

Coffee and tea were exotic and chic. As stimulants, they could be prescribed as medicinal by physicians, offering another legitimate excuse to eat early in the day. Unlike the expensive chocolate drunk by the Spanish nobility in the South, for most regular Europeans the introduction of coffee and tea meant alcohol had been replaced as the preferred morning beverage, which granted the Church the moral high ground to finally approve of dining in the morning. Breakfast finally went from a boorish repast of the working proletariat to a meal suitable for members of every level of society.

EIGHTEENTH CENTURY TO TODAY

Between the Early Modern Period (following the Middle Ages) and the mid-1700s, breakfast changed very little in Europe; the meal had changed even less in the infant America. When they did eat it, rich people ate meat and eggs, and poor people ate porridge or gruel, or stale bread and ale. By the end of the 18th century, dinner had already been pushed to 4:00 or 5:00 p.m., eventually pushing supper even later in the evening.[47] With the shift of the day's two meals toward a later time came the need to eat in those hours between waking and lunch—a meal to break the evening's fast. Physicians and the Church had little negative left to say about it and finally approved of the already firmly established custom. At long last, the modern breakfast made its triumphant debut.

By the beginning of Queen Victoria's reign in 1819, bacon and eggs had already become firmly fixed as a part of the everyday breakfast. Even among most of the English working class, bacon was ubiquitous; in fact, the only time it was not served was on sausage or ham day. In well-to-do English households, most days began with porridge, followed by bacon and eggs cooked in a variety of ways. These could be cooked beforehand and left in a chafing dish until the master and mistress arose to eat. Soon, the Victorian era witnessed the birth of Britain's greatest (perhaps only) culinary achievement: the Full Breakfast.[48]

Though the Full English breakfast is central to the British national identity, the meal itself is only a relatively recent construct. As the 18th-century tradition of a full breakfast was dying out in favor of the simpler coffee and rolls, the mythos of the "Full English"—an alternative to the Continental or American breakfasts of the day—began in earnest.

The Victorian era (and the Second Industrial Revolution) in the latter half of the 19th century brought about the rise of the bourgeois middle class. Besides becoming absolutely necessary for the working class headed for the morning shift, breakfast provided additional opportunities for the middle class to brandish newly acquired wealth. Like most meals, breakfasts reflected the increase in leisure time and disposable income not seen in previous eras. The *nouveau riche* brought a certain amount of sensible, working-class structure into daily society life, allowing the arrangement of mealtimes—including that of breakfast—to become more firmly established. But there was still (new) money to burn, and lavish three-course breakfasts of eggs, fish, cured pork products, hot cereals, fresh fruits, and toast with butter and jam with coffee and tea became a way for the parvenu and established socialites to while away the morning hours.[49]

These large morning spreads came to closely resemble what we think of today as brunch; the word "brunch" first came into use in the English language at around the same time. British journalist Guy Beringer, in a piece for *Hunter's Weekly* in 1895,[50] wrote persuasively that "[b]y eliminating the need to get up early on Sunday, brunch would make life brighter for Saturday-night carousers. It would promote human happiness in other ways as well. Brunch is cheerful, sociable and inciting. It is talk-compelling. It puts you in a good temper, it makes you satisfied with yourself and your fellow beings, it sweeps away the worries and cobwebs of the week."

Although it is technically a meal falling between the times of breakfast and lunch (hence the portmanteau), brunch usually consisted of breakfast foods, and this persists today. Without work to tend to, more time can be spent on elaborate versions of breakfast basics or other time-consuming dishes like Crêpes Suzettes—coincidentally invented the same year as the word "brunch." And as Beringer mentions, brunch is a meal best served on Sundays, which may be part of the reason why Sunday holidays like Mother's Day are celebrated with a brunch. Though an Englishman coined the word, brunch continues to take the form of high art in the United States, perhaps in lieu of the laudable Full English of Britain.

Early 19th-century Americans still typically enjoyed only two meals a day: a large breakfast at around 8:00 a.m. and a late-afternoon dinner. The time at which one had one's breakfast was largely dictated by one's affluence (or lack thereof): Poor people rose earlier to get straight to their chores and ate an hour or two later, while the wealthier classes slept in and enjoyed a leisurely morning, taking both of their meals later.[51] By the end of the 19th century, relatively balanced and sensible breakfast menus appear in cookbooks like Fannie Farmer's 1896 bestseller *The Boston Cooking School Cook Book*. Typical breakfasts in Farmer's book consist of eggs, meat or fish (apparently left over from the previous evening's supper), a fruit, a hot cereal, a potato (usually fried), and a bread product (often a muffin or biscuit). Each of her eighteen breakfast menus includes coffee.

Even in late-1800s America there were still those stalwart few clamoring on about what to eat for breakfast, or what *not* to eat, as the case may be. Cookbook author and professor of French cookery (and perhaps the first celebrity chef) Pierre Blot made very specific rules for breakfast: Eat as little as possible; do not have any liquor, no matter what one's age or gender; if one is going to have it (which one should not), eat only leftover meat (and cold, not warm); avoid warm cakes, muffins, or pastries, which are very bad for the stomach and teeth; drink only coffee, milk, water, or cocoa, but do not by any means drink tea for breakfast.[52] This omission of tea is reflected in Boston Cooking School founder Fannie Farmer's breakfast menus as well, though she makes no explanation for its absence and goes further to declare that the United States is not a tea-drinking country.[53]

Perhaps due to his propensity for wagging his finger at extravagance, Blot went from being touted by the *New York Times* as "the eminent gastronomist . . . whose name has become a household word" in 1867 to a social pariah whose death a mere seven years later would not even receive an obituary in the very paper that praised him so. It appeared that the fickle wealthy of New York preferred to leave the matter of cooking to their Irish servants.[54]

Outside of the big cities, American pioneers and farmers had been enjoying a variety of corn-based breakfasts. This was largely thanks to the thousands of years of diligent genetic modification that indigenous Mesoamericans had performed to increase the size and carbohydrate content of the large graminoid's fruiting structure—the spikelet, or ear. In a process of selective breeding, Mesoamericans domesticated the Mexican annual teosinte (*Zea mays* ssp. *parviglumis*) into maize (*Zea mays* ssp. *mays*) by selection of key mutations; up to 12 percent of its genetic material is derived from another subspecies, *Zea mays* ssp. *mexicana*, through a natural process called introgressive hybridization.[55] Of all New World crops, colonialists most readily accepted corn.

Hulled corn made into hominy was an inexpensive and filling breakfast commonly eaten with milk or maple syrup, or fried in pork drippings. The hulled corn was first treated with alkaline ash in a process called nixtamalization. The nixtamalization process, used by Mesoamericans since approximately 1500–1200 BCE, frees the niacin in the kernel, making it available for absorption by the human body, and preventing deficiency diseases such as pellagra. Pellagra is also characterized by protein deficiency due to the lack of two amino acids in early corn crops: lysine and tryptophan. Nixtamalization somewhat increases the bioavailability of these amino acids, but indigenous people also had long known that by balancing the maize in their diet with meat or other crops such beans, amaranth, and chia, that disease could be averted. What they did not realize was that this is the only way the complete array of amino acids may be acquired by the human body, and the way for normal protein synthesis to occur. Pellagra was virtually unknown among indigenous populations.

In the autobiographical novel *Little House in the Big Woods*, author Laura Ingalls Wilder goes into great detail describing her mother's nixtamalization techniques using fresh corn and wood ash from the fireplace. After husking the ears and cutting the kernels (a task performed by Wilder's father), her mother boiled the cut kernels with the ashes until the corn swelled and their skins slipped off easily. This took what is rather unscientifically described as "a long time." Then she turned the corn into a pot of cold water and she rubbed the skins off until all of the kernels were hulled, changing the water as it became cloudy.

Mrs. Ingalls may have learned the technique from Iroquoian Huron Indians, who in turn may have learned it from the Navajo tribe Hopi, believed to have been descended from ancient Puebloan cultures, and who continue to use the process today. The word comes from the Aztec language Nahuatl; a compound of *nextli* "ashes" and *tamalli* "unformed corn dough" (tamal). The word hominy is similarly derived from indigenous Americans, in this case the Powhatan (Virginia Algonquin) word *rockahommie*. In the 19th and early 20th century, trail food called "rockahominy" specifically referred to the roasted and coarse-ground nixtamalized corn, closer to today's hominy grits.

Corn has remained a sacred food of indigenous Americans, present in most aspects of everyday life and in ceremony, dating back to the first European contact. The delicate, tortilla-like Hopi dish *piki*, or paper-bread, is a ceremonial breakfast eaten by a man and woman on the morning of their wedding day, a practice that dates back to at least the 16th century (when Spaniards arrived), but probably much earlier.[56] Though it is not strictly a breakfast food, the act of eating *piki* on the morning of their wedding day is a critical part of the commitment ceremony for Hopi couples. The *piki* is made by finely grinding blue maize into a powder on a *metate*, which is mixed with water into a thin batter. The ashes of the greasewood shrub (*Sarcobatus vermiculatis*) are added to accentuate the blueness of the *piki*. The batter is smeared on a hot, flat rock greased with the oil of sunflower, squash, or watermelon seeds and it cooks almost instantaneously. The thin bread is quickly peeled off the rock and rolled tightly into scrolls two inches thick. *Piki* is said by American journalist Raymond Sokolov to be the "highest expression of Hopi cuisine, and the most intricate symbol of the intertwining of traditional Hopi life with corn." Ceremonial *piki* must always be sacred blue, to symbolize the heavens. A woman's suitability for marriage was judged solely on her *piki*.[57]

Untreated corn was also dried and ground into meal for baking and frying a variety of breads: cornbread, corn pone, johnnycakes (or hoecakes), and hush puppies. These indigenous American foods later became more closely associated with the working class in the American South. Corn meals were also used for a variety of porridges with a wide array of colloquial names: samp, Indian pudding, Indian mush, cornmeal mush, hasty pudding, pudding corn, coosh.

Use of hickory coal to smoke meats like ham, bacon, and sausage was also learned from indigenous people; Plains Indians hung meat at the top of their tipis to increase its contact with smoke. Smoking meats not only imparted a unique flavor to the meats, but also preserved them for long-term storage. American breakfast meats got their signature flavor from a combination of salting, smoking, and later, saltpeter. In the 19th century it was discovered that the addition of potassium nitrate to the curing salt maintained the meat's red color rather than the unappetizing gray of earlier cured meats.[58] Consumption of cured meat skyrocketed.

Salishan Indians (Flathead tribe) of Washington curing meat. Courtesy of the Library of Congress.

The advent of today's breakfast cereals was likely a response to the new habits of beginning one's day with an excess of meats and other rich foods. The so-called Jacksonian-era Clean Living Movement (a term coined in 1990 by social scientist Ruth Engs and a spinoff of the Popular Health Movement) was highly influential in mid-19th-century United States dietetics, introducing a regimen of personal hygiene, exercise, and vegetarianism, as well as elimination of stimulants from one's diet.[59] While it promoted a rational skepticism of the "authority" of established medical expertise, the Popular Health Movement also attempted to abolish all other intellectual elitism.

This may have been tangentially related to early 19th-century dietary re-former Sylvester Graham's glorification of brown bread—symbol of the common people—as more wholesome than the refined white bread of the college-educated (read: intellectually elite) middle class. (Ironically, by the latter half of the 20th century, the reverse would be true.) Backlash against Industrial-era conveniences like chemical leavening agents preferred by commercial bakers for the production of white bread led to a focus on wholesome, unprocessed foods in the mid-19th century, thought to promote mental and spiritual health as well as a more hygienic physical self. (Incidentally, two major groups of Clean Living proponents, the Mormon and Seventh Day Adventist Churches, emerged from this era.)

The end of the Clean Living Movement in the latter half of the 1800s also saw the creation of the first modern breakfast cereals, changing the American breakfast landscape forever. Contrary to modern marketing themes, it was the quest for health—not convenience—that drove the invention of breakfast cereal. In 1863, granola was invented by Dr. James Caleb Jackson, who called it "Granula" after the texture of the crisped and crumbled nuggets of bran-rich Graham flour.[60] Although it provided ample dietary fiber to alleviate painful gastric disorders brought on by an overindulgence in meat, Granula lacked the convenience of today's breakfast cereals; the large nuggets were very dense and required overnight soaking before eating. Jackson's views on health and diet influenced the health reform of Ellen White, who would go on to found the Seventh Day Adventist Church.

In 1894, flaked breakfast cereal was accidentally invented by Seventh Day Adventist John Harvey Kellogg. Seventh Day Adventists—known for being vegetarian health fanatics, among other things—founded the Battle Creek Sanitarium (originally opened as the Western Health Reform Institute) in Battle Creek, Michigan. It was the health resort for the social elite, and Corn Flakes would become their panacea.

Flaked cereal was developed entirely by happenstance, when a pot of cooked wheat was left unattended and went stale. With an eye on their bottom line, John Kellogg (the Sanitarium's superintendent) and his younger brother Will decided to try forcing the paste through rollers, hoping for usable sheets of dough. Instead, it dried into flakes, which were fortunately a big hit among the Sanitarium's clientele. The Kelloggs went into full-time packaged flaked cereal production using corn and various other grains. They had a patent for the technique two years later. That did not prevent the idea from being copied by others, including one C. W. Post, who noted the production details during an ill-conceived tour of the factory given at the Sanitarium. Post went on to found Post Cereals, Kellogg's top competitor. John Kellogg later developed a cereal similar to the Granula invented by Jackson thirty years earlier, but the name was changed to granola to avoid legal problems. Will Kellogg added sugar to Corn Flakes against John's protests in attempt to bolster sales, and then founded the Battle Creek Toasted Corn Flake Company, which eventually became the Kellogg Company. After the ensuing fraternal feud, John founded the Battle Creek Food Company.

Dietary reform often began with breakfast. With the ascent of the Clean Living Movement, mutton chops gave way to whole grain cereals. The expansion

John Harvey Kellogg, between ca. 1910 and 1915. Courtesy of the Library of Congress.

of the railroad in the latter 19th century meant that citrus fruits from Florida and California would become more available and affordable, and the work of microbiologist Ilya Mechnikov influenced Kellogg to explore the healthful effects of yogurt. John Kellogg's wife, Ella, went on to write numerous cookbooks on the benefits of a vegetarian diet, offering a litany of recipes for Graham gems and gluten porridge. Her breakfast offerings were "pretty and dainty" as well as "suited to the needs of the invalid."[61] The name Kellogg became synonymous with health and hygiene.[62]

Following the invention of ready-made cereals, a wide range of developments occurred that would deeply impact the cultural identity of breakfast. The 1920s and 1930s were a time of convenience and modernity in the kitchen, introducing many of the foods that modern Americans still associate with breakfast: Bis-quick (dry mix for biscuits and pancakes), Ballard's Oven Ready Buttermilk Bis-cuit (the first refrigerated cardboard tube with portioned biscuit dough, known by the brand name Pillsbury in the 1950s), Cream of Wheat instant semolina cereal, Quaker Oats quick-cooking oats, Sanka's instant decaffeinated coffee, and Lender's bagels.[63] Many of these instant and ready-made convenience foods became more necessary during the egg and meat rationing of World War II.

Cereal box prizes were first introduced to markets by Kellogg's in 1945 in the form of pin-back buttons inserted into Pep cereal. A year later, injection molding made the production of cheap, plastic toys possible, and cereal compa-nies quickly caught on. The addition of cartoon mascots like the Rice Krispies Elves (introduced in 1930s) firmly implanted cereal companies into the psyches of American children. Breakfast cereals soon began their descent into the nutri-tional wasteland of modern sugar cereals, matching marketing efforts directed toward the first kids of the Post–World War II baby boom generation.

The 1940s and 1950s experienced another boom, in the American diner craze. Though travelling café wagons and lunch cars had been around since the late 1800s, stationary diners—often little more than prefabricated tin cans resembling mobile homes—hit their stride after WWII, concurrently with the rise in suburban populations. Postwar, diners presented an attractive small busi-ness opportunity in urban and suburban areas around the northeastern United States. These were the first dining establishments to emphasize breakfast foods and offer them twenty-four hours a day.

Twenty-four-hour diners were more than a place for lonely hearts to ponder the bottom of their coffee cups, or for late-night revelers to wind down the eve-ning's imbibing; postwar diners were often sited near factories that operated at all hours, offering graveyard shift workers—a key component of their customer base—a place to enjoy hearty breakfast fare in the morning hours after their shifts had ended.

At home, breakfasts were becoming an afterthought, quickly thrown together to get the kids off to school. With the rise of feminism in the 1960s came an increased demand for foods that would move liberated mothers out of the kitchen. Instant oatmeal, Yoplait's sweetened, individually packaged yogurt cups, and Carnation's chocolate-flavored Instant Breakfast entered markets in the 1960s, while new sugar cereals continued to be introduced every year.[64] This may have been the market's predictable response to an increased demand, but was just as likely an advantageous coincidence that allowed American moth-ers to justify stepping away from the stove. Either way, American women were increasingly liberated from their kitchens and free to pursue the workplace and other endeavors.

Ever the kingpin of breakfast convenience foods, or perhaps sensing a sea change in the American family dynamic and seizing the opportunity, Kellogg's was the first to bring toaster pastries to the market in 1964, with their Pop-Tart. Post had developed the foil-wrapping technology and invented the packaged toaster pastry called "Country Squares" in 1963, but was foolish enough to announce their product to the press before it was actually ready to bring to market. Kellogg's, perhaps still bitter about losing the monopoly on cold breakfast cereals, was able to develop its own version in six months, and Pop-Tarts were so popular that Kellogg's could barely keep up with the demand.[65]

Country Squares never really took off, while Pop-Tarts continue to be a top seller for Kellogg's. In the early 1960s, with popular television bringing American audiences shows like *The Beverly Hillbillies* and *The Andy Griffith Show*'s slack-jawed bumpkin Gomer Pyle, the word "country" was less associated with wholesome, healthy living and more reminiscent of hayseeds with a penchant for pitchforks, banjoes, and "kissin' cousins"; meanwhile, "square" had been co-opted from the Beatnik vernacular to mean someone who is unhip and old-fashioned. Country Squares never stood a chance.[66]

Decades later, critics would clamor that what women were gaining in convenience could not mitigate the deterioration of public health that eventually arose from this increased reliance on prepackaged foods high in preservatives. Many authors, including Michael Pollan, have perhaps unintentionally implicated feminism for the decline in home cooking, citing Betty Friedan's *The Feminine Mystique* (1963), which equates cooking with oppression against women. Pollan's *In Defense of Food* goes on to explain that this belief was not necessarily shared by French feminists like Simone de Beauvoir, who considered cooking a form of "revelation and creation," or Julia Child, who detested the word "housewife" and never cottoned to condescending to viewers with such a label. In reality, the convenience of ready-made breakfast foods like cold cereal and frozen waffles were a help to housewives for several decades before they were a help to feminists stepping away from the stove. Even women who actually enjoyed cooking often fed cereal to their children; it is what their children wanted to eat (because of high sugar content and effective advertising during cartoons), but also because providing a cabinet of cereal for a child to pour herself fostered the child's burgeoning independence—a parenting theme promoted by eminent mid-century pediatrician Dr. Benjamin Spock.[67]

Convenience foods may have been a boon to busy, well-meaning housewives of the 1960s, but across America, members of the counterculture were becoming disenchanted with their separation from the natural world and the food chain. They began to identify with the back-to-the-land movement that had been quietly raging since the Great Depression. Responding to a new market, cereal makers gave granola a facelift; dried fruits and seeds were added to the toasted, sweetened grains, and granola became an overnight sensation with the ecology movement's new generation of health food consumers. Colloquially, the word "granola" is still largely evocative of hippies. The original Swiss health food, müesli, also grew in popularity as a result of this renewed interest in wholesome diets.

In the American South, a sort of anti-health-food movement had been holding strong. Comfort foods like biscuits with sorghum or cane syrup, fried fish, and grits had been part of the African American culinary identity for generations, yet the term "soul food" was not first printed until 1960, when the word "soul" was becoming a pop-culture synonym for "black."[68] For people who toiled in the fields from dawn until dusk, a calorie-dense breakfast was requisite, but even now that farm labor has dramatically decreased among African American Southerners, soul foods—including breakfasts—persist. This is due in part to strong cultural heritage that Americans of color associate with their traditional foods; soul food is part of their identity, to be shared with members of an extended family or church community.

Soul breakfasts also bore a great similarity to brunch—a meal over which many Southerners (New Orleanians, in particular) have claimed ownership. For French Quarter merchants who began their workday well before dawn, breakfast was eaten relatively late; Creole breakfast items like Eggs Sardou served alongside soul food dishes such as shrimp and grits are still central to the regional ethnicity. Like most brunches, these large breakfasts are normally reserved for Sundays and holidays when a more leisurely cooking and dining pace may be afforded.

Once necessary for sustaining long, grueling hours in indentured labor, traditionally prepared soul foods tend to be high in calories, fat, cholesterol, starch, and sodium. Soul food has been linked to high rates of heart disease, diabetes, and stroke in modern African Americans, but it may actually be the use of recycled cooking oil, rather than fried food itself, that is to blame. One study found that the degradation of reused cooking oil into polymers and polar compounds (which reabsorbed into the food) were responsible for increased rates of hypertension.[69]

By the early 1970s, producers of mainstream breakfast foods were eager to capitalize on the popularity of the new "Black is Beautiful" culture and used R&B musicians and black athletes to promote their products. Musical sensations the Jackson 5 starred in television commercials for cereal brands like Post Alpha Bits, while spoofing Quaker Oats' Life cereal on their 1972 television variety program *The Jackson 5 Show*. The exhibition basketball team The Harlem Globetrotters were used in a promotion for General Mills' Cocoa Puffs.

In the 1970s, breakfasts, like all meals, were informed by the economic challenges faced by many households. The School Breakfast Program (SBP) introduced federally subsidized breakfasts under the jurisdiction of the Child Nutrition Act of 1966; amendments to the Act in 1975 made the SBP permanent. Though participation rates were initially slow, the years between 1970 and 1980 experienced rapid growth in participation in the SBP, attributed by the USDA to an increase in the number of households in which the mother worked outside of the home—a phenomenon driven in part by the economy, and in part by women's increased desire for professional autonomy.[70]

The Special Supplemental Nutrition Program for Women, Infants and Children (abbreviated as WIC), enacted in 1972, is another federal spinoff of the Child Nutrition Act of 1966, created to address healthcare and nutritional needs of low-income pregnant women, breastfeeding women, and infants and children under the age of five. These programs helped children too young to benefit from the SBP, while also providing guidance to families on how to prepare balanced meals. WIC provides women with lists of foods that qualify under their program, which are provided free with vouchers. Since its inception, WIC has not allowed program participants to use vouchers to purchase Kellogg's Raisin Bran because it exceeds WIC's limit of 45 percent sugar.[71] This was a decision that understandably offended Kellogg's—they lobbied against WIC's sugar limits for more than twenty years on the grounds that raisins are fruit. Though raisins are naturally high in fructose, WIC has not budged on the issue; Kellogg's has since ceded, and began adding high-fructose corn syrup to Raisin Bran in 2010.

In response to the worldwide food crisis (in Ethiopia, India, and China, notably), vegetarianism—as an environmental and social responsibility, and a solution to worldwide famine—experienced a resurgence in popularity with Frances Moore Lappé's 1971 *Diet for a Small Planet*. Soon, whole grain pancakes and fruits replaced bacon and eggs on the breakfast tables of American families.

A focus on grain-based foods was emphasized by Adventist vegetarians of the late 19th century and modern adherents in the 1920s, but cereals were not the end-all and be-all of a vegetarian's breakfast. Back-to-the-land types in the 1970s brought an appreciation for the wonders and wide-ranging appeal of the soybean. Soy-based meat analogs were a vegetarian's dream come true, and patents for the first soy-based "bacon" were filed in 1974.[72] Even nonvegetarians were eager to eat lighter, though; a patent specifically for "process for preparing fabricated bacon"—the first turkey bacon—came in 1977.

The 1970s also witnessed the birth of the fast food drive-through lane and breakfast sandwiches like McDonald's Egg McMuffin. Eggs and sausage, ham, or bacon on an English muffin became a time-saving way to grab breakfast on one's way to work. Inhabitants of the British Isles typically opted for a breakfast roll instead of the Full Breakfast. The breakfast is not rolled in the style of an American breakfast burrito; rather, the ingredients of a Full English—sausages, bacon, white or black pudding, butter, mushrooms, tomatoes, and tomato sauce or brown sauce (everything but the beans) is served on a white roll. Though the take-out breakfast roll had been inspired by American fast food, the idea was actually a British one; bacon or sausages sold in a bread roll (a "bap," as they were known) dates back to the mid-19th century.[73]

In the 1980s, frozen breakfast foods grew more than any other frozen foods, due to the rapid price drop in microwave ovens. As cereal companies like Quaker Oats and Kellogg's had already begun cashing in on the whole grains trend in the 1970s, all that was left was to package the cereals in microwavable paper or plastic cups. Muffins were on the rise, both in popularity, and in size. Muffins were "what the world is looking for," said Richard J. Sharoff, the 1987 president of California-based bakery chain Vie de France. "They're a portable, good-tasting breakfast product with healthy connotations. You don't have to put them in the oven. There's no mess, and you can eat them on the run. They are the quintessential food of the 1980s."[74]

The marriage of European and California-style cuisine made other impacts on the breakfast table as well. In the late 1980s, quiches were popular at any meal, as was anything with avocados, goat cheese, and sun-dried tomatoes. These west-coast ingredients trickled into crepes and omelets, and increasingly, tofu scrambles, particularly as the decade moved into the health-crazed 1990s. By the end of the 20th century, bacon and eggs were back on the plate, thanks to zealous misinterpretation of the studies of Dr. Robert Atkins, which led approximately 10 percent of Americans to abandon carbohydrates. Fortunately for bakers, the Atkins Nutritionals Company filed for bankruptcy in 2005.

AROUND THE WORLD IN A MEAL

The fourteen-course *kaiseki* breakfast of traditional Japanese *ryokan* is an elaborate parade of tiny, perfectly balanced dishes, while most Italians have nothing more than a cup of coffee with buttered bread and jam. Although regional iterations obviously exist, breakfast foods do bear remarkable similarity around the world. Every morning, most everyone who eats breakfast will enjoy some variation on the theme of grain, dairy, and protein, washed down with something hot and caffeinated.

CEREALS

Recent discoveries of wild cereal residue on grinding stones in prehistoric Israel reveal that human ancestors in the Upper Paleolithic routinely processed grains for at least 12,000 years before agriculture. Oven-like hearths discovered at the same sites suggest that bread baking has been occurring as long.

Porridge

If there ever was a universal dish, it is, unequivocally, porridge. Once early cereal cultivation was developed in the Fertile Crescent and beyond, porridge soon became a mainstay. Porridges are inexpensive, easy to prepare, filling, and nutritious.

Emmer wheat, one of the Founder Crops that originally grew wild in the Fertile Crescent, was the basis of the ancient Roman *puls*, a thick porridge eaten with every meal. The Roman poet Ovid makes mention of *puls fabricia*—porridge with fat bacon—as an offering to the goddess of health and vitality, Carna. The ancient Greek porridge *kykeon*, which is made with barley and ricotta (and wine instead of water), closely resembles Roman statesman Marcus Cato's beloved *puls punica* (Punic porridge), though *kykeon* was thin enough to be drunk.

The preparation of *kykeon* was always women's work. Depending on her knowledge for herbs (read: propensity for witchcraft), a woman might yield a brew with any variety of effects, even powerful enough to send men to sleep—sometimes permanently. In the *Odyssey*, the witchy *kykeon* prepared by the "loveliest immortal" Circe allowed Odysseus's entire crew to be transformed into pigs. This may have been more than mere fiction; some scholars suggest that the Eleusinian Mysteries were so mysterious because the *kykeon* barley was infected by the ergot fungus. Alkaloids in ergot, it would be discovered in 1941, include lysergic acid amide (LSA), a chemical precursor to the hallucinogenic drug LSD. A variety of less mind-blowing barley porridges would eventually become the preferred breakfasts across Europe, Asia, and Africa.

Speaking of acid porridges, many developing countries around the world utilize lactic acid fermentation to render thin, insubstantial porridges both more nutritious and more palatable. Lactic acid fermentation, or lactofermentation, occurs when *Lactobacillus* bacteria convert sugars to lactate (lactic acid); this process results in the sourness of sourdough bread and yogurt. Fermenting increases the nutrient density of thick gruels threefold, greatly improving the nutrition of impoverished people. Fermenting also inhibits the proliferation of dangerous gram-negative pathogens such *E. coli* and *Salmonella*.

Most acid porridges are consumed as staple foods, particularly in the countries of Africa. Many are thin enough to be consumed as a beverage, but in rural Kenya, *uji* may be thinned and drunk in lieu of tea. In urban and affluent households, where mealtimes are more established, *uji* is eaten with bread and tea for breakfast. Outside of Africa, buttery oat porridge called "sowens" was lightly fermented before being cooked and served for breakfast on Christmas, New Year's Day, or Hallow-e'en in 16th-century Scotland, as mentioned by Scotland's national bard Robert Burns. In Europe today, a number of sour porridges are also eaten for breakfast, but rely on the addition of cultured dairy, not wild fermentation, to achieve the sour taste.

Porridges in the Western world usually consist of warm bowls of grains cooked to varying degrees (often beyond recognition), sweetened with sugar, honey, or syrup, spiced with sweet spices like cinnamon and nutmeg, and served with milk or cream and dried fruit like raisins or currants. While porridges are certainly not restricted to breakfast, sweet porridges seem to be almost universally so.

Of those who eat it for breakfast, most North Americans and northern Europeans start their day with porridges of oats, corn, or wheat. In North America, farina is usually associated with Cream of Wheat, and eaten with milk and sugar. Eastern Europeans are quite devoted to a buckwheat porridge called *kasha*, which is one of the oldest known Slavic dishes. The centrality of *kasha* to the Eastern European way of life is evinced by the Russian rhyming proverb, "*schi da kasha—pischa nasha*" ("cabbage soup and porridge are our sustenance"). This reverence for humble fare is not really tied to the food itself; like many Russian proverbs, it reflects the deeper pride of the Russian poor.

Similarly, the oat has played a monumental role in the history of Ireland. Today's so-called Irish oatmeal likely closely resembles the oatmeal that Gaelic rebels ate: whole, dried oat grains called "groats" cut with steel blades, thus the moniker "steel-cut oats." Unlike the rolled version that many Americans think of as oats, steel-cut oats are roughly the size and shape of a pinhead—another name for this type of oat. Rolling oats into flattened grains substantially reduces their cooking time; steel-cut oats require overnight soaking to accomplish the same result. Grinding oat groats into oatmeal is another way to economize cooking time. It is so regularly cooked into porridge that to most people, the word "oatmeal" refers to oat porridge; in the United States, rolled oats are most typically sold simply labeled as oatmeal.

In 16th-century Scotland, a thick, uncooked "parritch" (porridge) made of ground oats softened with cold water, sour milk, or buttermilk, or sometimes with mutton or beef broth, was called "crowdie." It was such a staple breakfast that the phrase "crowdie time" literally meant "breakfast time." (Being Scotland, it could also mean it was lunch or dinner time, too.) The Bard himself, Robert Burns, wrote in the 18th century a lamentation for the life of the married man doomed to eat crowdie for every meal:

Oh, that I had never been married,
I'd never had nae care;
Now I've gotten wife and bairns,
An' they cry crowdie evermair!
Once crowdie, twice crowdie,
Three times crowdie in a day![1]

Today, the oat porridge is called "brose," and can be made with split peas and greens like kale or nettles as an alternative to oats, and crowdie nowadays refers to cream cheese, often eaten with an oat scone called a "farl." To further confuse matters most splendidly, farl can be made from buttered brose that has been baked on a hot griddle and eaten for breakfast. Depending on whom one asked, and when, one could perhaps eat crowdie on a farl made of crowdie. The name overlap is likely due to the similarity in texture of the two crowdies.

Oatmeal was also, apparently, a favorite of Swedish devil worshippers in the 1670s. On the tails of European witch hysteria, English clergyman and philosopher Joseph Glanvill wrote in his 1681 *Sadducismus Triumphatus* of wild, Satanic sex orgies at Blockula, Sweden, in which Lucifer himself laid out for his witches a diabolical feast of "broth with colworts [cabbage] and bacon in it, oatmeal, bread spread with butter, milk and cheese." This meal was followed by dancing and other venereous acts.

By most accounts, oatmeal was still considered peasant fodder well into the 20th century. Quick-cooking rolled oats were introduced to American markets by the Quaker Oats Company in 1922, and hot cereal regained public favor. Once it was introduced in 1966, Quaker's instant oatmeal became a staple of busy households.

In 1987, medical journalist Robert Kowalski wrote *The 8-Week Cholesterol Cure*, wherein it was declared that eating oat bran was something of a magic bullet against cholesterol, triggering an oat bran craze that lasted for years.[2] Sales of Quaker's oat cereals went from one million pounds in 1987 to 20 million pounds in 1989. By 1990, however, sales dropped off precipitously when the *New England Journal of Medicine* published a Harvard study that found no significant differences between serum cholesterol levels of those who ate oat bran and those who did not. Within weeks of the study, Quaker's sales dropped by 50 percent. It would seem that people were happy to go back to their bacon and eggs.

Although they have typically been associated with soft-cooked grains, porridges can be made from legumes as well. The 18th-century children's nursery rhyme, *Pease Porridge Hot*, refers to a dish of dried split peas cooked until thick and soft. As the ditty goes, "pease porridge hot, pease porridge cold, pease porridge in the pot, nine days old." When it was hot, it was dinner; the next day, before the morning's fires were lit, the leftover pease-porridge-cold was for breakfast. Whether or not it actually made it to nine days old was a matter of what scraps (and how much) could be added from day to day to stretch the pot of porridge to the next meal.

Originally a medieval staple, pease pottage, as it was then called, dates back to the Norman occupation in England in the 12th century. "Pottage," from the

Old French *potage*, was common breakfast fare from the 9th century until the 17th century, after which the word "porridge" came into use. Pease pottage is quite similar to the barley and legume porridge called *tisana* mentioned in *Apicius* in the 4th century.

In the book of Genesis from the Bible, Esau, famished after his morning chores, exchanged his entire birthright to his brother Jacob for a serving of lentil (*Lens culinaris*) pottage. This tale would work its way into a 1422 sermon by English historian and theologian John Capgrave, wherein Jacob supplanted his brother Esau, buying his father's blessing for a "mese of potage."[3] Hence, after Capgrave's sermon about tragic myopia and the short-selling of one's soul, a "mess of pottage" would be synonymous with something of no value. Esau's familial position, both figuratively and literally, amounted to a hill of beans.

Fūl medames is a fava-based pease porridge of sorts, and the national breakfast of Egypt. The dish consists of slow-cooked, whole, or mashed favas (*Vicia faba*) with lemon juice, olive oil, onion, and parsley, sometimes seasoned with cumin or chili flake. In the Middle Ages, the preparation of fūl medames was dominated by those living around the Princess Baths near today's public fountain of Muhammad 'Ali Pasha in Cairo; hence the nickname for the specific bean used for the dish: *fūl hammām*, or "bath fava." During the day, the bath attendants kept the fires going to heat the water, but since wood was at a premium, they had garbage as fuel. In a tragic case of aromatherapy gone wrong, eventually large dumps grew around the baths. The valuable coals left at the end of each day could not be wasted; rather, large pots were filled with fūl hammām and kept simmering all night. In the morning, the fūl was ready to be sold to the citizens of Cairo. In modern Cairo and throughout the Levant, fūl medames is still often sold by street vendors and fūl shops with bread and pickled vegetables; however, every Egyptian will declare that their family has the best recipe. Thankfully, no one cooks them using burned garbage anymore.

Tunisians enjoy a similar breakfast stew called *lablābī*, which happens to be their national dish as well, and a favorite of stevedores toiling long hours on the docks of Tunis.[4] Traditional recipes used hyacinth bean (*Lablab purpureus*), which is poisonous unless boiled in several changes of water. Most modern recipes simply use chickpeas (*Cicer arietinum*) or occasionally favas to save the trouble. According to one folkloric source, the name of the dish is onomatopoeic; lablābī's spiciness causes one to make the same noise as rams in coitus.[5]

Throughout South Asia, legume porridges called *dal* are commonly eaten at every meal, breakfast included. With the colonialism of the British East India Company from 1752–1851, dal made its way westward. The 1877 Canadian householder's guide *The Home Cook Book* includes a simple recipe for "breakfast dal" by cooking dal—"an Indian lentil," the recipe author known only as Mrs. Keer explains, with butter and onion.[6] To those wavering Victorian housewives reluctant to try such exotic, pungent fare, Mrs. Keer offers assurance: "[I]t is necessary to say that [you] need not fear to follow the recipe, as the modicum of well-cooked onion prescribed is in reality hardly appreciable to smell or taste, the dal apparently absorbing and counteracting its flavor." Cookbook author and temperance enthusiast Ella Kellogg (wife of John Harvey Kellogg) would add in 1893 that lentils "have a stronger flavor than any of the other legumes, and their taste is not so generally liked until one has become accustomed to it." She does, however, endorse their use for purees and soups and the like, and includes a recipe for a sort of dal similar to Mrs. Keer's—adding cream and omitting the onion—to serve as a "very palatable toast" for breakfast.[7]

Throughout East Asia, rice and millet porridges called *congee* are typically eaten for breakfast. Congees originated in China, dating back to the Zhou dynasty in 1000 BCE; in fact, the Chinese character for *zhou* (粥) means "gruel." In the south of China, rice is the predominant grain for congee; in the north, where rice crops do not thrive, sorghum, barley, millet, and wheat are more common.

Today, *jook* is the ubiquitous Chinese rice gruel, eaten for breakfast by most people, rich or poor. So goes the Chinese saying: "eat a good (hearty) meal for breakfast, enough food for lunch, and not much for dinner," and this is perhaps why jook is typically served with a variety of toppings, including shredded dried pork (*rousong*), fish, chicken, bamboo shoots, salted duck, or century eggs (*pidan*), as well as pickled things like fermented tofu (*sufu*) and mustard plant (*zha cai*).[8] As a breakfast, congee is usually eaten with fried dough sticks called *youtiao*.

Myriad regional variations of breakfast congee exist across Asia, tailored to the specific palates (and wallets) of the people. Cantonese-style congee called *bai zhou* is cooked even longer than jook, until the rice disintegrates into a thick, white porridge; Vietnamese *cháo* fortified with quivering spoonsful of coagulated pig's blood is a delicacy.

In Japan, the morning rice gruel (*asagayu*) depends on the season. In summer, cold *asagayu* may be served with pickled vegetables or preserved plum; a specialty of the 400-year-old Hyotei inn in Kyoto, *uzuragayu* is served with quail meat and eggs in the winter as part of the inn's renowned *kaiseki* breakfast. In the centuries-old Japanese tradition of writing a *jisei*, or "death poem" on one's deathbed, one poet, Kusamaru (1784–1836) was so inspired by his rice gruel breakfast that it was his last thought before passing:

Asagayu no　　　　　　My morning porridge
za kara mi ni iku　　　　and then I'll go see
yanagi kana　　　　　　the willow blossom.

Corn porridges have been eaten in the New World for millennia. Maize was deified by indigenous Americans as early as the Olmec civilization (ca. 1400–400 BCE), and was readily accepted into the European diet following the Spanish conquests of the 16th century. *Atole* has been prepared since pre-Columbian times; the Maya were buried with containers of atole to sustain them through their trip to the Underworld. It consists of thrice-ground maize meal cooked into a warm, drinkable gruel, traditionally flavored with herbs, toasted and ground squash seeds, honey, dried chilies, or dried leaves and flowers of the anise-scented Mexican marigold (*Tagetes lucida*). The Zapotecs of the Oaxaca Valley (late 6th century BCE) drank their *atole* flavored with toasted cacao seeds and allspice as *champurrado*, but once Spaniards brought exotic spices to the New World in the 16th century, cinnamon became another integral ingredient. Today, chocolate champurrado is a thick drink enjoyed for breakfast with another gift from the Spanish: sticks of sweet, fried pastries called *churros*.

As a staple food, porridge has been synonymous with peasantry, but perhaps inaccurately; recent evidence suggests that eating porridge can lead to higher earning potential, especially for men. A thirty-year study of Guatemalan children between 1969 and 1977 showed that boys who included atole as part of their daily breakfast in the first two years of their lives grew up to earn 46 percent higher wages than their placebo-eating peers (who were given skim milk and sugar instead of the porridge).[9] The two sample groups ate breakfasts containing equal micronutrients, so it was concluded that it was the protein and carbohydrates of the atole that ultimately led to success.

Native Americans had also been eating maize for thousands of years, in every conceivable way, porridge included. Cornmeal mush, or Indian pudding, would eventually become a staple breakfast dish of American settlers, though most colonists to the New World refused to accept Native American foods until they had been assimilated into the diets of their European countrymen and then returned to America reinterpreted. Indian corn was initially only added to the colonial diet by necessity, after attempts to grow European wheat had failed. Eventually, wheat adapted to stateside soils and climate, but by then corn had become firmly entrenched in the new American diet.

Precolonial Iroquois Indians of the northeastern United States, for whom breakfast was the only regular meal, made several varieties of cornmeal porridge—some with hickory nuts and meats, some with pumpkin and sugar. Dried cornmeal was such a mainstay that many Iroquois hunting parties travelled with nothing else to eat. One would simply swallow a few spoonsful of fine, dried meal, wash it down with a draught of water, and the corn porridge would cook itself in the heat of the stomach, swelling to fill the belly completely. The Iroquois could thus abate hunger without even stopping to light a fire.

A porridge called samp had been eaten by New England colonists since shortly after they arrived in America. The dish, which gained an endorsement from 17th-century Native American language scholar Roger Williams (with a slight caveat and suggested modification to the recipe), was described as "the Indian corne, beaten and boild, and eaten hot or cold with milk or butter, which are mercies beyond the Natives plaine water, and which is a dish exceedingly wholesome for the English bodies."[10]

Similar to samp, hasty pudding leftover from supper could be sliced into cakes after it congealed overnight, fried in pork drippings, and eaten with molasses or maple syrup for breakfast. This was Mary Johnson Bailey Lincoln's suggestion, who recommended frying any of the mushes in her 1884 *Mrs. Johnson's Boston Cook Book: What to Do and What Not to Do in Cooking*. "When eaten with bacon, they make a nice relish for breakfast."[11]

Another cornmeal porridge can be made by boiling stale cornbread. Cush-cush is a Louisiana breakfast dish that was standard camp fare for Confederate soldiers during the Civil War (1861–1865). Ironically, the dish likely originated in Barbados as the cornmeal mush "cou-cou" and came to America via African slaves. Cornmeal mush is still eaten for breakfast in America today, primarily in the U.S. South in the form of grits. A traditional breakfast of grits with pan-fried ham and red-eye gravy made from rendered ham drippings and brewed coffee is such an emblem of the South that in 2002, the State of Georgia declared grits its official prepared food.

Breakfast Cereal

Though hot cereals had been eaten for centuries, cold breakfast cereals, or just "cereal," was not invented until the late 1800s. The last half of the 19th century saw a wave of morally driven health crusades that had deep implications for breakfast. The first of these, the Jacksonian-era Clean Living Movement (1830–1860), saw the birth of the Sanitarium as the cure-all, as well as a new focus on eating whole grains without chemical additives. Broadly prescribed lifestyle changes included the abstention from meat, alcohol, caffeine, tobacco, and in some cases, sex. Bacon and eggs, pancakes with syrup, and hot coffee were now considered as "injurious" to one's health as masturbation.

One prominent figure to emerge from this movement, physician and hydropathist Sylvester Graham, advocated a shift to simple cereal-based breakfasts. Graham was particularly adamant about the risks of eating processed flours and developed his own flour made from the entire wheat seed, rather than the endosperm alone.

Dr. James Caleb Jackson, founder of the Our Home on the Hillside health spa in New York, baked small multigrain biscuits of Graham flour, oats, and cornmeal to supplement the institutional breakfast. Realizing he was on to something, Jackson reformulated his cereal, trying again by creating wafers of just Graham flour, which he crumbled and twice-baked like zwieback. These exceedingly firm nuggets, which he named Granula (but were called "wheat rocks" by some people), required an overnight soak before they were palatable; this, for many, defeated the purpose. The cries of housewives demanding the convenience of ready-to-eat cereals were evidently heard, as Jackson was able to advertise the cereal as "ready for immediate table use" by the 1880s. Among other salubrities recommended at the time, Granula was purported to be of the utmost prophylactic against disease; "a most excellent health food," the papers called it.[12]

At the same time, John Kellogg filed the patent for "Flaked Cereals and Process of Preparing Same."[13] Prior to that, the well-known Adventist superintendent of the Battle Creek Sanitarium in Michigan had experimented with grinding his own cereals and zwiebacks into a product that could be chewed by those with dental problems (of which there were many at the time). As the story goes, in 1894, John Harvey and his brother Will Keith Kellogg accidentally invented the cereal that would make them famous when a pan of cooking wheat was forgotten on the stove. Trying to save money by not wasting product, they ran the paste of overcooked wheat through a set of steel rollers. They named the flaked cereal Granose Flakes, and marketing began in 1895. Shortly after receiving the patent, more than fifty tons of Granose cereal had been manufactured and sold, primarily through mail order.

As competition among other companies began to ramp up, the Kelloggs focused on corn, and in 1898 they released their Sanitas Toasted Corn Flakes. Due to the high fat content of corn, it was prone to going rancid quickly. Despite John's protests, Will Kellogg added sugar—considered by John to be worse than meat for one's health—to increase palatability and sales; being a preservative, sugar also increased shelf life. The breakfast market began to change.

Child eating Puffed Rice cereal, 1918. Courtesy of the Library of Congress.

With rationing over after World War II, Kellogg's and other cereal companies began adding even more sugar to their cereals to increase their palatability to children, an emerging new market. At the same time, women were entering the workforce, and because cereal still carried the image of health (associated with sanitaria) and could be prepared by the unskilled hands of children, women were now free to leave breakfast to the kids, to whom cereal companies began advertising directly. By the end of the 1940s, the sugar content of breakfast cereals was so high they could hardly be called healthy anymore, but children—by now a clear driving force of markets—could not have been happier about it.

In the 1970s, many cereal makers came under public scrutiny as a diet high in sugar was blamed for a rising number of ailments. Sugar Crisp was renamed to Golden Crisp in the early 1980s, just as Kellogg's similar cereal Sugar Smacks were renamed to Honey Smacks, and Sugar Pops were changed to the wholesome-sounding Corn Pops. In an attempt to distance themselves from an unhealthy image, many other companies also dropped the word "sugar" from their products. This nutritional whitewashing may have been successful in sales, but the actual sugar content of these cereals has never been altered.

Some healthy cereals did become available again, in response to the health food craze of the 1960s and 1970s. Similar to Kellogg, Swiss nutritionist Bircher-Benner was a proponent of clean living, and created the cereal called Bircher müesli in 1906 to serve as a breakfast meal at his sanitarium in Zürich. The food, made of uncooked rolled oats, nuts, and dried fruit, had been inspired by a dish served to his wife while she hiked the Swiss Alps. With the addition of müesli's dried fruits and nuts to the toasted and crumbled oat and wheat cereal trademarked by Kellogg in the late 1880s, granola enjoyed a resurgence in popularity.

Though the high sugar content of cereal may undermine general health goals, cereal does provide a crucial source of vitamins, minerals, and micronutrients for many children. In the 1930s, after debilitating nutritional deficiency diseases like pellagra and rickets had plagued children for generations, the American Medical Association and the U.S. Food and Drug Administration endorsed a standardized fortification program to add niacin, thiamin, iron, and riboflavin to cereal products. In the 1940s, Vitamin D and calcium were added. Thanks to the fortification of cereals, pellagra has been eliminated in the United States. Today, more than 90 percent of American children eat cereal for breakfast.

Bread

According to recent findings, humans had been eating bread for at least 12,000 years before the domestication of cereal crops, coinciding with the birth of art and religion; some could say that humans have been eating bread for as long as they have been human.[14]

In ancient Greece, all meals consisted of bread and the accompaniments to bread known as "everything else" (*opson*). Rich or poor, emmer wheat bread (*artos* for the rich) or unleavened barley cakes (*maza* for the poor) were dunked into undiluted wine—*akratis*—and eaten for the morning meal, *akratisma*. Greek rhetorician Athenaeus noted that Homer used *ariston* to mean the morning meal (and not the midday meal, as it was otherwise recognized) in both the *Iliad* and the *Odyssey*. Athenaeus also observed that the comic playwrights Antiphanes and Cantharus considered *akratisma* but a snack to tide one over until the cook or slaves finished preparing ariston, implying either that the two words were interchangeable, or that breakfast had two courses.

The Gallo-Roman historian Gregory of Tours noted in the 6th century that French peasants and laborers ate a hunk of bread soaked in wine for breakfast every morning; in another of his texts, a transient priest is offered bread for breakfast by his peasant host, who asks the priest to bestow a blessing on the bread. The peasant would carry a piece of the blessed bread with him to work, to help him resist the Devil's offense, which would attempt to coerce him into throwing his cart and oxen into the river at the bridge crossing.[15]

By the 18th century, bread and butter were standard morning fare, even among those reticent to admit needing to eat breakfast. Richer foods were certainly available in the morning, but were considered unhealthy, both physically and spiritually. In his 1712 treatise on the schooling of young men, *Some Thoughts Concerning Education*, English philosopher and physician John Locke wrote of diets that are especially suited to children, that "a good piece of well-made and well-baked brown bread, sometimes with and sometimes without butter or cheese, would be often the best breakfast for my young master." Though he was a well-known follower of the tradition of Francis Bacon, Locke warned against giving youngsters any highly seasoned foods, and salted meats in particular.

Romans first came up with the concept of toasting bread as a means of extending its shelf life; the word "toast" comes from the Latin *tostus*, meaning scorched or dried with heat. The concept traveled throughout Europe, eventually landing in the British Isles; by the 16th century, it became fashionable in England to add toasted bread to drinks, hence the notion of a toast to someone's honor with a beverage. In the 18th century, when tea was commonplace in Britain, it was a natural mate for the light aristocratic breakfast. When colonists arrived in America, so did toast, made on hearths or wood stoves, with or without the aid of a wrought iron toast rack.

In the late 1800s, with vegetarianism on the rise among the newly formed Seventh Day Adventist Church in Battle Creek, Michigan, toasts—particularly brittle, double-baked zwieback toast—enjoyed the breakfast spotlight as a means by which nourishment could be quickly and affordably derived, in addition to being an ideal delivery system for other foods. The concept of serving foods like stews or porridges atop a slice of stale bread was hardly new; in lieu of tableware (which had yet to be invented), "trenchers" had been the norm throughout the Middle Ages. Wealthy classes often ate only the food on top and threw the trencher to the dogs or to the poor.

Zwieback gained popularity among the Seventh Day Adventists and other Clean Living Movement adherents. *Every-day Dishes and Every-day Work* by Ella Kellogg listed numerous recipes for breakfast toasts, including those with stewed lentils, warm grapes, or creamed tomatoes; "[t]he foundation of all these toasts is zwieback," she wrote. Today, zwieback in America is mostly used as a snack for teething babies, but in Italy the zwieback-like *fette biscottate*—a hard, double-baked sweet bread eaten with butter and jam—is regularly served with coffee for a light *prima calazione* or "first breakfast."

Milk toast is another classic. Throughout the 19th and early 20th century, toast served in warm, sweetened milk was a common children's breakfast, and like many foods for children, enjoys a comfort cult following. Preeminent food writer M. F. K. Fisher has described milk toast as a "warm, mild, soothing thing, full of innocent strength" and "a small modern miracle of gastronomy."[16]

French Toast

The first written mention of French toast by name occurred in *The Accomplisht Cook* (1660), but rather than today's rich, custardy affair, this was essentially a recipe for bread soaked in wine, similar to the ancient Greek breakfast *akratisma* or the English *sowpes dorry* ("golden sops") from the 14th century cookbook *Forme of Cury*. Most early recipes for anything resembling today's eggy French toast were intended for dessert, as is the French *pain perdu*.

Recipes from 14th-century Germany for *arme Ritter*, or "poor knights" suggest that "French" toast is really a misnomer. Arme Ritter was food for German soldiers who could afford only eggs for protein. Before World War I, it was even known in the United States as "German toast." In 1905, recipes for German toast appeared in ladies' magazines as a "delectable dish" for breakfast. Within five years, the new French label was used to remove the association with Germans after the war.

Rolls and Muffins

Several types of small, round breads lend themselves well to breakfast. Among them, English muffins, bagels, and biscuits stand out as being both a suitable bread on their own (often served toasted, with butter and jam or another simple spread) as well as serving as the platform for any variety of breakfast sandwiches.

English Muffins

As opposed to American muffins, which are chemically leavened quick bread, English muffins are yeast-leavened bread rolls that are cooked on a hot griddle instead of being baked in an oven. In the United Kingdom they are simply called "muffins."

During the reign of the first King George (1714–1727), muffins were toasted on forks, which had just begun gaining widespread use in Great Britain. Interestingly, during the time of George's reign muffins were not called muffins yet, nor did the word appear in Samuel Johnson's 1755 *A Dictionary of the*

English Language, as pointed out by Charles Dickens in his essay "Dainty Breads," featured in volume 4 of his journal *All the Year Round.*[17]

It is unclear why the word "muffin" was missing from the English dictionary when it appears in other published works of the time. One thing is clear, however; the muffin was for breakfast. "And taking some muffin, I'll have breakfasted before these *Pray madams* and *Pray my dears,* have seated," wrote English author Samuel Richardson in his 1753 epistolary novel, *The History of Sir Charles Grandison.* Breakfast muffins began appearing in American texts shortly after, gaining the "English" descriptor in the early 19th century, during which time Americans and Canadians had also learned the English technique of splitting, toasting, and buttering their muffins (and began to differentiate from the small, cake-like muffins of America). By 1841, *The Knickerbocker* (also known as *New York Monthly Magazine*) called the English muffin "that dream of farinaceous enjoyment." Today, English muffins are usually served toasted and spread with butter and jam, or with eggs, cheese, and breakfast meats as a sandwich.

Bagels

Bagels are a well-loved symbol of the Jews of New York. By the 14th century, Jewish artisans and traders had brought bagels and pretzels from the West to Kraków, Poland, independently of Germans who were introducing the ring-shaped breads to Polish markets. Centuries later, Jews brought the bagel to America from Europe.

Although it is true that in the 1890s, Ashkenazi Jews were the only people in the United States eating them, bagels had never really been a central culinary Jewish icon until they were popularized in the urban areas of the Northeast, specifically, in the Jewish delis of New York, which were also patronized by gentiles. When bagels with lox and *shmear* (cream cheese) became strictly for breakfast is unclear. They make an appearance on the breakfast table in playwright Max Shulman's 1954 comedy *The Tender Trap,* but other than that they are not widely mentioned in American writing before the 1960s, when Lender's mechanized, frozen bagels, previously only available at his Connecticut bakery, swept American grocery stores.[18]

Though Harry Lender was, himself, a Jewish baker originally from Poland, his Americanized version of the bagel—sweeter and softer than traditional bagels—appealed to the American gentile palate that had become accustomed to factory-made white bread. Lender's bagels were far removed from what most Ashkenazi Jews considered a real bagel; they were not too ethnic for the

American masses. Furthermore, buyers did not need to venture outside of the safety of their neighborhood supermarket to obtain them. Soon, blueberry bagels replaced Jewish pumpernickel, and in the 1980s Kraft Foods bought the Lender's Frozen Bagel company as the perfect partner to their Philadelphia Cream Cheese.

Biscuits and Scones

Like the English muffin, the biscuit is another bread of muddled etymology. Outside of the United States, the biscuit is a crisp cookie, but in America it is a small, round quick bread like a scone or the Scottish farl. Rusk, a twice-baked biscuit, was very dry and was usually broken into one's coffee or tea at breakfast. American biscuits are eaten hot, buttered with jam or honey, or with sausage-studded milk gravy, as they do in the South. Scones were typically eaten for tea, but the potato ("tattie") scone and oaten farl—both favorites of poet Robert Burns—are still part of a full Scottish breakfast or Ulster fry.

Biscuits emerged as a bread distinct from a crisp cookie or cracker in the early 19th century. Before the American Civil War, yeast was somewhat expensive and difficult to store, but chemical leaveners such as saleratus (sodium

Making biscuits, 1939. Courtesy of the Library of Congress.

bicarbonate, or baking soda) and pearlash (potassium carbonate) were afford-able, if sometimes bitter and unpleasant. Chemical leaveners, for all their short-comings, had one thing going for them: they were fast. In her 1837 *Directions for Cookery in its Various Branches*, cookbook author and etiquette specialist Eliza Leslie describes the preparation of several biscuits; of those, her soda biscuits are a dead ringer for modern American biscuits:

> Melt half a pound of butter in a pint of warm milk, adding a tea-spoonful of soda; and stir in by degrees half a pound of sugar. Then sift into a pan two pounds of flour; make a hole in the middle; pour in the milk, etc., and mix it with the flour into a dough. Put it on your paste-board, and knead it long and hard till it be-comes very light. Roll it out into a sheet half an inch thick. Cut it into little round cakes with the top of a wine glass, or with a tin cutter of that size; prick the tops; lay them on tins sprinkled with flour, or in shallow iron pans; and bake them of a light brown in a quick oven; they will be done in a few minutes. These biscuits keep very well.[19]

It is a good thing that these biscuits keep well, because this recipe makes ap-proximately nine dozen of them.

For a plantation worker in the South, breakfast was necessarily the most sub-stantial of the day's meals. Biscuits with "country" or "white" gravy scratched together from sausage, pan drippings, flour, and milk were affordably made from the foodstuffs that were in low supply after the American Revolutionary War. Biscuits and gravy are still emblematic of Southern cooking.

Similar to biscuits and gravy is creamed chipped beef on toast. Since World War II, American soldiers have referred to the dish by the dysphemistic "shit on a shingle," or S.O.S. for short. This might sound harsh, but many veterans had fond memories of S.O.S., and as a breakfast item, it has been popular in the Mid-Atlantic and Northeast regions of the United States since the 1930s. Creamed chipped beef on toast is often enjoyed on a biscuit or English muffin in lieu of the more accurately shingle-like toast, but many of the chain restaurants that featured the dish on their menus have since switched to country gravy.

Despite claims that biscuits keep well, most home cooks simply prefer freshly baked biscuits. That said, many home cooks do not want to prepare them from scratch. In 1930, a Louisville, Kentucky, baker named Lively Willoughby came up with a way to store premade biscuit dough in a cardboard tube that could be stored in the refrigerator. After a few failed attempts that resulted in explosions of dough being scraped off the ceiling, Willoughby developed a technique that successfully contained ready-to-bake, pre-portioned dough. He sold his idea to Ballard & Ballard Flour Company, who was purchased by Pillsbury twenty years later. Today, many home cooks opt for the convenience of ready-made biscuit dough, which, according to the original 1931 advertisement, can be baked "while the bacon broils or the table is being set. . . . Now, in less time than you need for making toast, you can serve hot biscuits for breakfast, whether you have a cook or not."

Sandwiches

Breakfast sandwiches of scrambled or fried eggs, cured meats, and cheese, served on English muffins or biscuits (sometimes on bagels or croissants), are a convenient—and therefore popular—way to eat in the morning, but the breakfast sandwich experienced a somewhat stunted genesis. All of its components—bread, egg, cheese, smoked meat—had been on the same breakfast plate for hundreds of years before anyone thought to stack them together, even after the sandwich had become a fairly regular part of most English diets. After the Civil War, variations on what would later be known as the breakfast sandwich (though not yet eaten for breakfast) were becoming firmly entrenched in the American culinary dialect. American pioneers ate ham and egg sandwiches on their westward journeys, but were not strictly eaten in the morning. The first recipe for a true breakfast sandwich, written in 1897, appears in cookbook author Maud C. Cooke's delightfully garish *Breakfast, Dinner and Supper, or What to Eat and How to Prepare It.*[20]

> Breakfast Sandwich.—Use stale bread. Spread each slice with chopped meat; cover with another slice and press together. Cut each sandwich in halves and place them on a plate. Have ready a pint of milk, salted and mixed with 1 beaten egg. Pour this over the sandwiches and let stand a few moments. Put a heaping teaspoonful of butter into a frying pan and when it begins to brown place the sandwiches carefully upon it. When nicely browned on one side add a little more butter, turn, and brown the other side.

Sadly, outside of the United States, most breakfast sandwiches are not nearly as sumptuous as Maud Cooke's Monte Cristo–style hot sandwich. Many Scandinavians and other northern Europeans eat an open-faced breakfast sandwich called *butterbrot*, or "buttered bread," with a spread of fruit preserves, honey, chocolate-hazelnut spread, or a meat-based spread such as liverwurst. Cheese or thinly sliced cured meats like ham or salami are also fairly standard. The French eat slices of baguette with butter and jam (*tartines*) with coffee; the Italian version is nearly identical, but the bread, *fette biscottate*, is a hard and lightly sweetened zwieback or a bread roll (*panino*). Yeast spreads like Marmite and

Scandinavian breakfast featuring butterbrot, 2011. Courtesy of Ewan-M, Creative Commons.

Vegemite are eaten on bread or rolls in Australia and New Zealand. In the Middle East and southern Europe, a platter of fresh-baked flatbread with spreadable yogurt cheese called *labneh* or crumbly feta cheese, olives, figs, and cucumbers are offered at the breakfast table, unchanged by thousands of years of history.

With fast food giant McDonald's introduction of the Egg McMuffin in 1972, the rest of the world would quickly develop a taste for the American version of the breakfast sandwich. Soon, biscuits or English muffins with eggs, American processed cheese, and ham or sausage could be enjoyed by every corner of the globe. In Hong Kong, the Egg McMuffin is served twenty-four hours a day because eggs are not strictly breakfast fare to the Chinese.

In the American Southwest, the burrito has supplanted the sandwich as a preferred convenient breakfast food. In 1977, in rural Lake Arthur, New Mexico (forty minutes south of Roswell), a housekeeper named Maria Rubio was rolling a burrito for her husband's breakfast, when she noticed the face of Jesus Christ in a char mark on the tortilla. She saw the visage as a sign from God, and the Miracle Tortilla was soon drawing crowds from all around, eager for a chance to see the holy burrito for themselves. Rubio quit her maid job to set up the "Shrine of the Holy Tortilla" in her home. Eventually, she moved the shrine to a shed in her back yard, where it was graced with more spots due to the desert heat; in 2005, Rubio's granddaughter took the divine breakfast burrito to school for show-and-tell, where it was accidentally dropped, shattering to pieces. The shrine has since been closed, and the remaining shards of the Miracle Tortilla have been retired to a drawer in the Rubio home.

The hand-held breakfast reached the apex of absurdity at the turn of the 21st century, with the introduction of Jimmy Dean Pancakes & Sausage on a Stick by the consumer goods company the Sara Lee Corporation. It was available in such flavors as Original, (artificially flavored) Blueberry, and Chocolate Chip, both in "stick" and in stick-less "mini" form. On his television program *The Daily Show*, political satirist Jon Stewart said of the new breakfast product, "finally, the classic taste of chocolate chip pancake wrapped sausage, with the convenience of a stick." Due to poor sales, the chocolate chip flavor was discontinued a few years later.

Pancakes and Waffles

When they are not wrapped around sausages and stabbed onto a stick, pancakes are a prevailing breakfast food. The Greeks made *tagenites* with wheat flour, wine, and curdled milk, fried them in olive oil, and served them with honey for breakfast, but these were considered to cause crude humors by 3rd-century physician Galen.[21]

One 16th-century recipe from *Good Huswifes Handmaide for the Kitchin* is quite rich, consisting of a staggering *pint* of heavy cream, four or five egg yolks, and a mere handful each of sugar and flour. The batter is seasoned with ginger and cinnamon (a common way to show off one's wealth in the early modern period), leavened with ale, then fried in brown butter. Twenty years later, writer Gervase Markham's *The English Huswife* (1615) included a comparatively austere recipe using water instead of milk or cream, and only two or three egg yolks; Markham adds a greater wealth of spices, adding mace, cloves, and nutmeg, but omits the sugar, instead opting to serve the pancakes with "sugar strowed upon them."[22] "There be some which mixe Pancakes with new milke or cream," Markham comments, possibly in a coy intimation at the anonymous *Good Huswifes* author, "but that makes them tough, cloying, and not so crispe, pleasant and savory as running water."[23] Having tested it himself, food historian Ken Albala reports in his comprehensive *Pancake: A Global History* (2008) that this recipe is "remarkably dull and ponderous" and found that combining it with the earlier, more decadent recipe yielded pleasant results, not unlike the modern pancake.[24]

Most early American recipe books (penned by English authors in the New World) include recipes for very thin pancakes that result from batters heavy on egg and dairy and light on flour, as seen in the earliest recipe. It was likely from

Hannah Glasse's *The Art of Cookery* (1747), which included recipes for pancake batter with enough flour to achieve "a proper thickness," that most early Americans learned to cook pancakes.[25] The first truly American cookbook, Amelia Simmons's 1796 classic *American Cookery*, features several recipes for "pan cakes," though these do not appear until the second edition of the book. Her "Federal Pan Cake" is an amalgam of the English pancakes from other cookbooks and her own maize-based Indian Slapjack.[26]

Of course, the cornmeal-based hoecakes and johnnycakes had been eaten since long before the colonists arrived. Cornmeal flatbreads called *pone* were prepared by the Algonquian Indians who already inhabited the Atlantic seaboard before the arrival of colonists from England; corn pone is still eaten for breakfast in the South. In the South, johnnycakes were also called hoecakes for the special flat hoes typically used for growing cotton, which did double duty as griddles. Hoecakes were made of a slightly thicker dough; in New England, similar pancakes were made using a thinner batter, and had been called johnnycakes since the 1730s.

In most cases, these maize pancakes are made from cooked cornmeal mush, rather than dry cornmeal mixed into a batter. This technique was reported by

Teamsters with the Federal Army of the Potomac making hoecakes in front of their tent, 1862. (AP Photo/Mathew B. Brady)

the earliest colonists in the 17th century, and two hundred years later, johnny-cakes were considered a specialty of freed slave cooks; it is likely that African slaves learned the recipe from the early Native American slaves. During his rare stays at Mt. Vernon, George Washington's favorite breakfast was reportedly three of these simple cakes, "swimming in butter and honey."

By the 19th century, buttermilk pancakes, too, became a typical American breakfast. In her *Godey's Lady's Book Collection of Receipts and Household Hints* (an 1870 collection of recipes from *Godey's Lady's Book* magazine), Sarah Annie Frost gives a recipe for "buttermilk breakfast cakes" that reads like a typical modern pancake batter recipe, minus the eggs.[27] The batter is leavened with the acid-base reaction of baking soda and buttermilk, and baked on a griddle. Most of Frost's breakfast quick bread recipes are remarkably similar to those of today. Hers all use sour milk and baking soda for the breakfast versions, rather than a proper leavening, which is a great time-saver; however, she offers the caveat that they are "neither as good nor [as] healthy."[28]

Another classic American pancake addition, the blueberry, is native to North America; in fact, one species, the New Jersey blueberry (*Vaccinium caesariense*) is specifically indigenous to the place its name implies. Strangely, no one thought to put blueberries into pancakes (or write about it) until the end of the 19th century. American children's author Sarah Chauncey Woolsey (under the pen name Susan Coolidge) included in her story *Eyebright* (1879) a scene in which the titular girl, while visiting a country house in coastal Maine, is met with a new dining experience:

> Did any of you ever eat blueberry flapjacks? I imagine not, unless you have summered on the coast of Maine. They are a kind of greasy pancake, in which blueberries are stirred till the cakes are about the color of a bruise. They are served swimming in melted butter and sugar, and in any other place or air would be certain indigestion, if not sudden death, to any person partaking of them. But, somehow, in that place and that air they are not only harmless but seem quite delicious as well. Eyebright thought so. She ate a great many flapjacks, thought them extremely nice, and slept like a top afterward, with never a bad dream to mar her rest.[29]

It did not take long for blueberry pancakes to travel outside of New England to the rest of the country; today, few American breakfast restaurants would dare expect to stay in business without them on the menu. Unlike the flapjacks eaten by Eyebright, early recipes instruct the cook to stir in blueberries very gently, to keep the juicy berries intact (and to avoid turning the pancakes the hue of a contusion). This is first seen in the recipe for blueberry griddle cakes included in *Miss Parloa's Young Housekeeper* (1894), written by pioneer of the "Domestic Science" movement, Maria Parloa.[30]

Most early cookbooks placed pancakes with waffles. Both breakfast cakes are flat, made of batter, fried with a little fat, and eaten with syrup or honey, but because waffles are cooked in a honeycomb-pocked iron rather than a flat griddle, most experts agree that they are not the same as pancakes at all.

The earliest (14th century) waffles really were more wafer-like, and the similarity in names is no coincidence; they consisted of little more than pressed, unleavened bread dough, and were much crispier than the fluffy, modern version. Throughout 16th-century Holland, waffles were sold by street vendors who were mandated by law to keep a distance of six feet from one another. They were enjoyed by aristocrat and peasant alike; as always, the poor ate their dull version made of rye, and the wealthy enjoyed wheaten waffles enriched with milk and eggs.

The Dutch brought waffles to America in the 1620s, but "waffle" did not come into English usage until the 18th century, with royal chef Robert Smith's 1725 *Court Cookery*. Soon, the waffle craze took off in New York, and waffle parties (or sometimes "frolics") were a fashionable way to socialize from the mid-1700s until the early 1900s; incidentally, this is when waffles became a breakfast standby. Sweet and savory toppings were enjoyed on waffles, ranging from the expected butter and maple syrup or honey to, of all things, kidney stew.

In the early New York jazz era, musicians chose not to decide between sweet and savory, instead opting for both. Having finished playing their gigs too late for dinner, yet too early for breakfast, they ate waffles with fried chicken and maple syrup on top. Though this combination of fried chicken and waffles was purportedly invented by the Harlem restaurant Roscoe's in 1938, chicken and waffles appear in literary sources from the late 19th century in Philadelphia, and recipes show up in cookbooks of the same time and place. In *Mrs. Rorer's Philadelphia Cook Book: A Manual of Home Economics* (1886), domestic scientist Sarah Tyson Heston Rorer offers fried chicken and waffles together on a supper menu, but three years earlier, home economist Estelle Woods Wilcox's *The Dixie Cook-Book* had already suggested serving them together for a proper Southern lady's breakfast.[31]

Breakfast Cakes and Other Pastries

If the batter from pancakes or waffles is baked in a tin instead of poured straight onto a griddle, muffins are the result; if poured into a loaf pan, one produces a coffee cake. The batters used for all of these are nearly indistinguishable, varying only by the amount of liquid and cooking time involved. These were usually grouped together as breakfast foods in cookbooks starting in the mid-19th century. Prior to that, some breakfast cakes were listed with desserts or "confectionary cakes" rather than among other breakfast dishes; one such cake by professed housekeeper Charlotte Mason is included among other "ordinary" or "plain" cakes in *The Lady's Assistant for Regulating and Supplying Her Table* (1777):

> An ordinary Breakfast Cake. Rub a pound and a half of butter into half a peck of flower [*sic*], three pounds of currants, half a pound of sugar, a quarter of an ounce of mace, cinnamon, and nutmeg together, a little salt, a pint and a half of warmed cream, or milk, a quarter of a pint of brandy, five eggs, a pint of good ale-yeast; mix it well together, bake it in a moderate oven. This cake will keep good a quarter of a year.[32]

This recipe reads more like one for biscuits or yeasted scones, and even with a jolly half cup of brandy added, it is unlikely that this cake would still be very good after three months. The use of cinnamon, nutmeg, and mace, though, are reminiscent of more modern coffee cakes.

For those preferring their cake a bit more temperate, tastemaker Sarah Josepha Buell Hale has another offering from her 1839 *The Good Housekeeper, Or, The Way to Live Well and to Be Well While We Live.* Her breakfast and tea cakes, though not nearly as sweet or brandied as Mason's (and resembling today's breakfast muffins), come with a warning:

> If I thought there was any hope of the advice being followed, I would say do not eat warm cakes at all; cold or toasted bread is far better for the constitution. But as most people will have warm bread of some kind, a part of the time, at least, I consider it better to give directions for the sorts which seem likely to do the least injury; only adding here, that those persons will be *least* likely to be injured who eat the smallest quantity of hot cakes in proportion to their cold bread, which our customs allow.[33]

Hale notes that her Breakfast Cake (which, like Mason's, is more like a biscuit than any cake one would encounter today), could be baked with sour milk and baking powder to be "less likely to injure the health" than those raised with yeast. A more salutary breakfast cake appears in M. Tarbox Colbrath's *What to Get for Breakfast* in 1882. The "East-Wind Gems" are made from Graham flour, which, like many high-fiber foods, had some flatulent effect, as her book includes a disclaimer with the recipe. "You need not fear the east wind they may have imbibed, for the hot oven counteracts its mischievous influence, and they are not only hygienic, but taste good."[34]

Coffee cake has been eaten for breakfast since the latter half of the 19th century, originating from the European streusel-strewn batter cakes, particularly *aranygaluska* of Hungarian Jews and the earlier German *streuselkuchen* and *kaffeekuchen*. Dutch *ontbijtkoek* is another variation, differing primarily in its use of rye flour, but adding the familiar sweet spices cinnamon, nutmeg, mace, and cloves to the brown sugar streusel sprinkled on top (*streusel* is the German word for "a sprinkling"). A specialty of Groningen in the northeastern tip of the Netherlands, the *oudewijvenkoek*, or "old hag's cake" is lightly flavored with anise seed and eaten in thick, butter-smeared slices for breakfast. The name is said to come from the palatability of the soft bread to the dentally challenged elderly.

Pastry

With their higher fat content and flakier, lighter texture, pastries have long been a decadent alternative to simple breads. By way of the Babylonians, the technology and ingredients to produce pastry were in place in ancient Egyptian kitchens, along with the professional bakers to wield them, but sweet breads like croissants did not become a part of the breakfast menu until the mid-1800s.

Today, the croissant is a mainstay of the French *petit déjeuner*, but it was not introduced to France (or the breakfast table) until the mid-19th century, when Austrian artillery officer August Zang opened his *Boulangerie Viennoise* (Viennese bakery) in Paris in the late 1830s. The *kipferl*, a popular item in Zang's bakery, was renamed "croissant" by the French for its crescent shape. By 1869, it was considered a breakfast staple, and in an 1872 issue of his weekly journal *All the Year Round*, in "The Cupboard Papers, VIII: The Sweet Art," Charles Dickens calls the Austrian "the perfect baker" (though in mentioning Switzerland, he offers that he had "eaten some delightful little rolls in the heart of the hills") and includes "the dainty croissant on the boudoir table" among his plethora of other delectable European breakfast breads.[35] Serendipitously for the croissant, chocolate and coffee were also beginning to be taken in the chambers before facing the day.

In 1915, "patisserie savant" Lauritz C. Klitteng brought the Danish pastry from his bakery in Læsø, Denmark to the wedding of U.S. president Woodrow Wilson. Two years later, an article in the *Oakland Tribune* described Klitteng's pastry rather favorably: "you just tuck a small morsel under the tongue, roll up the eyes, say 'Ah-h' as though there were a sky-rocket present, and it fades away and trickles down to the barbed-wire entanglements of the soul, a subtle something that clings like an opium eater's dream. In other words, Danish pastry is said to be good eating."[36]

Soon, the pastry began appearing in bakeries and restaurants in New York City, where it was filled with fruits like apples or berries, or sweetened baker's cheese; by 1930, the Danish pastry was on breakfast menus in eateries across America.

Doughnuts

Ring-shaped foods and fried dough share a long history. According to Aristophanes, ancient Greeks were enjoying a ring-shaped bread made of flour and honey called *dispyrus*—a baked precursor to the doughnut—since at least the 5th century BCE. Unfortunately for the Greeks, coffee would not be introduced to them for another two thousand years, so in proper ancient Greek form, they dunked their doughnuts in wine instead.

Fried dough is eaten for breakfast throughout Asia, usually as an accompaniment to congee; unsweetened *youtiao* have been eaten in China since the 11th-century Song Dynasty. In Taiwan, chewy *youtiao* with sweetened condensed milk and coffee is a common commuter's breakfast. The Cantonese name translates to "oil-fried devil," in an act of defiance against Chancellor Qin Hui, widely regarded as a turncoat to the Song Dynasty's beloved General Yue Fei. The shape of the doughnut—two long pieces of dough joined in the center—is said to represent the shape of the Chancellor joined at the hip with his similarly double-crossing wife. Frying and eating the dough is a symbolic punishment doled out to the traitorous couple.

Early Germanic people had perfected fried dough as early as the 10th and 11th centuries, when *oliebollen* ("oil balls") were eaten to stave off the Teutonic goddess Perchta. Perchta was vengeful and particular: On her day (which occurred during the Yule, at the end of the "twelve-nights," or the twelve days between Christmas and the New Year), anyone who partook of foods other than her favorite fish and porridge (sometimes thickened into dumplings, depending on the region) would have their belly sliced open, stuffed with straw and bricks, and sewn back shut. Eating greasy oliebollen prevented this; her blade would simply slide right off one's belly.

By 1850, doughnuts were specifically prepared for breakfast, under the pseudonym "fried breakfast cakes," as seen in Sarah Annie Frost's *The Godey's Lady's Book Receipts and Household Hints*.[37] Though a bit sweeter than her fried breakfast cakes, Frost's recipe for doughnuts, "an excellent fried cake," as she calls it, is nearly identical. Her recipe for "old-fashioned doughnuts" uses yeast rather than baking soda; confusingly, in today's doughnut shops, "old-fashioned" refers to a specific cake-type doughnut, not the yeast-risen variety.[38]

A century after the first American doughnut recipes were published, heart-throb Clark Gable appeared in the 1934 film *It Happened One Night*, and dunking doughnuts in one's coffee became a customary way of enjoying two breakfast standbys simultaneously. Three years later, Krispy Kreme opened its flagship doughnut shop in Winston-Salem, North Carolina; in 1950, Dunkin' Donuts opened the first of its chain in Quincy, Massachusetts. With over half its sales in coffee, not doughnuts, Dunkin' Donuts likens itself more as a competitor with coffee giant Starbucks than to Krispy Kreme or Tim Hortons, the Canadian doughnut chain that opened in 1964. Thanks to Dunkin' Donuts' wildly successful advertising campaign in the 1980s, however, to most Americans, it will always be "time to make the donuts."

DAIRY

Dairy products have been part of the human diet since the beginning of the Neolithic period. Dairy spread from southwestern Asia to India, but by the 14th century the Ming Dynasty Chinese avoided dairy as a way to distance themselves from the "heathen" Mongols. Cultural differences aside, most East Asians simply cannot digest raw milk, along with approximately 60–70 percent of adult humans. A gene mutation allows some milk drinkers to tolerate lactose, and continued lifelong exposure to dairy may have also trained the human body to process it without trouble. For some people, fermenting dairy products with live cultures abates this problem.

Yogurt

Yogurt made from the cultured milk of cows, sheep, goats, yaks, camels, and buffalo is eaten everywhere—its consumption dates back to around 8,000 years ago. Most scholars agree that the first cultured dairy products were probably made unintentionally, from feral bacteria living in bags made from goatskin that transformed milk into thick curds.

As early as 500 BCE, yogurt with honey was already known in India as *amrta*, or ambrosia—"food of the gods," appearing in Vedic Sanskrit texts. Pliny the Elder noted that

[i]t is a remarkable circumstance, that the barbarous nations which subsist on milk have been for so many ages either ignorant of the merits of cheese, or else

have totally disregarded it; and yet they understand how to thicken milk and form therefrom an acrid kind of milk with a pleasant flavor.[39]

By the turn of the 11th century AD, the first written records of the word "yogurt" appear in medieval Islamic texts written by Turkic scholars from what would become the Ottoman Empire. In the 16th century, King Francis I of France suffered from a debilitating and theretofore untreatable case of diarrhea, when an Ottoman doctor cured the King's flux with sheep's milk yogurt. Delighted at his recovery, Francis declared yogurt *"le lait de vie eternelle,"* or "milk of eternal life."

During the same late-19th-century health boom of the American cereal magnates, Russian biologist and Nobel Laureate Ilya Ilyich Mechnikov made great strides in understanding the beneficial effects of lactic acid on human health. Based on his observations of the diets of Bulgarian centenarians, Mechnikov claimed that regularly ingesting lactofermented foods would prolong one's life, and drank "sour milk" every day. Following Mechnikov's lead, John Harvey Kellogg heartily endorsed yogurt, and served it at Battle Creek Sanitarium, to be eaten first thing in the morning for breakfast, and then taken again an hour

Turkic woman and boy selling yogurt and rice porridge for New Year's festival, between 1865 and 1872. Courtesy of the Library of Congress.

later, a different way. "The Yogurt enema . . . produces remarkably rapid curative effects," he claimed.[10]

When Mechnikov died in 1916 at the age of seventy-one, his claims of yogurt's powers of longevity began to be doubted by some Americans; however, the effects on digestion and the intestines had continued to show promise, and the probiotic craze was already firmly under way among spa-hopping health fanatics. Yogurt's popularity in the United States skyrocketed when it began to be produced commercially in the 1930s and 1940s by East Coast companies Columbo and Sons Creamery in Massachusetts and Danone (renamed Dannon) in New York. In 1947, Dannon began to produce yogurt in a single-serving size with strawberry preserves already in the cup, being the first company to give Americans yogurt with "fruit in the bottom."

In many cultures (pardon the pun), yogurt is strained for twenty-four hours to remove some of the whey and achieve a thicker consistency; in the United States, this is often called "Greek" yogurt. If yogurt is strained past the "Greek" stage an additional twenty-four hours, *labneh*—or yogurt cheese—is the product. Labneh is rolled into balls, partially dried, and stored in olive oil to preserve. Eaten with flat bread, olives, cucumbers, figs, and dates, labneh has served as the morning protein throughout the eastern Mediterranean, North Africa, and the Levant for thousands of years.

Cheese

By around 4500 BCE, Neolithic migration had brought dairying from the Fertile Crescent to the Middle East, Europe, and India. Wherever these early farmers traveled, cheese making soon followed. Cheese making (and lactose tolerance) was already widespread throughout Mesopotamia by the time Genesis was written (5th–6th century BCE).

By the time of Greek physician Martial and Roman philosopher Pliny the Elder in the 1st century, smoked goats' milk cheeses from Luna and Vestini (now near the Italian regions of Liguria and Abruzzo, respectively) were eaten for breakfast. Martial notes in Book XIII of his *Epigrams* that the cheese from Luna, marked with the emblem of the moon in tribute to Diana, "will serve your slaves a thousand times for breakfast" and of Vestine cheese that "in case you desire to break your fast economically, without meat, this mass of cheese comes to you from the flocks of the Vestini."

Halloumi, a semi-firm, unripened, brined cheese made of sheep's and goats' milk has been a Cypriot specialty since the Byzantine era. Across the Levant, a breakfast of fried halloumi cheese is eaten on flatbread drizzled with honey; Arabs prefer it with olives and *za'atar* (a mix of oregano, basil, thyme, sesame seeds, sumac, and salt). While cheese was enjoying its infancy in the cradle of civilization, the Celts were perfecting their own cheese and introducing their techniques all over Europe. Celtic cheeses made from cows' milk were already in France, Belgium, Switzerland, and the Balkan Peninsula by the time the Romans invaded Europe in the 1st century, and was imported back to Rome after the invasions.

The 16th century saw a great expansion of cheese—or at least of written descriptions of it—just as breakfast began to lose some of its stigma for the English. By the 1700s, cheese and bread were commonplace at the breakfast table. In his 1622 *The Compleat Gentleman*, English poet Henry Peacham talks of boorish Spartans "having for breakfast a browne loafe, and a mouldie cheese, or (which is ten times worse) a dish of Irish butter."[41]

Throughout Europe today, breakfast would not be complete without a platter of cheeses, cured meats, and bread. In Germany, there is a unique tradition of eating rather strong *Frühstückskäse*, literally translated as "breakfast cheese." A relish called *Handkäse mit Musik* ("hand cheese with music") is made by marinating the breakfast cheese in vinegar and topping with onions, and has been eaten in the Odenwald region of Hessen, Germany, for at least 400 years. This relative of famously odoriferous Limburger is named for its having been shaped by hand; the music, it is said, comes "after."

Cheese was sometimes eaten with eggs in 19th-century America, though it certainly had not become the staple it was in Europe, perhaps in part due to the Clean Living Movement's insistence on breakfast foods with a more evacuative effect. *The New Century Cook Book*, compiled by the Wesley Hospital Bazaar Committee in 1899, included an intriguing recipe for "Mr. G.M.D.'s Cheese Fondu [*sic*] for Breakfast."[42] It is not necessarily that the recipe itself is remarkable, but that it is a recipe for Welsh rarebit under a different name. Other recipes for rarebits appear in cookbooks of the time, but never for breakfast. It is difficult to understand why not; the dish called "golden buck" takes the Welsh rarebit's rich cheese custard on toasted bread and does it one better, topping the whole affair with breakfast-appropriate poached eggs, yet this was not a breakfast dish. The Yorkshire rarebit goes further still, slipping slices of bacon between the cheese sauce and egg, and yet it was a supper item. Incredulity aside, a simpler version of the rarebit—the humble cheese on toast—persists today as a staple of time-strapped breakfasters throughout the United States and Great Britain.

CHAPTER 2

Potted Cheeses

Many milder, younger, or "fresh" cheeses are eaten for breakfast in northern
Europe and North America. Because they have not been pressed or aged into
cakes or wheels, they require cold storage in containers or "pots." In Europe,
quark (from the Russian *tvorog*) is made by heating soured milk until the proteins denature; the soft curds are strained to remove some of the whey, and then
the product is creamed. The texture, like thickened sour cream, is soft enough
to be spread on crispbread, which is usually how it is eaten for breakfast. Similar
to yogurt parfaits in the United States, in Europe, quark is also sometimes eaten
with müesli and fruit.

Some people eat cottage cheese with fruit (usually canned crushed pineapple or peaches), while others prefer it with tomatoes or toast, seasoned with
salt and pepper. The style in which one eats their cottage cheese appears to be
something of a personal divide; people always seem to eat it one way and balk
at the other. People today rarely eat it alone, as "curds and whey," had by the
arachnophobic Little Miss Muffet in the 16th-century nursery rhyme penned by
her father, physician (and entomologist) Thomas Moffet.

By the late 1800s, cottage cheese started appearing in bills of fare and menu
planners as a healthy breakfast food, rather than strictly for tea or as a side dish
for supper. At around the same time, American author Marion Harland offers in
Breakfast, Luncheon and Tea (1875) instructions for creating a shortcut version
of the "famous English cream cheese" by beating cottage cheese until smooth
with a bit of butter and sweet cream. The earlier, more complicated versions involved mixing new milk and cream with a bit of rennet to set it, layering on salt,
then applying a weight or press and allowing the mix to drain in a cheesecloth
to remove the whey until sufficiently thickened. Though cream cheese was often
mentioned as a specialty of Newport, Lincolnshire (on the central east coast of
England), the earliest recipes are actually from Scotland.

Another method for making cream cheese required filling an ox's or cow's
bladder with fresh cream and hanging it in the cellar for three weeks to allow
the whey to drain and the remaining solids to curdle. To avoid the unappetizing
flavor of urine, the softer exterior of the cheese was scraped off, and then the remaining product could be molded or potted. "It will eat at first like butter, having the taste of cheese," described agrarian Robert Maxwell in the mid-1700s.[43]

By the 1840s, Americans had already developed a taste for cream cheese,
but by then it was Philadelphia, not Lincolnshire, that had the reputation for
quality. In 1872, thirty years after American cookbooks began extolling the
virtues of cream cheese (while lamenting its short shelf life), a dairyman named

William Lawrence embarked on its first commercial production. Though his factory was located in Chester, New York, the product was named Philadelphia Cream Cheese in 1880 to capitalize on the city's gourmand notoriety. Lawrence sold his trademark to the Phenix Cheese Company in 1903, and Phenix merged with Kraft Cheese Company twenty-five years later. [44] Kraft still owns the Philadelphia trademark, and has continued to dominate the cream cheese market ever since.

As a modern breakfast food, cream cheese is a favorite spread for bagels but not much else, despite the insistence of Kraft's advertisements to "butter your bread with Philly instead." Regardless, the bagel stronghold is enough to keep cream cheese relevant as a breakfast food; since the 1950s the "New York breakfast" has been effectively defined as a bagel with smoked salmon and cream cheese.

EGGS

Bird eggs have been an important source of energy for humans since prehistory. Nest robbing was a relatively risky, but worthwhile, way of obtaining protein. Besides bread, no food was more heavily relied upon in the Middle Ages than the egg. In the 13th century, Italian physician Aldebrandino da Siena wrote in *Le Régime du Corps* (*Plan of the Body*) that the eggs of chickens or partridges were best, because besides being the most nutritious, they "engender the best blood and are most suitable to human nature." Next in line according to Aldebrandino were duck eggs, which "nourish poorly"; followed by goose, which nourished fine but were "gross and heavy." Ostrich eggs—one of which is equivalent to two dozen chicken eggs—were preferred less than goose, but worst of all were peacock eggs, because they are "heavy and bad smelling, and engender bad and poisonous humours."[45]

Egg cookery reached fantastic heights in the 15th and 16th centuries. During the Renaissance, European households could not always afford meat, but eggs could be produced every day without much land, and by the mid-1500s, eggs were no longer banned on meatless days. By the 17th century, French and Italian cookbooks featured more than a hundred ways to enjoy eggs.

In 19th-century America, too, eggs were served in a variety of ways, alongside other dishes, much as they are today. They were simultaneously sophisticated and affordable, an uncommon combination of qualities in those days. Cookbook author Marion Harland championed these properties of the egg. "'Elegant and frugal!' I shall have more hope of American housewives when they learn to have faith in this combination of adjectives."[46] She called eggs "nutritious, popular, and never (if we except the cases of omelettes, thickened with uncooked flour and fried eggs, drenched with fat) an unelegant or homely dish."[47]

In England, however, eggs did not become a major breakfast food until after World War I. In Edwardian and Victorian times of cheap food and plentiful servants, the egg was overshadowed by richer, meatier dishes like sautéed mutton kidneys and veal in jelly. After the war, when cooks and ingredients were hard to come by, eggs stood in as an affordable, available, and easily prepared breakfast food, but they never regained the status they enjoyed in their Renaissance glory days.

Boiled

Boiling in the shell is among the simplest ways to cook an egg; it requires no ingredients but water and takes little skill. Hard-boiled eggs are one of the earliest convenience foods, portable and with a long shelf life. Although the U.S. Department of Agriculture recommends that hard-boiled eggs should be refrigerated immediately, and consumed within one week for safety, this was not always common convention. On the contrary, boiling was once a way to *extend* the storage capacity of eggs. In 1838, English agriculturist Walter B. Dickson offered these tips:

> Another way to preserve eggs is, to have them cooked in boiling water the same day they are laid. On taking them out of the water they are marked with red ink, to record their date, and put away in a cool place, where they will keep, it is said, for several months. . . . At the end of three or four months, however, the membrane lining the shell becomes much thickened, and the eggs lose their flavour.[48]

Loss of flavor, not safety, was the reason to eat the eggs within four months. The authors add that if the eggs were boiled the same day as they are laid that "the taste is said to be so well preserved that the nicest people may be made to believe that they are new-laid."

If an egg is cooked such that its white is just set (yet the yolk is still runny), it is said to be coddled. This is most easily accomplished by adding an unbroken egg to boiling water (or an egg coddler), then turning off the burner and allowing the egg to cook in the latent heat as the water cools. Originally, coddled egg recipes called for lightly beaten egg to be cooked in hot milk and butter in a double boiler, but by the end of the 19th century, the term started to refer to eggs cooked in the shell until "the white (is) soft and jelly-like and the yolk soft but not liquid," writes Sallie Joy White, Boston's first female journalist, in *Cookery in the Public Schools* (1890).[49]

Soft-boiled eggs are cooked until the white is set, while the yolk remains runny; these are usually eaten from eggcups, which are highly collectible. Soft-boiled eggs are often served with toast, sometimes cut into strips for dipping into the runny yolk. In England, this simple breakfast is known as egg with toast "soldiers" or just "egg soldiers." It is unknown why the toast strips are called soldiers; the earliest citation is from the 1966 *Oxford English Dictionary*. One popular (if obvious) explanation is that they were named for their vague resemblance to upright soldiers in a day when many children played with toy army men. This dish is still a nostalgic comfort food for many English; incidentally, the term "soft boiled" refers to someone who is soft hearted or sentimental, in appropriately stark opposite to the callous and tough "hard-boiled" person (usually used to describe detectives).

At the end of the 19th century, many breakfast recipes used hard-boiled eggs in ways unheard of today. Phillis Browne treated the egg with the utmost respect in *The Dictionary of Dainty Breakfasts* (1899).[50] Among the myriad "fundamental dishes" that include poached and fried eggs are a number of "trifling accessories" for which plain boiled eggs "should be properly regarded."[51] Ironically, among the so-called fundamental breakfast dishes are the more frivolous preparations, such "Eggs à l'Aurore," which consist of toast poured with hot white sauce mixed with finely diced hard-boiled egg whites, sprinkled with breadcrumbs and the hard-cooked yolks (run through a sieve), garnished with croutons and parsley, and presented with slices of tomato.

If eggs are boiled a very long time, perhaps six or more hours (with or without onion skins), the Sephardic Judeo-Spanish dish *huevos haminados*, or hamine eggs is created, also known as *beid hamine* in Egypt. The long cooking process allows the Maillard reaction to brown the egg whites inside the shell, creating a mahogany-colored treat with a meaty, nutty flavor and a tender, creamy texture. It is sold as a street food for a Saturday breakfast in many parts of the Middle East and Levant, alongside tomato salad, fried eggplant, and the pickled mango condiment called *anba*.

Poached

Eggs broken into a hot liquid for cooking have been eaten since at least the days of the 2nd-century Roman physician Galen, who wrote of *oa pnikta* (eggs poached in white wine). Aldebrandino da Siena wrote in the late 13th century that "poached eggs strengthen natural warmth, especially when they are cooked to neither hard nor soft, because the water eliminates their harmfulness, and they are better eaten that way than any other way."[52] A recipe for "Pochee" appears in *Forme of Cury* (1390), featuring eggs served in a sauce made from egg yolk and milk, and since the recipe was written by "the chief master cooks of King Richard II," it was seasoned with expensive saffron and ginger.

By the 17th century, many physicians and other dietary advisers had begun recommending eating a breakfast of poached eggs without the rich custard, but seasoned simply with vinegar, salt, and pepper. In *The English House-Wife* (1615), Gervase Markham took the next step by instructing the addition of vinegar to the raw egg prior to adding it to the pan of boiling water. Cookbooks from the 18th century onward advise adding vinegar to the boiling water instead; acidulated water causes the albumen of the egg to seize up sufficiently to produce a soft, neatly contained mass rather than the feathery shards seen in Chinese egg drop soup.

Today, the most well-known way to enjoy a poached egg for breakfast is the Benedict, harkening back to the 14th-century tendency to serve the eggs with a rich custard. Eggs Benedict is a dish of poached eggs served atop sliced or Canadian bacon and toasted English muffins, draped in Hollandaise sauce prepared from egg yolks, melted butter, and lemon juice. There are several conflicting accounts of the invention of the dish, all of which place its conception in New York. The earliest of these stories claims that it was created in the Waldorf-Astoria Hotel in 1894. In the same year, however, it was already on the menu of the University Club in San Francisco. In the January–June 1894 issue of *Overland Monthly*, two gentlemen are enjoying a luncheon "which consisted of Blue Points, potted char, eggs *à la Benedict*, and a remarkable Maraschino jelly."[53] Within only three years, the Philadelphia-based magazine *Table Talk* (volume 12) published a recipe in response to a letter from Savannah, Georgia, requesting it. The recipe called for ham, poached eggs, and Hollandaise on toast; in 1898, *Eggs and How to Use Them* presented the arrangement on today's familiar English muffin instead.[54]

If the ham is substituted with spinach, the dish is known as eggs Florentine. *Eggs and How to Use Them* distinguishes eggs Florentine as being served on an artichoke bottom with diced chicken and mushrooms. If the two versions are combined—poached eggs, spinach, and Hollandaise served on an artichoke bottom—the result is eggs Sardou. Eggs Sardou was invented at Antoine's in 1892, when superstar playwright Victorien Sardou visited the New Orleans restaurant, where it still appears on the menu.

Cured

In China, salted duck eggs (*xián yā dàn*) are eaten as a condiment to the break-fast jook (congee). These cured eggs have a runny, salty white, and a firm, bright-orange yolk. The eggs are prepared by curing in brine or by packing them in salted charcoal paste (in the Philippines they often use salt mixed with clay from an anthill or termite mound). The eggs are dipped in the salty paste, arranged in a wooden box lined with newspaper, and left to cure for twelve to fourteen days; they are then wiped clean and boiled in nets, fifty eggs at a time. Duck eggs are typically used because they have thicker shells and withstand mass cooking better than chicken eggs.

Similarly, Century eggs, or *pidan*, are another long-cured egg eaten with congee. The 600-year-old process for creating them is not unlike that of the salt-cured duck egg, but in addition to salt, wood ash and quicklime are added to boiling tea to make a paste. The alkaline mud is mixed with rice husks and caked on the egg, and these are stacked in clay jars to cure for several months. For those wishing to rush the process, lead oxide may be added to the mix; this obviously results in a product that is poisonous, so zinc oxide is used to the same effect by the more scrupulous of the impatient manufacturers. When they are ready to eat, the white of the egg has turned to a translucent, dark-brown jelly and the yolk is a mucky, blackish green with a creamy texture and the tan-talizing aroma of sulfur and ammonia.

Roasted and Baked

Roasting in the shell was probably an early way of cooking eggs, alongside meats. It was a favored method of the Celts, and Martial confirms that the Ro-mans were well acquainted with eggs roasted in hot ashes in the 1st century. In modern Sephardic societies, roasted eggs are eaten on Sabbath morning. These are the same *huevos haminados* resulting from a six-hour simmer; they can be prepared either in a pot of water or in the coals, but are either way left to cook overnight in the dying fire to ensure that the Jewish commandment that prohib-its cooking on Shabbat will not be broken.

In the 15th century, Italian Renaissance writer Bartolomeo Platina described the technique of famous cook Maestro Martino of Como on the art of cooking eggs on a spit. "Pierce eggs lengthwise on a well-heated spit, and roast near the fire as if it were meat. They have to be eaten hot. This is a stupid concoction, one of the absurdities and games of cooks."[55] Though it does not necessarily demonstrate that spit-roasted eggs were eaten for breakfast, it does speak to the one-upmanship of Renaissance egg cookery.

English poet Alexander Pope said in the 18th century that "[t]he vulgar boil, the learned roast an egg," though the practice had evidently died out some time earlier. When and why this style of egg fell out of fashion remains unclear, though it is plausible that roasting in the hot ashes of a wood fire ceased in 16th-century England when, due to wood shortages, coal became the fuel of choice.

Eggs "roasted rare in embers make the thickest and strongest blood," noted Dr. Thomas Moffet in *Health's Improvement* (1655).[56] Two centuries later, *Eggs: Facts and Fancies About Them* (1890) presents a compelling case for bringing roasted eggs back, with a bit of a warning: "People . . . have discovered anew this delightful way of serving eggs. A soft, velvet-like substance results, which cannot be obtained by any other method of cooking. Unless the shells are slightly pricked, a sudden explosion may surprise the watchers round the camp-fire."[57] To avoid the dangers of hot eggshell shrapnel, one may follow the advice of self-described "Gastronomer" Ange Denis M'Quin, who explained in *Tabella Cibaria* (1820) that "the cottager half buries his eggs in an upright position in hot ashes upon the hearth; and when a clear dew-drop oozes on the top of the shell, the eggs are fit to be eaten."[58]

Shirred eggs are first cracked open and then baked in a ramekin or gratin dish, or perhaps a pot-sherd, which is where 19th-century literary critic Richard Grant White supposed the use of "shirred" originated. His appears to be the first written use of the word to describe the dish known in France as *oeufs cocotte* ("eggs in a casserole"). Interestingly, the first written recipe for *oeufs* cooked in "*Les Cocottes*" appears in English, written by royal chef Louis Eustache Ude to introduce French cooking to average English households.[59]

Robert May's 17th-century *Accomplisht Cook* provides instructions for baking eggs in a pan of butter and sauced with fried onions, or "Eggs in Moon shine." If one were to poach the eggs in hot oil or melted butter, this was "Eggs in Moon shine, otherways." Eggs were also baked in a sauce of onions thickened with bread, which dates back to the Middle Ages. Hannah Glasse featured a recipe for eggs in bread sauce in *Art of Cookery Made Plain and Easy* (1747), and by the end of the 19th century it was a favorite breakfast dish in American households.

Beaten

Once eggs have been cracked and beaten, they can be cooked several ways, or they can be simply stirred into hot rice as they do in Japan for *tamago kake go-*

han, or "egg sauce over rice." The egg partially cooks in the rice's heat but stays a bit raw, appealing to the Japanese love of *nebaneba*—gooey and slimy foods.

Omelet, Frittata, and Tortilla

The earliest omelets are thought to have been cooked in ancient Iran. Consisting of egg batter combined with chopped herbs, fried into a firm, flat disc, and served in wedges, it was nearly indistinguishable from modern *kookoo sabzi* eaten on the morning of *Nowruz* (Persian New Year). From Persian *kookoo* (also called *eggah*), the concept of the omelet spread through the Middle East and North Africa to Europe, impressing itself onto Spanish and Italian culinary tradition with the *tortilla* and *frittata*, respectively.

The proper French *omelette* was first mentioned in the medieval housewife's guidebook *Le Ménagier de Paris* in 1393 as either *alumete* or *alumelle*; there is even a recipe for a heavily herbed version that may have been inspired by Persian *kookoo*, but was also very similar to the botanical *erbolat*—or "herbolade" (a "confection of herbs"), from *Forme of Cury*, published three years earlier. [60]

By the 1830s, omelets were considered a fine breakfast for the upper and middle classes of England and America. Fancier versions with cheese, bacon, or fresh herbs were included in English and American books of French cookery during the mid-19th century. The American Denver omelet, made with peppers, onions, and diced ham, came from the western sandwich of the pioneers, which was essentially the Denver omelet served on sourdough. After the railroad was built in Utah in 1870, the southwestern region of the United States was connected by rail to the rest of the country, and the Denver name was ascribed to the western omelet shortly thereafter. The Denver omelet is nearly indistinguishable from the *omelette à l'Espagniole* or "Spanish style" omelet from *Eggs, and How to Use Them* (1898).

In the Philippines, people eat an omelet similar to the western version. The breakfast *torta* (not to be confused with the Mexican sandwich) is an omelet stuffed with any number of things: usually leftovers of some type of meat like ground beef, pork patty, or even crabs, as well as vegetables like tomatoes, onions, eggplant, or potatoes. This dish was introduced by the Spanish, who brought their nightshade vegetables and the *tortilla* during their 16th-century conquests, but the Spanish likely did not enjoy the dish with garlic fried rice and banana ketchup the way Filipinos do today.

The Spanish tortilla (not to be confused with the Mexican flat bread) is usually prepared with waxy potatoes and served in thick wedges as an afternoon *tapa*. The original Italian version, the frittata, was also traditionally a midday food co-opted to the North American breakfast table only as recently as the 1920s. Like the Spanish tortilla, frittata is usually served in wedges, and not always hot.

Quiche

If the raw frittata mixture is poured into a pastry shell, a quiche is created. Recipes for savory custards baked in a pastry shell with herbs or meats date back to at least 14th-century England. Though the word is French and considered by most to be a French dish, quiche originated in the western Germanic kingdom of Lothringen (renamed Lorraine by the French in 1766). Indeed, the most well-known variety is quiche Lorraine, made of beaten eggs mixed with fine *lardons* of bacon. Modern quiches may include spinach, cheese, mushrooms, broccoli, or other vegetables, but to be a true quiche Lorraine, there must be bacon.

By the 1950s, the American cookbook *The Joy of Cooking* included quiche among other breakfast dishes, but quiche's popularity reached its zenith in the 1970s. In 1982, humorist and screenwriter Bruce Feirstein wrote *Real Men Don't Eat Quiche*. The book satirically cast quiche as an overtly feminine food in the context of American culture, and may have been successful at it; the book sat on the *New York Times* bestsellers list for more than a year and in the 1980s quiche's popularity plummeted.

Scrambled

Scrambled eggs were fashionable in 18th-century France, but before that, they were often included with pastry recipes, as a sweet dish flavored with candied lemon peel or marmalade. Various cookbooks by the 17th-century father of modern French cookery, François-Pierre La Varenne, included a few savory treatments, including scrambled eggs with cheese, or cooked with meat broth and served on toast.

Scrambled eggs were sometimes called "rumbled" eggs, particularly in Scotland; another name, buttered eggs, persisted as synonymy into the 19th century, even after "scrambled" eggs came into written use in 1864. To minimize confusion, Scottish author and feminist Margaret Dods helpfully noted in *The Cook and Housewife's Manual* (1862) that buttered eggs are "the Scotch rumbled eggs, and the French *oeufs brouillés*."[61] Her basic recipe calls for an unusually complicated technique, asking that the cook "*skink* [pour] the mixture backwards and forwards, setting it on the fire occasionally, but keeping it constantly briskly agitated till thickened."[62] A spoon might have been easier.

Scrambled eggs in the 18th and 19th centuries were usually eaten on toast, and by the turn of the 20th century they were served at breakfast with numerous accompaniments to enhance the flavor. *The Dictionary of Dainty Breakfasts* (1899) offers one important tip on scrambled or buttered eggs: "[t]hey should never taste of [V]aseline."[63] Barring any hint of petroleum jelly, the book suggests cooking them with a variety of other ingredients, such as tomatoes, curry, anchovies, and pâté de foie gras.

Fried

"Anybody, almost, can fry an egg wrong. It takes some skill to fry one exactly right," wrote Martha McCulloch-Williams in *Dishes & Beverages of the Old South* (1913).[64] Truer words were never written, though McCulloch-Williams likely never knew how true they were; the eggs she ate were fried by her Mammy, rather than herself. To fry an egg without breaking the yolk would be a simple enough task unless it needs to be flipped. Though it is one of the most basic abilities of even a greasy spoon line cook, many chefs today consider a properly cooked egg to be an effective gauge of culinary skill. The difficulty of frying an egg on both sides is belied in its colloquial nickname: "over easy." If a fried egg is cooked on only one side, it is called "sunny-side up."

Fried eggs enjoy as long a history as most other cooked eggs. The ancient Greeks enjoyed *oa tagenista*, or eggs fried in a *tagenon*—a clay skillet similar to the tagine used in the Mediterranean today. In the 14th century, the *Piers Plowman*, William Langland's great allegorical narrative poem, talks of "wilde brawen [boar] and egges yfryed with grece," evidence that fried eggs with ham are firmly entrenched in English culinary history.[65]

Since the early 1900s, children in England, the United States, and Canada have enjoyed a breakfast called eggs-in-the-basket, also known as egg-in-the-hole, among myriad other names.[66] The dish is prepared by cutting a hole in the center of a piece of bread. The bread is fried or toasted in a pan with butter, and an egg is cracked into the hole to fry in the center of the toast. Because of the simplicity of its preparation, the dish is a campsite classic, earning mention in a 1950 issue of *Boys' Life Magazine* as "nest eggs."

Huevos rancheros, or "ranch-style eggs" is a traditional Mexican dinner dish made of fried (sometimes scrambled) eggs in a spicy chili sauce, served on a corn tortilla. Between the 1930s and 1950s, American tourism to Mexico tripled, and huevos rancheros began appearing on Mexican hotel breakfast menus to appeal to northern appetites for eggs in the morning and today, huevos rancheros is an American breakfast dish.

MEAT

Whether it was hunted or scavenged, early humans were lucky to obtain meat. Once humans began domesticating animals in the Neolithic, meat became a more predictable source of protein, and the sedentism that accompanied the period promoted the concept of drying meat near fire for long-term food storage. When salt and smoke were added to the equation, flavor could be enhanced considerably while extending shelf life, and cured meat was born.

Meat was never such a popular breakfast food as it was during the 1800s and early 1900s. In 1908, *Mrs. Gillette's Cook Book: Fifty Years of Practical Housekeeping* (written by *White House Cookbook* author Fanny Lemira Gillette) suggests an astonishing array of suitable viands for "a comfortable breakfast":

> Broiled chops, broiled beefsteak, broiled chicken, broiled fish, broiled quail on toast, broiled Hamburger steak, fried veal cutlets breaded, fried ham and eggs, fried chops, fried liver and bacon, fried sausages, fried oysters, fried pigs' feet, fried pork tenderloin, fried chicken, fried tripe, fried tomatoes with mutton chops, fried steak, fricasseed tripe, fricasseed kidneys, corned beef hash, codfish balls, creamed codfish, stewed meats on toast, creamed dried beef, poached eggs on toast, oysters on toast, salmon on toast, omelets of various kinds, eggs cooked in many ways.[67]

Meat, throughout history, has been afforded by only the world's wealthiest people. This remains true today in most of the world, though some impoverished Americans find that mass-produced fast food meats are still more affordable than fresh produce or cereals. In affluent northern European countries, meats are eaten for breakfast nearly daily; in developing countries, meat is a rare luxury.

Pork

For breakfast, there is perhaps no more versatile meat than pork. In the 17th century, Samuel Pepys wrote in his diary of breakfasting on a "Coller of brawne," a cut of pork close to the shoulder that typically yields spare ribs and chops.[68] Prehistoric inhabitants of Europe utilized smoke to cure ham and bacon, and the technology was firmly in place by the time English missionary Saint Boniface was warned to stick to boiled and smoked bacon while traveling among the "heathen" tribes of Germany in the 8th century.

Bacon

For those who do not reject pork, bacon has been a breakfast favorite since the 17th century. Though most 19th-century physicians considered meat too heavy for the morning (particularly following the medieval and modern eras' unofficial ban on breakfast, as well as the Clean Living Movement's penchant for whole grains), at least some doctors found a dose of bacon in the morning to be harmless, if not healthful. In 1890, bariatric physician Isaac Burney Yeo counterintuitively declared that "[b]roiled fat bacon at breakfast is, with many persons, an easily-digested form of fat."[69] Of course, being an obesity specialist, Dr. Yeo may have had a financial interest in promoting the consumption of bacon fat.

During the Victorian era of food surplus and plentiful household staff, daily bacon was a given. It could be prepared ahead of time and kept warm in a chafing dish until the master and lady of the house rose for breakfast. In the American West, bacon was a staple of the frontier. Cured bacon was lightweight and versatile, a must for the wagon trail. Travel writer and claim-staker Lansford Hastings advised in 1845 that for the trek to Oregon, the emigrant should provide himself with, among other things, a minimum of 150 pounds of bacon. The bacon most pioneers carried was a slab of fatback, stored in a barrel of brine. Most pioneers had coffee and bacon every morning, with warm bacon fat smeared across a biscuit or a piece of cornbread left over from the previous night's dinner.

In the early 1920s, the totemic "bacon and eggs" was popularized by public relations pioneer and nephew of Sigmund Freud, Edward Bernays. To promote sales of bacon on the heels of Adventist health fanaticism (when the typical breakfast was coffee, a roll, and orange juice), he surveyed 5,000 physicians and reported the recommendations that "a hearty breakfast" is better for the health of the American people than a light breakfast. Bernays then extrapolated the results, creating a PR frenzy with his announcement that doctors recommend bacon and eggs as a hearty and truly American breakfast. Newspapers ran with it, and bacon sales increased in the United States as a result of Bernays' tactics of recruiting third-party experts. Perhaps not coincidentally, the American Heart Association was founded in 1924.

Ham

Like American and English bacon, ham-like Canadian bacon—the relatively lean, back bacon trimmed of its fat—became common on breakfast tables at the turn of the 20th century, especially when served with an English muffin, a poached egg, and Hollandaise sauce, as eggs Benedict. In the late 1800s, Canadian bacon had established for itself a reputation for quality, and began to edge cheaper American bacon out of British markets. Canadian hogs fed on peas, yielding a firmer, leaner product that sold for a higher price in England, whereas American hogs were often fattened on corn, or—noted derisively by Canadian agricultural journals of the time—on acorns. Incidentally, acorn-fattened pork is now the most expensive in the world, selling for upwards of $100 per pound.

Ham was a mainstay of Colonial homes, and in 1775, traveling clergyman Andrew Burnaby wrote of the excellence of Virginia ham, noting that "[i]n several parts of Virginia the ancient custom of eating meat at breakfast still continues . . . it is the custom to have a plate of cold ham upon the table; and there is scarcely a Virginian lady who breakfasts without it."[70] Ham remains a favorite accompaniment to grits and biscuits in the South, and to eggs everywhere.

Sausage

Undoubtedly, the utility of early charcuterie was a reason for its prevalence; *Apicius* (4th century) included an entire chapter dedicated to it.[71] Highly seasoned, smoked sausages masked the ill odors of meat past its expiration date, if the spices and smoke did not kill some pathogens outright. The sausage met an untimely (and fortunately, temporary) end when Constantine I banned it in the 4th century for being made of blood (forbidden by the Bible) and for the meat's resemblance to a certain pagan fertility totem. This is not, however, the etymology of the British sausage known as the "banger."

Although Europeans had perfected sausage-making over the millennia, the first to be specifically called breakfast sausages did not begin popping up in American and English cookbooks and ladies' magazines until the end of the 19th century. The addition of sage to the uncured pork distinguished breakfast sausage then, just as it does today, but it is unclear why; perhaps the strong flavor of sage helped mask the odors of meat going bad without refrigeration, or the antibacterial effects of the aromatic mint relative could have prevented illness. Breakfast sausage, or country sausage, as it is also known in the United States, has remained an important source of protein in a traditional farmer's breakfast. In rural and urban areas alike, cooked, crumbled sausage is stirred into gravy and eaten on biscuits, forming what many would consider the base of the culinary heritage of the South. Sausage patties, too, are often eaten on biscuits or English muffins as sandwiches (with or without eggs and cheese), a common item on fast food breakfast menus.

Beef and Mutton

Breakfasting on beef, for the affluent, was a nearly daily occurrence. Rich, meaty breakfasts would eventually fall out of favor thanks to the tireless efforts of dieticians, but caloric austerity did not hit home for most working-class people until wartime rationing in the early 20th century.

In the Victorian golden age of breakfast, the problem may not have been *what* people were eating so much as *how* the foods were prepared. In 1864, health reformer and hydropathist Thomas Low Nichols disdained that "butter and lard are so cheap that they are used with great profusion, and the best viands and vegetables are rendered indigestible."[72] Nichols suspected that the "nice things which Americans eat for breakfast" were not so much to blame for the growing rates of illness as were the great amounts of grease used to prepare them.[73]

The idle upper classes and white-collar "brain workers" required lighter fare in the morning than laborers; this is just as true today as it was a hundred years ago. Farmers and lumberjacks paid little heed to the likes of Nichols, Graham, and Kellogg, and continued filling up on chicken fried steaks with cream gravy well into the 21st century. The antithesis of the hygienic brown bread and grapefruit breakfast served at the sanitaria, the breaded and fried beefsteaks began appearing in regional American cookbooks in the 19th century. Mary Randolph's 1838 *The Virginia Housewife* features a recipe for veal cutlets that somewhat resembles chicken fried steak, and was very likely inspired by the traditional *wiener schnitzel* introduced by German and Austrian immigrants arriving in Texas in the 1830s.

Chicken fried steak (or country fried steak, as the dish is known east of the Red River) was quickly adopted in the Southwest as a way to utilize tougher cuts of the abundant range-raised beef available to ranchers. Cowboy cooks perfected the recipe, and during their heyday from the end of the Civil War to the 1880s, they were the first to serve the steaks as a proper chuck wagon breakfast with gravy, fried potatoes, biscuits, and boiled coffee. By the 1930s, most recipes for the dish accompanied one for cream gravy, which is the way it is most often eaten for breakfast today, both on the farm and in truck stop diners across North America.

In affluent households of the Colonial and Victorian eras, lamb chops were a favorite. They "are a convenient, simple, and dainty breakfast, being readily accomplished, requiring only nicety and attention," wrote M. Tarbox Colbrath.[74] Colbrath was not the only cookbook author to consider the daintiness of the lamb chop; in his 1885 *Breakfast Dainties*, Thomas Jefferson Murrey notes that "dainty lamb chops require but a moment's cooking," and suggests serving them with sweet butter and French peas.[75]

Mutton seems to have been more predominant in England than stateside. On what she calls "the great cold mutton question" (presumably, whether or not one should eat it), English cookbook author Mary Hooper wrote of mutton in 1873 that "for potted meat, mince to be eaten with eggs, *rissoles* [pastry-covered meatballs], or a dry hash or curry, nothing can be more suitable for making a change from the everlasting bacon and eggs of the national breakfast."[76]

World War II soured many Americans and British on mutton. Servicemen came home from war with a bad taste in their mouths from the vast quantities of canned mutton they were fed while abroad, the quality of which was scarcely fit for dogs. The flavor of mutton, to many, was the foul taste of war. In 2004, Charles, the Prince of Wales, launched the Mutton Renaissance Campaign to attempt to reinvigorate the British taste for the meat, but despite His Royal Gusto, mutton chops are seldom seen on breakfast menus these days.

Poultry

In Victorian and Edwardian times, before World War I eliminated cooking staff from many English kitchens, chicken breakfasts were still a fairly common occurrence in wealthier households. In the late 19th century, many cookbooks included recipes for using up leftovers from a chicken dinner. Chicken à la king (under a different alias), fricassees, and croquettes were all fair game as dainty options for the breakfast table. In *Common Sense in the Household: A Manual of Practical Housewifery* (1871), Marion Harland included a recipe for a ragoût of turkey that was apparently intended to make use of Thanksgiving leftovers, as it includes a spiced sauce sweetened with cranberry or currant jelly, and instructions to "[l]eave out the stuffing entirely; it is no improvement to the flavor, and disfigures the appearance of the ragoût."[77]

Before in-home refrigeration was widely available, however, most people did not typically eat poultry in the morning. This is because poultry were typically killed right before dressing, a task that was impractical to complete early in the morning or the night prior. Poultry was also not usually smoked or cured, so large stores of fowl were uncommon before cold storage became commonplace.

Chicken breakfasts were a rare delicacy, one that was coveted enough by Civil War infantrymen that several written works mention it specifically. In one story, the soldier was sustained through a bloody battle by keeping his mind on his precious chicken breakfast. Two grueling days later, he finally did enjoy the chicken that he had tied to his backpack; even though he did not have any salt, it had been "highly seasoned" with gunpowder. In another, three Yankee soldiers make a plan to steal chickens in the night from a Confederate barn, risking life and limb to do so. The three were successful, enjoying the chicken breakfast they desired, except for one of them; after being hit in the back of the head with a crowbar during their escape from the farmer, he could only drink the broth because it hurt too much to chew.[78]

Following the Civil War, fried chicken became stigmatized as a food for black people. Ironically, though deep frying was likely brought to the United States from West Africa by slaves, fried chicken was too expensive to be more than a rare treat for most black people. Nonetheless, fried chicken did begin to appear in breakfast cookbooks by the late-19th century, thanks largely to the new availability of home refrigeration, affordable flour, cast iron cookware, and lard. *Breakfast Dainties* (1885) distinguished the Southern style of fried chicken as breaded with flour before frying in pork fat and finished with white gravy.

Nowadays, no fried chicken would be served for breakfast without waffles or biscuits, a trend that took more than a century to catch on. Though home economist Estelle Woods Wilcox presented fried chicken and waffles as a Southern lady's breakfast in *The Dixie Cook-Book* in the 1880s, outside of the South the pairing has only been a regular offering for the past few decades. And despite the explosion of fried chicken-biscuit sandwiches on mainstream fast food menus over the past few years, the concept of fried chicken at breakfast is still quite foreign to many Americans. In a 2008 piece for *Time* magazine, comedian Joel Stein wrote about the recent addition of the chicken biscuit to the McDonald's breakfast menu that "[t]he biscuit is soft and buttery, and while I don't love chicken, this is at least clearly decent, non-McNugget chicken, boldly presented without sauce. . . . Yet I still don't feel that it's breakfast."[79]

In response to health concerns, bacon and sausages made from turkey became more widely available in the 1980s, but as Andrew F. Smith notes in *The Turkey: An American Story* (2006), even though turkey sausage, for example, contains only 20 percent of the calories of pork sausage, turkey products in general contain roughly twice the sodium as the pork products they are intended to replace. The flavor of the turkey bacon is more reminiscent of ham than bacon, but for millions of dieters and pork-abstainers, turkey bacon is a godsend.

Seafood

For hungry 1st-century fishermen, a hot fish breakfast was also a godsend. Along with bread, it is one of the only breakfast foods mentioned in the Bible, in an early post-mortem appearance by Jesus. After having spent all night fishing in the Sea of Galilee, the disciples rowed upon the shore to see Jesus cooking fish beside a fire. According to the gospel of John, "Jesus said to them, 'Come and [have] breakfast.'"[80]

Kippers are a cold-smoked herring, split along the belly and flattened before drying. Medieval Germans and eastern Scandinavians ate plenty of smoked herring, and by the 16th century, "red heryng" are mentioned specifically for breakfast, at least on fish days. Red, or "bacon'd" herring refers to smoked, or kippered herring, and was regarded then and for several more centuries as something quite special. During meatless Lent, it was a substitute for bacon.

That the name "kipper" comes from the Old English *cypera,* meaning a male salmon (and also related to the copper color of a spawning salmon), is evidence that the fish used was not always herring. Smoked salmon was still breakfast for many people, even after kippers became synonymous with herring. The lox of today's bagels, however, was a purely American invention, surfacing in the 19th century. Smokehouses opened all over New England, preserving a variety of fish. A few decades later, the transcontinental railroad in 1869 allowed traders to bring the Pacific Northwest's prolific salmon runs (cured with smoke and expensive salt afforded by the lucrative fur trade) directly to the East Coast, just in time for native Atlantic salmon runs to begin their decline.

Four years before the transcontinental railroad, English cookbook author Georgiana Hill detailed a simplified recipe for curing salmon that relies on brown sugar, with a little salt and saltpeter before smoking, providing an interesting peek into what was known as the "London cure" technique among Jewish immigrants to England, but with the addition of sugar typically found in the American Indian tradition.[81]

By the end of the 18th century in the Midwest and West, pan-fried fish had a place on the breakfast table among eggs and hoecakes; in the South, it was served with grits—unless one lived in the Low Country of Georgia and South Carolina, where shrimp has been the preferred accompaniment to grits since at least the 1890s. Of a fried fish breakfast, M. Tarbox Colbrath wrote that it "is very popular and often very convenient, yet very badly performed by many, and has more failures than any other cooking operation."[82]

In Jamaica, the Sunday breakfast called *ackee* and salt fish is the national dish. The ackee fruit, introduced to Jamaica by West African slaves before the 1770s, is related to the lychee but has a flavor and texture resembling scrambled eggs when cooked. The salted cod must be soaked in water to soften; the dish is then prepared by sautéing the salt fish with boiled ackee, onions, fiery Scotch bonnet chilies, and tomatoes, then seasoned with pepper and paprika. Salt fish caught on for breakfast outside the Caribbean, as well. American abolitionist and author of domestic manuals Lydia Maria Child wrote in *The Frugal Housewife: Dedicated to Those Who Are Not Ashamed of Economy* (1829) that "[t]here is no way of preparing salt fish for breakfast, so nice as to roll it up in little balls, after it is mixed with mashed potatoes; dip it into an egg, and fry it brown."[83]

For the Japanese, fish requires no such frippery. A simple piece of grilled or broiled fish with a little salt is part of a traditional Japanese *asagohan*, usually eaten with rice and miso soup, pickles, and perhaps a bit of rolled omelet; this has been the tradition for centuries. Of course, for the Japanese, seafood at breakfast does not necessarily stop at grilled fish. Cod or herring roe—served still in its bilobal sac—is another traditional breakfast, particularly during New Year.

Offal and Other Protein

For centuries, offal—literally derived from "off-fall," as in, "that which falls off the butcher's block," in Middle Dutch—has vacillated between being fancy comestibles for the wealthy and the waste parts suitable only for the lowest rung of society. Grilled mutton kidneys were on the first-class breakfast menu of the *Titanic* in 1912, while tripe *menudo* is a peasant dish firmly embedded in generations of Mexican heritage.

Fried sweetbreads or stewed kidneys served atop waffles in lieu of syrup began appearing on breakfast menus at around the turn of the 20th century. Kidney stew is still eaten on waffles for Sunday brunch in Baltimore, Maryland, but offal was never as popular on the British and American breakfast table as it was during the 19th century. Cookbooks ranging from frugal housewife's manuals to sophisticated hotel steward's guides abound with recipes for calf's liver, lamb's tongue, stewed tripe, and sheep's brains.

Brains were a particularly welcome addition because they were affordable, available year-round, and temptingly delicate. Brains could be dipped in egg and breadcrumbs for frying, they could be battered into fritters, or served with white sauce on toast. Still eaten in parts of the Midwest, brains and eggs are often scrambled together, or eaten as an omelet, based on the Portuguese *omolete de mioleira*. Brain cakes were a "good way of dealing with cooked brains left from the previous day," according to *The Dictionary of Dainty Breakfasts*.[84] "When sheep's brains are fried for breakfast," author Phillis Browne helpfully adds, "the rest of the head can be converted into brawn."[85]

"Brawn" in the old English sense referred to pretty much any pork that was boiled or pickled, noted in the lists of breakfast meats supped upon by the likes of Earl and Lady of Northumberland in the 15th century, as well as Samuel

Pepys in the 1660s. Later, it came to mean a head cheese—not a cheese at all, but a meat terrine in aspic—made from the head of a pig. However, as Browne notes, "[a] clever cook can make brawn of almost anything; yet nothing that is not absolutely dainty should be put into it."[86]

Originating in Westphalia, the same German region that perfected ham two thousand years ago, *pon haus*—or "scrapple" as it has been known since the addition of cornmeal at the turn of the 19th century—was also brought to the United States by the Pennsylvania "Dutch," and it remains a primarily rural food of the Mid-Atlantic states. Scrapple is essentially a cornmeal mush mixed with scraps of pork offal, and thickened with buckwheat flour. The book *Buckeye Cookery, and Practical Housekeeping: Compiled from Original Recipes* (1877) deems scrapple "nice sliced and fried for breakfast in winter" and this is precisely the way it is eaten today.[87]

Tripe is another of the butcher's castoffs to make it to the breakfast table, though for some reason it did not seem to attain the same level of appreciation by upper classes as liver, brains, and kidneys. Consisting of the lining of a cow's stomach, rubbery tripe requires long stewing or boiling to be edible. This is likely why most uses for tripe are, in fact, stews. Mexican menudo (made from cow's feet and tripe), requiring four to seven hours of cooking, was likely first eaten left over from the previous night's dinner. In restaurants, it typically only appears on weekend breakfast menus; this is possibly because of its time-consuming preparation, but may also be related to its reputation as hangover food.

In Vietnam, offal is commonly added to the breakfast *phở*. The brothy soup is made by boiling oxtails with charred ginger, shallots, and star anise, and beef tendon and tripe are commonly added with the noodles. Vietnamese culture expert and scholar Hữu Ngọc has declared phở to be his country's "contribution to human happiness"; as the national dish of Vietnam, it is frequently called the "soul of the nation."[88]

Of course, not only warm-blooded animals contribute their viscera to the breakfast table. For those with a palate for *chinmi* ("rare tastes"), *shiokara*—slivered cuttlefish served in the fermented entrails of sea cucumbers—may be found in tiny dishes alongside bowls of rice and miso soup in a traditional Japanese breakfast. Shiokara is reportedly so pungent that it is an acquired taste even for native Japanese; like most offal and fermented dishes of this type, it was probably eaten first out of necessity.

Even insects had a place on the breakfast table. In 1700, British emissary to Morocco Jezreel Jones wrote of the Moroccan Jews[89] that along with roasted eggs, baked chicken, and bread seasoned with cumin and anise seeds,

[t]hey esteem honey as a wholesome breakfast, and the most delicious that which is in the Comb, with the young bees in it, before they come out of their cases, whilst they still look milk-white, and resemble (being taken out) gentles, such as fishers use: These I have often eat of, but they seem'd insipid to my palate, and sometimes I found they gave me the heart-burn.[90]

Jones failed to mention that while chewing the sweet beeswax, the bee larvae produce a popping sensation in the mouth.

SOUP, STEW, AND LEFTOVERS (OTHER THINGS IN BOWLS)

Soups and Stews

Americans tend to forgo soups and stews until lunch or later; this appears to be but one of the national quirks that puts the United States out of step with the rest of the world. Elsewhere, plenty of people begin their day with a bowl of soup. The traditional Japanese breakfast features miso soup, and the rice soup–porridge hybrid jook is firmly engrained in the culinary heritage of China. For centuries, Mediterranean peasants had a bowl of soup with their watered-down claret wine in the morning.

As a way to stretch foodstuffs, soups and stews are essential to the diets of the poor, which could be why soups are the national foods of so many developing countries. Noodle soups are eaten for breakfast throughout Asia, reaching far beyond the "soul of Vietnam," phở. In southern Burma, where fresh fish is plentiful, a catfish chowder called *mohinga* is considered by many to be the national dish. Based on archaeological evidence, mohinga may have been prepared since as early as the 1st century, and has been hawked by street vendors as an "all-day breakfast" for at least a century.

In the western-style diners of Hong Kong, the Chinese interpretation of American food often results in strange new creations. One such bizarre item found on every *cha chaan teng* breakfast menu is ham and macaroni soup. The bowl of clear broth suspending elbow macaroni and sliced ham—usually sandwich-style deli ham, but SPAM also features prominently—is so popular that McDonald's added the soup to its Hong Kong breakfast menu in 2005.

Lamb and mutton stews have long been eaten for breakfast as well, in both Asia and the Mediterranean. The Anglo-Indian soup mulligatawny, which often included mutton, began its illustrious career as breakfast food for British colonialists in the 19th century, while being bumped from the dinner table. Indian cooking enthusiast Arthur Robert Kenney-Herbert noted in his *Culinary*

Jottings, a Treatise for Anglo-Indian Exiles (1885) that "[a]lthough a well-considered curry, or mulligatunny . . . are still very frequently given at breakfast or at luncheon, they no longer occupy a position in the dinner menu."[91]

Early American colonists enjoyed simpler stews. Historian Gideon Hiram Hollister wrote in 1855 that the breakfast of 17th-century farmers in Connecticut "often consisted mainly of a hearty soup made of salted meat and beans, seasoned with savory herbs. This dish was called 'bean porridge,' and has long been the fruitful subject of verse."[92] *Mrs. Lincoln's Boston Cookbook* of 1884 included a recipe for the stew based on beans and corned beef. The recipe contributor wrote that the "men folk" would carry a pot of the stew out to their early-morning lumberjacking excursions, and that "with their brown bread [the men] enjoyed this strong food as no modern epicure can his costly French dishes."[93]

A century or so later, the first French-speaking Acadian settlers to emigrate from Canada to Louisiana brought the tradition of sipping bouillon for breakfast with them. Since 1946, Brennan's Restaurant in New Orleans has reflected this tradition by including French-inspired turtle, oyster, and onion soups as well as a Creole seafood gumbo on its famous three-course breakfast menu, where it remains today.

Leftovers

Along with soups, the poor have relied on dinner leftovers for morning sustenance because they had little else to eat; however, economy of time, too, has long been a driving force behind breakfast choices. Dishes that are cumbersome and time-consuming are rarely prepared fresh in the morning, but are often eaten as leftovers from the previous evening.

Fried rice is an especially typical breakfast throughout Asia. Sweet-sour tamarind and jaggery (palm sugar) were added to Chinese soy sauce to make *kecap manis* (the cognate to ketchup), which still distinguishes Indonesian *nasi goreng* from Chinese fried rice. Leftover rice eventually found its way to Great Britain. No respectable Victorian or Georgian household would rise without a silver platter piled with kedgeree. At its core, the dish is simply cooked rice mixed with flaked leftover fish (sometimes smoked), moistened with butter. Cookbook author Mrs. Beeton added a teaspoon of mustard powder and two soft-boiled eggs; other cookbooks suggested adding saffron, cayenne, or curry powder for heat and color. *The Thorough Good Cook* (1896), by suggesting the addition of grated Parmesan cheese, launched kedgeree's descent into fusion cuisine.

In the Victorian era, Georgiana Hill's *The Breakfast Book* (1865) unveiled an array of other uses for leftovers. Variations on the meatball such as rissoles, dolpettes, and croquettes, made of "any kind of cold meat," each satisfied the criteria for any proper breakfast: dainty and economical. Hash made from leftover roast or corned beef mixed with diced, leftover potatoes was perfectly fine on its own, too, served simply on toast or garnished with poached eggs. Somewhat more complicated than a poached egg, Georgiana Hill (in a sentiment echoed by Eliza Leslie) posits that for a family breakfast, "[h]ashed calf's head should have the brains made into small cakes fried for a garnish."[94] Her family-friendly brain cakes sound marginally less horrifying once the recipe is read: "beat the blanched brains to a smooth paste, add shred sage, seasoning, and egg, sufficient to give them the requisite consistency; fry them of a fine brown."[95]

In England, if one had leftovers of a roast dinner, one could enjoy a breakfast of bubble and squeak. The name of the dish is onomatopoeic; said Mr. Beeswing ("an epicure") in Sir George Webbe Dasent's 1872 "Lady Sweetapple, or Three to One," he and his private school classmates were sometimes served the dish for breakfast "thirty or forty years ago," and that

> with us bubble-and-squeak was no metaphor; it was an awful reality. Still I have not told you what bubble-and-squeak is. Well, it is the remains of that badly-corned cow-beef cut into slices, and fried with greens or cabbage. I believe that it contains about five parts of nutriment to ninety-five of innutritious matter. All the good has been boiled and fried out of it; it tastes like leather and smells like cabbage; and a boy, if he has good teeth, no taste, and no sense of smell, may eat it for half an hour, and rise up taking nothing away with him except an indigestion.[96]

Georgiana Hill called bubble and squeak "an inelegant and not over-wholesome dish." Despite so many critics, bubble and squeak is still firmly attached to the Full English breakfast.

FRUITS AND VEGETABLES

"The American breakfast," wrote Marion Harland, "should be a pleasing medium between the heavy cold beef and game pie of the English and the . . . too light morning refreshment of the French."[97] This is a fair judgment that goes humorously unsupported by the recipes in her 1885 *Breakfast, Luncheon and Tea*, in which it seems that every breakfast dish is either a croquette, made of offal, or both. In fact, the only use for a vegetable in her breakfast chapter is as a potato croquette, breaded and fried in lard.

It is difficult to imagine a time when a breakfast of fried kidneys was a "pleasing medium" between beef pie and a slice of baguette with jam, when fruits and vegetables were so plentiful. Even once breakfast became more regularly established toward the last half of the 17th century, fruits and vegetables seem to have largely maintained a back seat to meats, eggs, and baked goods.

Fruit

In television commercials, a breakfast table is often displayed with a bowl of cereal, perhaps some eggs and bacon, or a piece of toast. Typically pictured alongside the wealth of proteins and cereals are various fruits: banana or strawberry slices in the Cheerios, a halved grapefruit, a glass of orange juice. "Part of this complete breakfast," the ads always assert, though fruit's contribution to the meal's completeness is only a relatively recent phenomenon.

As breakfast began its triumphant return, however, fruit did not seem to join the party right away. Aside from the odd baked apple, sliced tomato, or dram of whiskey "infused with berries that grow among the heath," fruits were more or less absent from cookery books and bills of fare.[98] If one wanted fruit at breakfast, jam on bread sufficed. Although the word "frugal" is derived from the Latin word meaning "to live on fruits," most guides to household thrift still focused breakfasts centrally on meats and relegated fruit to a condiment.

By the 1830s, that started to change. Going against the convention that fruits were best served as dessert, William Andrus Alcott, an American educator and physician (and third cousin to children's author Louisa May) believed "the breakfast hour is the most appropriate time for fruits."[99] Marion Harland added forty years later that "[t]he sight of the fruit-dish or basket upon the breakfast table has become so common of late years that its absence, rather than its presence, in the season of ripe fruits would be remarked, and felt even painfully by some."[100] Others chimed in, well into the end of the 19th century.

John Harvey Kellogg wrote in 1891 that at breakfast, he would "often take fruit, either in its natural state or freshly stewed."[101] He also enjoyed the salutary effects of baked sweet apples with his oatmeal. After two hundred years of cider production, orchards eventually produced thousands of varieties of apples good enough to eat; most often, though, these apples were still cooked before eating at breakfast.

In *The Young House-keeper, Or, Thoughts on Food and Cookery* (1838), William Andrus Alcott revealed himself to be quite the apple devotee, spending seventeen entire pages enthusing over the humble pome. "No healthy man shall want for strength to labor, simply because he ate nothing for breakfast but apples," he declared.[102] Sour baked apples were a pleasant accoutrement to hash for breakfast, noted Emma Pike Ewing, a woman famous for teaching southern whites how to cook after the Civil War had freed their slaves. Baking apples might seem straightforward enough, but not so, warned Ewing. "An apple baked quickly, with all the heat it can bear, is very different from one baked in a moderate oven. The former is spicy and full of spirit, while the latter tastes as if all life had been worried out of it by slow torture."[103]

Applesauce was another favorite, for a number of reasons. First, it could be prepared well in advance and put up in pots (or in jars, when home canning came into active practice in the 1880s). Second, it was ideal food for the infirm. In the 1850s, if a woman was undergoing hydropathic treatment for "diseases peculiar to women" such as menstruation and other "morbid affections of the uterus which embitter the existence of so many women," "[a]t breakfast and tea, she may take perfectly ripe fruit, or stewed apples, or apple sauce, with her bread, instead of butter."[104]

For those not recovering from childbirth, there were more robust ways to eat apples for breakfast. The "Letters from Mr. Toulmin of Kentucky" published in *Monthly Magazine and British Register* (volume 9, 1800) tell of roadside lodgings in Pennsylvania that provided travelers with such breakfasts as "tea, coffee, and a mutton-chop, broiled ham, or some such thing," but most remarkable to Superior Court Judge Harry Toulmin was that "one day, indeed, apple-pye was added."[105] Apple pie, along with other types of pie, was served at breakfast throughout New England and mountainous regions of the South, a tradition that tragically subsided by the end of the 19th century.

Though it is the national symbol, rich, spiced apple pies seem to have fallen out of American favor as a breakfast food; however, numerous adaptations of the apple pie remain. Toaster pastries have always included an apple flavor, and apple Danishes, strudels, and coffee cakes still appear in coffee shops across the country. Apple-currant was one of the four original flavors of frosted Pop Tart released by Kellogg's in 1967. Today's envelopes of apple-cinnamon–flavored instant oatmeal may be a far cry from John Harvey Kellogg's hearty breakfast of baked sweet apples with oatmeal, but they nonetheless reflect the apple's lasting American heritage.

Because of the lingering sensationalism of the Jacksonian-era Clean Living Movement (of which Kellogg was a major player), sometimes what was popular was confused with what was healthy. This is how citrus fruits caught on. "It is fashionable, and therefore considered a wise sanitary measure, to eat oranges as a prelude to the regular business of the morning meal," wrote Marion Harland in 1875.[106] Hygiene books of the time also claimed that "eating an orange or two before breakfast is a pleasant and often effectual way of overcoming moderate habitual constipation," and was undoubtedly more pleasant than one of Kellogg's yogurt enemas.[107]

In 1823, roughly 330 years after Columbus brought oranges to Florida, French nobleman Odet Philippe brought grapefruits to the Sunshine State. It took around forty years for farmers to discover a seedless variety, and another sixty years to find a coral-pink variety preferred today. In the 1920s, scientists began work on sweetening the fruit and changing its cell structure so that it would not squirt juice in the eye of the breakfaster. Like all new foods, when grapefruit first hit markets, it was a faddish treat for the wealthy. By the turn of the 20th century, numerous dietetic journals claimed that when eaten in the morning and evening, grapefruit cured a variety of chronic diseases and bilious temperament.

During the influenza epidemic of 1919, markets were swept bare of the citrus in ten days when a successful advertising campaign convinced consumers that the grapefruit "flu diet" could cure the disease. After the subsequent grapefruit diet craze of the 1930s waned, grapefruit returned as a bright accompaniment to a more balanced breakfast. Much as they are today, most grapefruits were simply eaten on the half-shell, raw, perhaps with a sprinkle of sugar. In the late 1940s, however, recipes for broiled grapefruit—"a delightful morning appetite sharpener," suggested one article in a 1951 issue of *Women's Home Companion*—began to appear in cookbooks and ladies' magazines.[108]

A similar breakfast dish of bananas "baked to a state like candy" came earlier, though the recipe was from an 1889 hotel steward's handbook and would not have been intended for average homes.[109] Bananas did, however, make an easy ascent from expensive trifle to daily staple before the turn of the 20th century; now, bananas are the world's most popular fruit. One reason for this meteoric rise was the banana's transportability; bananas could be picked unripe and firm enough to ship, and then ripened to individual preference in the home. Even more importantly, bananas have a year-round growing season.

In 1910, an advertisement showed cereal being sprinkled onto a banana for breakfast; soon, bananas were sliced onto bowls of cereal instead, served hot or cold with milk and sugar. In 1963, Kellogg's unveiled its Corn Flakes with Instant Bananas. "Just add milk . . . presto! Real tasty banana slices!" touted the ads. Unfortunately, the reconstituted bananas were not considered "real tasty" enough, and they turned the milk beige. The product was discontinued three years later.

Despite a century of advertisers' attempts to convince consumers that bananas can be enjoyed at any time of day and in many different recipes, in America, they are still mostly eaten on cereal. Bananas were not the only food to find their way into breakfast cereals. Almost forty years before its ill-fated Instant

Bananas, Kellogg's introduced Raisin Bran (or Sultana Bran, in Australia and New Zealand) to American markets. Today, raisins and other dried fruits are added to numerous packaged breakfast cereals.

For many, the only fruit eaten at breakfast is preserved: jam, jelly, compote, conserve, and marmalade. Though the Scots did not invent marmalade (*Apicius* included recipes for fruit preserves in the 4th century), they were the first to eat it specifically for breakfast. To the cold, early morning stomach, a slice of orange peel "condite (candied) with sugar, and taken fasting in a small quantity" was a panacea recommended by physician Sir Thomas Elyot.[110] Before this endorsement, a dram of whiskey was what warmed most Scottish stomachs in the morning, chased by ale with a slice of toast. When tea drinking caught on in Scotland in the early 18th century, some people replaced the ale with tea; others replaced the dram as well, instead opting for a bit of tummy-warming candied orange peel or marmalade.

Brigadier Mackintosh of Borlum was not blown away about this change. "When I came to my friend's house in a morning, I used to be ask'd, if I had my morning draught yet? I am now ask'd, if I have yet had my tea," he bristled in 1729. "And in lieu of the . . . strong ale and toast, and after a Dram of good wholesome Scots Spirits, there is now . . . marmalet, cream, and cold tea."[111]

English literary giant Samuel "Doctor" Johnson had no such disdain for marmalade; rather, he mentioned it specifically as one of the delights of the Scottish breakfast table. In 1774, he wrote that "[i]f an epicure could remove by a wish, in quest of sensual gratifications, wherever he had supped, he would breakfast in Scotland."[112] This was in part, no doubt, because of their habit of serving tea with "not only butter, but honey, conserves and marmalades." "Marmalade" often meant a very thick, tart pulp of quinces (a fragrant pome resembling a fuzzy pear), but during Johnson's time, the word just as often referred to a jam made with the juice and slivered rinds of citrus.

Vegetables

In 1660, Pepys dined on "a breakfast of Radyshes at the Pursers cabin" while sailing with King Charles II's escorts to England, but aside from Pepys's experimentation with tap-rooted crucifers, not many members of the English upper crust ate vegetables in the modern era, especially not for breakfast.[113] John Evelyn, a gardener, friend of Pepys, and fellow diarist, wrote extensively on the benefits of adding roughage to the diet, but before him, most people—physicians included—believed that vegetables were indigestible or worse: pabulum for the poor.

As it turned out, the English had simply not caught on to what the rest of the world was eating. Raw or pickled vegetables like carrots, cucumbers, and olives had been eaten for breakfast with bread, olive oil, and cheese in the Middle East and Levant for millennia. In Israel, a cucumber and tomato salad is still standard breakfast fare. In ancient Egypt, pharaoh and slave alike ate onion relishes with their breads. Vegetables were eaten with jook in ancient China, and pickled *tsukemono* have an important place in the Japanese kaiseki breakfast. In Korea, eggplant salads, seaweed, and pickled burdock root are eaten with the morning's rice and *kimchi*—the spicy, fermented pickle of cabbage, scallions, garlic, and chili flakes whose earliest version dates back to at least the 7th century BCE.

In the early 18th century, Scottish physician and vegetarian proselyte George Cheyne promoted "vegetable foods" for breakfast, but by the middle of the 19th century, only those embarking on prescriptive diets due to illness typically ate breakfasts consisting entirely of vegetables. Generally, though, even Americans showed greater acceptance for vegetables at breakfast than the English. In the first quarter of the 19th century, vegetables started trickling in a bit more steadily: mushrooms, parsley, and onions were added to omelets, an occasional salad might be served with the heartier fare, and the odd fried or stewed eggplant might make an appearance.

Tomatoes landed on the breakfast table in America several hundred years after hitching a ride on Hernán Cortés's fleet in 1519. Even though the crop was indigenous to America, like corn, tomatoes were not eaten by colonists until they had been filtered through the culinary traditions of Europe and England for a few hundred years. By the 1820s, however, the United States found itself in a new tomato mania. In *The Kentucky Housewife* (1839), cookbook author Lettice Bryan suggested eating thick slices of raw tomatoes seasoned "highly with salt, pepper and vinegar. This is a delicious breakfast dish."[114] In New England, where the flavor of fresh tomatoes may never have matched those of the South, broiled, rather than fresh, tomatoes were a more common part of breakfast menus.

Aside from the addition of diced tomatoes to an omelet, salsa in a breakfast burrito, or fried as part of a Full English, tomatoes are most often eaten for breakfast in the form of sauce; namely, as ketchup. In 1804, American horticulturist James Mease observed that the "love-apple" makes "a fine catsup," and eight years later, his was the first published recipe for the condiment.[115] By the 1940s, ketchup's best breakfast partners were well established: scrambled eggs and fried potatoes.

Potatoes were introduced to the European diet at the end of the 16th century, but it was not until the late 18th century that the tuber began to stand in as a staple food. Like the tomato and corn, the potato was an American crop, yet it did not begin to replace corn as the colonies' favorite breakfast starch until the turn of the 19th century.

American cookbook authors were generally more appreciative of the potato's virtues than their English counterparts. In 1847, Eliza Leslie listed potato dishes in her *Lady's New Receipt-Book* on more than half of her breakfast menus. (Some were for sweet potatoes, which are botanically unrelated, but her sentiment was clear.) Unlike the English *The Breakfast Book* (1882), which included only one vegetable dish (fried potatoes and bacon), American Thomas Jefferson Murrey's *Breakfast Dainties* (1885) includes six different potato recipes, and a bevy of other vegetable dishes. Two years after Murrey's fried Lyonnaise potatoes with browned onions, American cooking teacher Maria Parloa published the first recipe for "hashed and browned potatoes," or hash browns.[116]

The hash browns of today, typically made with shredded (rather than diced) potatoes, were likely inspired by Swiss *Rösti*, the traditional farmer's breakfast from Switzerland's capital Bern. Like Jewish latkes, Rösti can be served with apples or onions; unlike latkes, bacon is another commonly added ingredient. By the 1970s, hash brown patties were mostly shredded and even available frozen, thanks to Oregon-based potato company Ore-Ida. In 1973, Ore-Ida filed the first patent for an "Apparatus for Producing Prepared Hash Brown Potato Product." Five years later, the golden, fried patty was added to the McDonald's breakfast menu.[117]

The hash browns of yore, made from diced or chopped potatoes fried in butter or bacon fat, with or without browned onions, are usually known in today's vernacular as "home fries." Though the name implies that they are cooked and eaten in one's abode, home fries are a staple of breakfast diners and greasy spoons across the country.

Of the various modes of cooking potatoes, there has emerged over the past two hundred years a clear favorite. "Fried potatoes of any kind are excellent," wrote Mary Hooper in her *Handbook for the Breakfast Table* (1873).[118] More than a century later, fried potatoes are still the preferred vegetable of America and Britain, and the most common one eaten at breakfast.

BEVERAGES

In the roughly nine thousand years between the invention of wine and the invention of coffee, surprisingly little changed in the world of breakfast beverages; in the five hundred years between the invention of coffee and the drive-through espresso shack, even less has changed.

Booze

Abstinence in the days of Classical Antiquity was rare, yet most Greeks and Romans insisted that the only civilized way to drink wine was mixed with water. The Ancient Greeks enjoyed a light repast of bread dipped in diluted wine, or *ariston*; by the classical period of the 5th century BCE, when ariston was moved to lunchtime, the breakfast wine was no longer diluted.

Most Greeks thought it barbaric to drink undiluted wine, but it is possible that the neat *akratos* was not actually meant to be drunk. In the 2nd century BCE, Athenaeus explains in his *Deipnosophistae* (*The Banquet of the Learned*) that "we call it akratismos, because we eat pieces of bread sopped in unmixed (akratos) wine"; by then, it was a tradition that had carried on for three hundred years.[119] According to historian Maguelonne Toussaint-Samat, the wine into which 5th-century Greeks dipped their bread for breakfast was undiluted as an expiatory pre-meal offering to the gods, not to become intoxicated. Eating bread dipped in unmixed wine, much as the Eucharist communion rite, was a way of saying grace before beginning the day.

In the Middle Ages, with water quality leaving much to be desired, the safest potables were often the potent ones. The tradition of drinking ale at breakfast continued through the Elizabethan period, and "[e]ven well into [the 18th] century ale was a common drink for breakfast among those who affected the manners of the old school," wrote 19th-century beer historians in *The Curiosities of Ale & Beer: An Entertaining History*.[120] Although Good Queen Bess herself famously enjoyed a jug of ale with her morning oat cakes, Benjamin Franklin was less enamored of the habit, particularly on a workday. "My companion at the press drank every day a pint before breakfast, a pint at breakfast with his bread and cheese, a pint between breakfast and dinner," Franklin complained. "I thought it a detestable custom; but it was necessary, he suppos'd, to drink strong beer, that he might be strong to labor."[121]

Like Franklin's printer colleagues, 18th-century farmers appreciated ale at breakfast as well. For many, however, the draught was sweetened and mixed with cereals and milk or eggs into a drinkable porridge called a "caudle"—a handy way of getting one's ale and oatcake all in one convenient package. Conversely, the milk and eggs could be curdled with beer or wine to make a posset.

Possets were similar to hot eggnog (with ale or wine instead of brandy), and people drank them immediately before bed and again upon rising, as a sort of breakfast before breakfast. They could also be taken in lieu of a proper meal, by those too ill to eat solids. One 18th-century herbal prescribes a medicinal breakfast posset to be taken on the full moon to cure "both old and young of convulsions Hysterick vapours fitts and falling sickness."[122]

Caudles were typically the thicker of the two breakfast drinks. The earliest caudle recipe, from the 14th century, consisted of "wine, amidon (wheat starch), seedless raisins put therein and sugar," but rather than forming the basis of a wholesome breakfast, the additives were intended to "cut down the strength of the wine."[123] By the 15th century, recipes for caudles became slightly more complex, consisting of the same wine but additionally enriching the brew with milk and eggs, using ground almonds, bread, or oatcakes to thicken, and seasoning with luxurious spices like saffron or ginger.

An inclusion of caudle in Eliza Smith's *The Compleat Housewife* (1727)—the first cookery book published in the United States—demonstrates that the drink was popular enough to travel to America with the colonists, but within a hundred years, the caudle and posset were transferred from breakfast to dessert.

The widespread adoption of caffeinated beverages in 18th-century Europe eliminated most alcohol at breakfast. One such casualty was the dram of whiskey, dropped when tea and marmalade swept the British Isles, to the aforementioned dismay of Brigadier Mackintosh of Borlum. The small tipple, meant to warm the belly and stir the appetite upon waking, was one of Samuel Johnson's favorite parts of a Scottish breakfast. After the morning dram, which was drunk nearly always ("no man is so abstemious as to refuse the morning dram," noted Dr. Johnson), came the breakfast. Should one overindulge on the rich Scottish victuals, the dram was also sometimes enjoyed as a medicinal digestif; one early 19th-century author mentions that breakfast, "according to the fashion of the times, was finished by a small dram of whiskey, swallowed neat, as a settler to the various substantialities."[124]

Caffeine

The late 16th and early 17th centuries were a very busy time for Europeans. Three different caffeinated beverages had just been discovered, and all arrived within a few decades of each other. Less than a century after chocolate was wrenched from the cold, dead hands of Montezuma, Europe was beside itself with joy, and tea and coffee were right around the corner. In the trinity of stimulants, chocolate was Europe's first, prompting Swedish botanist Carl Linnaeus to give the plant the Greek name *Theobroma*, meaning "food of the gods," but for millennia to the Aztecs, chocolate was actually a drink of the gods.

Within fifty years of first contact with Spanish conquistadors, chocolate had gone from an alien beverage to an intimate affair taken in the boudoir before facing each day. Just as breakfast was coming back into acceptance in the 17th century, chocolate was there. The Catholic Church even changed the rules for chocolate. As Roman fervor for the exquisite beverage came to a boiling point, the question arose of whether or not chocolate should be considered a liquid, and not a food—thereby allowing chocolate during a fast. Cardinal Francis Maria Brancaccio declared in 1662 that "*Liquidum non frangit jejunum,*" meaning "liquid does not break the fast," which most people were happy to interpret as "chocolate does not count."[125]

By the 18th century, drinking chocolate before breakfast (or with the coffee or tea) was universal among Europeans and Americans. While chocolate was still a staple breakfast of Mexico past the turn of the 19th century, "it is to be regretted that it is not more used in the United States. During the winter, it certainly is a preferable breakfast to coffee," discussed one domestic manual. "When properly boiled with milk, it certainly is preferable to any other breakfast."[126]

More than 150 years later, the Carnation Company was wont to agree. In 1964, the Washington-based evaporated milk company released its Instant Breakfast, which came in three flavors: plain, coffee, and chocolate; today, there are four different chocolate flavors, and plain and coffee have been discontinued. The vitamin and protein-enriched powder was intended to be mixed into a glass of milk as a substitute for food. "Each glass delivers as much protein as two eggs, as much mineral nourishment as two strips of crisp bacon, more energy than two slices of buttered toast, and even Vitamin C," touted the advertisements in the 1960s. Modern ads for the "rich, intense" dark chocolate flavor claim the breakfast drink has "as many antioxidants as a cup of . . . green tea."

Tea had experienced the same millennia-long affair with Asians as chocolate had with the Aztecs; similar to chocolate, tea only made it to Europe as recently as the 16th century. Catherine of Braganza of Portugal created a tea fad in the 17th century when, upon marrying King Charles II, she brought a chest of it to England with the rest of her impressive dowry. By the 18th century, the stimulating brew found its way onto commoner breakfast tables, much to the delight of Samuel Johnson, who wrote that "with tea welcomes the morning."[127]

By the turn of the 19th century, when tea drinking had become firmly established throughout Europe, the British Isles, and America, most experts agreed that tea was relatively harmless if taken with food; however, many people still opted for tea or coffee in lieu of a proper breakfast. Because of the appetite-suppressing effects of caffeine, this was not only a relatively easy way to stave off hunger until dinner (the noon meal), but it saved money and time. If the energy was not needed for labor, food in the morning was not a necessity—a flashback from the early modern era. "[T]o those leading an easy life, and little exposed to severe exercise, a tea breakfast is not only agreeable, but perhaps, now-a-days, the best that can be taken," wrote agricultural scientist Sir John Sinclair in 1817.[128]

Although chocolate was an acceptable substitute for tea, coffee rarely sat in tea's stead. Along with chocolate and tea, coffee arrived in Europe in the 16th century and by the 17th century, when breakfast was regaining its stride among the social elite of Europe and America, coffee was ready for its spotlight.

In 1710, it was the French who first brewed coffee using an infusion method and filtration, rather than the Turk style of boiling coffee into a muddy sludge. By the second half of the 18th century, café au lait—coffee with milk—and sugar had become de rigueur at breakfast. It was "the nicest thing in the world," declared the Marquise de Sévigné. French historian Pierre Jean-Baptiste Legrand d'Aussy noticed in the late 18th century that "[s]ince 1750 . . . the consumption of coffee in France has tripled. . . . There is no shop girl, no cook, no chambermaid, who, in the morning, does not have a café au lait for breakfast."[129] This would remain an accurate statement forever after, and before the 18th century concluded, it would be true for much of the world over.

By the 18th century, the trend toward coffee alone for breakfast was beginning to surface. Most people could not afford a luxurious, multi-course breakfast to while away the morning, but more importantly, coffee's appetite-suppressing qualities made skipping the meal physically tolerable. In France and Italy, people generally ate little more than a bit of bread or pastry with their coffee, and in the 1830s, a new item arrived in France that would pair even better with the morning coffee: the cigarette.

Clean Living proponents like Kellogg strongly advocated coffee substitutes. Coincidentally, Kellogg's archrival Charles Post profited handsomely from coffee substitutes. Before he got into the cereal market, Post made a fortune selling the eponymous Postum, a roasted grain beverage made from wheat and molasses. When the product was introduced in 1895, it spawned a half dozen other cereal-based coffee substitutes within a few years.

Sales of coffee substitutes soared further during the rationing of World War II, and one old-fashioned stand-in stood out. Chicory, made from the roasted root of a blue-flowered roadside weed (Cichorium intybus), has been a substitute for coffee in France, Germany, and other northern European countries since the 1700s. In 1873 three testers of a "chicory breakfast" found it to be "destitute of the agreeable and refreshing aroma so characteristic of coffee," but the beverage soldiered on.[130] By the 19th century, adulterating coffee with chicory had become a trick employed by unscrupulous coffee-sellers, but thanks to the French, chicory is still the secret ingredient in New Orleans–style café au lait.

On the heels of cereal-based coffee substitutes came instant coffee, first hitting markets in 1910. High-volume, freeze-dried coffee became available after World War II, and along with the myriad other convenience breakfast foods released in the era, became indispensable to busy housewives.

During the 1980s and 1990s, to say that espresso was popular in Seattle would be something of an understatement, but in Italy, where the beverage originated in the late 19th century, caffè latte, or coffee with milk, still dominated the breakfast table. It was Americans who substituted the Italian coffee with espresso and shortened the name to "latte." Like fast food, the latte was eventually co-opted into car culture; soon, gas station convenience stores were outfitted with instant latte machines, and drive-through espresso stands dotted parking lots across America.

Juice

Fruit juice was not a typical breakfast beverage past the early 1800s, and even then, it was only the fermented juice of grapes and apples that received much notice. Thanks to the tireless efforts of California citrus advertiser Albert Lasker in the 1920s, the parents of the baby boomers were the first generation to grow up drinking orange juice at breakfast.

A few serendipitous events occurred to nudge Lasker's campaign toward success. First, there was an orange surplus in California that had many orchard owners cutting down trees to control the market. Second came the advent of household refrigeration; third, pasteurization had just started being used on milk. Fourth, the influenza epidemic of 1918–1919 had killed 20–40 million people worldwide, of whom approximately 675,000 were Americans; doctors began recommending milk and juice to patients to prevent illness, and parents scrambled to provide these to their children. Lasker's "drink your fruit" ad campaign helped orange juice to outcompete apples, prunes, and plums for placement on the breakfast table.

The juice from grapefruits is another morning favorite. It increases the bioavailability of caffeine, which is a nice coincidence for the early adopters of grapefruit juice at breakfast. Along with orange juice, grapefruit juice became available bottled in the early 1920s, and before 1930 it was available canned as well. According to a 1941 ad in *LIFE* magazine, "[a]s a breakfast starter, the wide-awake, tangy taste of Florida's canned grapefruit juice just can't be beat."

For those who enjoy a curdled stomach first thing in the morning, "another good breakfast for someone in a hurry is a glass of orange juice and a glass of milk," suggested *For Young Souls* in 1941.[131] The advice book for teenaged Christians goes on to suggest beating honey, nutmeg, and a raw egg yolk into a glass of orange or grapefruit juice for a morning "pep cocktail." Other juices came out in the 1930s and 1940s as well, both as an accompaniment to food and in lieu of it. "Just open a can and breakfast is different!" promised Libby's pineapple juice. "Landsakes, boy, have a glass of this," demanded an advertorial for Heinz tomato juice. "It's a good tonic for boys, at any age." Prune and un-fermented grape and apple juices, however, despite an earnest advertising effort, just never reached the level of popularity as citrus and tomato juices.

During the prosperous times after World War II, when America had fruit to spare, blender companies like Waring began to include recipes for banana and pineapple smoothies with their appliances. Fruit puree breakfasts had been recommended to dieters since the 1930s, but the smoothie did not experience a real surge in popularity until the health food craze of the mid-1960s. By blend-ing fresh or frozen fruit with juice, dairy products like milk or yogurt, protein powders, and nut milks—or sometimes just ice, if one were watching her waist-line—smoothies continue to serve as a liquid breakfast, available at any of the thousands of juice and smoothie bars that have opened since the 1970s.

Despite its fairly recent addition to the average breakfast, the image of the glistening tumbler of orange juice alongside a bowl of cereal and heaping plate of bacon, eggs, and toast presents an idealized picture of the table in the break-fast nook, which, at the turn of the 20th century, made its first appearance in American homes.

BREAKFAST AT HOME

Before the advent of dining out, all meals, breakfast included, were eaten in the home, but even after restaurants came into fashion, most breakfasts were eaten at home. Before breakfast became a widely acceptable meal in 17th-century England, little nibbles of breakfast were still often taken in the bedchamber before greeting the day. By the 18th century, grander homes featured breakfast rooms or parlors where morning guests could be entertained, or where the family of the house might take toast and tea. Breakfast parlors were an architectural feature of colonial homes in America, as well. By the turn of the 20th century, the cozy breakfast nook was all the rage in American Craftsman–style homes.

American lives became more complicated after the onset of the Industrial Revolution, but in many ways, breakfast became less so. Modern appliances began to surface after the widespread adoption of electricity at the end of the 19th century; soon, average households benefitted from timesaving technologies like stoves that needed no fire and iceless iceboxes.

During and after World War II, women entered the workforce in droves. With the need for working mothers and fathers to sleep in on weekends, breakfast became the first meal a child learned to prepare without adult supervision; once postwar children could be left to fend for themselves in the morning, cereal companies jumped at the chance to market directly to undiscerning tots, changing the nutritional landscape of breakfast forever.

BREAKFAST IN BED

In the 17th century, before it was a much-written-about meal, breakfast was typically eaten in the bedroom. The bedroom, however, was far from private; in fact, it had only been used primarily for sleeping since the mid-16th century.[1] Most bedrooms had seating areas and were even used for entertaining. Women wanting privacy were prone to breakfasting in their dressing or withdrawing chambers off the bedrooms, alone but for the company of the lady's maid. With this in mind, it is entirely possible that breakfast was eaten regularly for far longer than supposed by historians; what happened in the bedchambers stayed in the bedchambers.

Breakfasts taken in bed were simple: possets of ale, tea, toast. In the 17th and early 18th century, posset pots were kept bedside, and were sipped from before retiring and again before rising. The pots resembled a squat, two-handled teapot. Curdled cream and eggs floated to the top and were spooned like custard, and the warm, spiced ale was sipped from the spout like a straw.

By the 18th century, breakfasting in bed was typically an affectation of the mollycoddled aristocracy but was also advised for the infirm and for pregnant women of "delicate constitutions and irritable habits."[2] By the 19th century, breakfast in bed was a way to pamper someone on a special occasion such as a birthday, much as it is today. Though it is a nice indulgence, there was one downside to breakfast in bed, according to one disgruntled mistress in 1847:

> Only the worst of breakfasting in bed is, that bother take it! the crumbs will get all over the sheets, and if one happens to have dry toast, they are so hard, and do scrub a poor body so, that really one might just as well lie upon sandpaper for the comfort of the thing; and drat it, do what you will, you can't get them out of the bed again, until the things are taken off and well shaken.[3]

One can hardly pity the person for whom crumbs in the bed are the worst part of the day. Fortunately, this mistress likely had hired help to shake the crumbs out of her sheets.

THE VICTORIAN AND GILDED AGE
BREAKFAST ROOMS AND MORNING PARLORS

In the late 1740s, many upper-class English and new colonial Americans had begun adding separate breakfast rooms to their homes. As breakfast became part of the accepted lifestyle, it became another way to advertise one's wealth, and this was reflected in architectural choices. Breakfast rooms in country houses were not just used for the meal, but as morning sitting rooms as well. These were often located adjacent to dining rooms (or in some cases, directly connected to a lady's bedchamber), and could be used as an anteroom during a large party. The preferred orientation of a morning room in gloomy England was on the east side of the home, in hopes of capturing some fleeting rays of sunlight to brighten one's day.

By the 19th century, creating and decorating a breakfast parlor became a pastime for ladies of comfortable circumstances. An 1893 article in *The Decorator and Furnisher* describes a few options for decorating "Dainty Breakfast Rooms," each more resplendent than the last. One had a theme of Swiss dot, gilded furnishings, and blue ribbons, with a denim floor and black goatskin rugs; another, a little girl's dream of apple blossoms, pink and white silks, and ribbons, complete with sachet powder in the chair seats and a canary in a white cage. More mature examples focused on cherry wood finishes or terra cotta color schemes. "Why not use a little spare time, money and energy, in arranging a breakfast room. It will give you thorough enjoyment three hundred and

White House breakfast room, ca. 1905–1945. Courtesy of the Library of Congress.

sixty-five days during a year," implored article author Harriet E. Clark.[1] If a lady were to go to the trouble of outfitting a room for the purpose, she had better have something nice to serve. "Perhaps I ought to add that a carelessly cooked breakfast would spoil the appearance of a breakfast room," clarifies Ms. Clark.

If a housewife was especially resourceful, she need not do without a breakfast room merely because her house was tight on space. All she needed was a knack for sewing, a bolt of pretty fabric, and a handy husband. She could sew a screen and arrange her furniture "as to have one room serve first as a large and airy sleeping-room; then, in the morning, it may be used as sitting-room one side of the screen, and breakfast-room the other," suggested educator Catharine Beecher in her 1869 *American Woman's Home*.[5]

Setting the Breakfast Table

The 19th-century breakfast table did not suffer a broody woman. The entire tone of the day for all members of the family would be set by the demeanor of the lady of the house at breakfast time. "Here, as everywhere, upon the mother devolves the burden of the family well-being," wrote domestic expert Christine Terhune Herrick in 1891.[6] A good place to start, she suggested in *What to Eat, How to Serve It*, was with a spotless room and a properly set table. "The table should always appear at its best at breakfast-time," Herrick insisted, adding a clever tip that "[a] colored cloth is economical as well as pretty, for it does not show every spot or splash with the readiness of a white cloth."[7] By following her simple tips, there was little chance to foul things up, and there was plenty to gain. "With the fresh room, the bright cloth, the shining glass and silver, the vase of flowers, the appetizing food, one must be either very dyspeptic or a confirmed pessimist who does not feel a slight rise of spirits as he takes his place at the breakfast-table."[8]

Whether the lady of the house performed this work alone or with help was largely a matter of her means. In wealthy households, the house's staff of servants set up an elaborate breakfast. In poorer families, the wife of the house prepared food alone or with the help of her daughters, if she was lucky enough to have any. Most middle-class families, however, had but two servants: the maid-of-all-work and the housewife.

According to 19th-century servant's guides, to prepare for breakfast, the maid-of-all-work (or "the girl," as she was ignobly called in the United States) began at daybreak by starting the kitchen fire, sweeping the ashes and cinders from the hearth (saving and redistributing cinders onto the fire), bringing hot water to the mistress's bedroom door, then starting the real work of cleaning the breakfast parlor. One book, *Household Work, or the Duties of Female Servants* (1850) goes into hair-splitting detail, written in the voice of the shrewd mistress, a question-and-answer format as though she were interviewing a prospective maid-of-all-work for the job. One can imagine the raised eyebrow on the mistress as she grills her prospective helper:

> Q. Before you meddle with the curtains or the breakfast-table, I hope you take care that your hands are clean.
> A. Yes, ma'am.[9]

After two hours of cleaning and prepping the breakfast parlor, she would wash her hands again and don a fresh apron; then she was ready to set the breakfast table. The cooking had not even begun.

Entire chapters of books were devoted to the proper way to set a breakfast table. Besides the food, which was plentiful and of innumerable variety, there was the staggering array of objects to accompany it. Long gone were the wooden or stale bread trenchers of the Middle Ages. Besides the expected china tableware—plates, bowls, and teacups—there was a sugar dish and tongs, there were egg cups and egg spoons (in the 1890s, an egg coddler would appear on the table as well), salt cellars, mustard pot in case there should be meat, the cayenne-pepper cruet for seasoning at the table, a dish and silver knife for butter, and a pot of hot milk for the coffee. There should be a carving knife and fork for the beefsteaks or roast.

Next came preparing the breakfast itself. Mary Foote Henderson, an American aristocrat and reputedly excellent hostess, noted that the French ate very little (if anything) and that the Englishman, for whom breakfast was a very informal meal, was "not mercilessly expected at the table simply because it is the breakfast-hour."[10] For an American breakfast, she insisted on arranging everything on the table at once, unless porridge was to be served. Henderson recommended oat porridge because Queen Victoria had given it to her own children, but also because while the family was eating their porridge, the remaining dishes could be prepared. For all else, there was a place for everything, and everything—coffee urn, bacon and eggs, melon balls, etc.—in its place. "Do not have them askew. It is quite as easy for an attendant to place a dish in a straight line as in an oblique angle with every other dish on the table."[11]

Hot buttered toast, being the latest rage in the 19th century, was requisite on the breakfast table. In the days before electric toasters, it took a fair amount of effort to toast bread properly. It was ideally to be made from slightly stale bread, was buttered and strung up on long-handled forks, then held in the fire until just browned. This was to be done immediately before the family sat down to breakfast, timed perfectly. "It may have exasperated maid and mistress alike when the toast sat on the table, perfectly browned with just the right amount of butter spread, and no one thought to eat it," stated historian Andrea Broomfield in her 2007 *Food and Cooking in Victorian England.* "But even more exasperating must have been those unfortunate mornings when the toast was burned and soggy from too much butter and the master then asked his wife to pass it to him along with another cup of tea."[12]

As such, this simple piece of heated bread held much sway over the morning; toast was a testament to a servant's culinary prowess and ability to perform her duties adequately, and to a mistress's ability to run her household and manage its staff successfully. Toast, it would seem, was a test. This is perhaps why Victorian cookbook authors devoted so many pages to toast. In the 1891 *The Modern Housewife* (written from the fictional perspective of a clueless housewife, Eloise, who requests advice from the domestic sage Hortense), author and French chef Alexis Soyer opens with a recipe for toast. If a housewife could not master the simple (yet not so simple) task of making toast, she had no hope at all. "[I]n cookery," Soyer wrote, "there are no trifles."[13]

Soyer's factually inaccurate pun aside, all of breakfast was important. The housewife's duty was to ensure that her family life ran smoothly and that her husband (and children, to a lesser extent) was happy; if breakfast was not served on time, the mistress alone bore the husband's judgment. "When it is possible to get the master to enjoy an eight o'clock breakfast, household matters go on charmingly," wrote Isabella Beeton in her *Every-day Cookery and Household Guide.*[14] It was simply best for the housewife to see to it that her family enjoyed a punctual breakfast, and to do so with what Herrick called a "bright and sunny" countenance.[15] If she did not, her husband might reasonably turn his attention to his newspaper rather than his bride, a threat to housewives well into the middle of the 20th century.

For the gentleman of the house, the newspaper was an important item on the breakfast table, and by the late 18th century, most American and British men took their morning meal with the paper. "On Newspapers," an essay published in *The Scots Magazine* in 1797, extolled the joys of the daily journal. "Even the breakfast table is indebted to the presence of this lively guest."[16] American journalists wrote thirty years later that "[t]here is something delightful in a newspaper, with a quiet breakfast."[17] In the early 19th century, some journals, such as *The Idler, and Breakfast-Table Companion,* appear to have been published entirely for the purpose of early morning entertainment. The newspaper was the world, brought to the breakfast table.

By the end of the Victorian era, eating together as a family, at a decent hour, was beginning to lose importance. "As a consequence," wrote domestic science expert Christine Terhune Herrick, "what should be one of the family gathering-places becomes little better than a hotel breakfast-room, where the guests come and go as suits themselves."[18] At the same time, however, a new way to enjoy breakfast with family and friends was coming into fashion: the breakfast party.

Breakfast Parties

On weekends, with the pressure of workdays and school behind her for the week, the mistress might host a breakfast party. There were numerous occasions to hold a breakfast party, such as hosting guests from out of town, or to introduce young people casually to encourage courtship. While attending one herself in the 1850s, author Harriet Beecher Stowe remarked that they were not common in America, but she thought them "the most delightful form of social life." British poet and celebrated conversationalist Thomas Babington Macaulay replied to her, expatiating on their merits, that "[d]inner parties are mere formalities; but you invite a man to breakfast because you want to see him."[19]

Finally, the harried morning meal could be enjoyed at a leisurely pace—once all the work was done, that is. As is the case today, some ambitious women took things a bit far. Breakfast parties were supposed to be somewhat casual affairs, yet some domestic experts nonetheless recommended dressing the table in white linen or stitched tablecloths, bowls overflowing with flowers, and an endless array of foods that was likely intended to complement the hostess's breakfast parlor more than please the guest's palate.

Party planners of the era outlined an exhausting menu for the breakfast party: first a fruit course featuring sugared berries or peaches with cream, for example; then an oyster course, as croquettes, perhaps; next came stewed kidneys, say, or sweetbreads *vol-au-vent* (in creamy mushroom sauce); lastly, a meat course of lamb chops or beef tenderloins with potatoes. Next would come a cold game pie, then a mayonnaise-dressed salad, followed by dessert of cold sweets. The meal would be concluded with a cheese course if it were not served with the salad. Bread or rolls should make their rounds throughout the meal, and coffee, chocolate, or tea should be frequently poured by the hostess. One might conclude that after such a meal, no guest would endeavor to complete any other task for the rest of the day.

Unlike luncheons, where only women would be invited, both men and women were welcome to a breakfast party, providing an opportunity for the sexes to mingle socially. The ideal number of guests was between six and twelve, which was "pleasanter than a crush," wrote Christine Terhune Herrick.[20] Mary Foote Henderson liked breakfast parties because they are "very fashionable, being less expensive than dinners, and just as satisfactory to guests," and noted with piqued enthusiasm that they were popular among "the *literati*" of England.[21]

Oliver Wendell Holmes's 1858 *Breakfast Table* series was not about breakfast per se, but reflected this trend of intellectual discourse over the breakfast table, as seen in the breakfast parties held by French politicos and the English literati alike. A prominent American poet at the time, Holmes attended a fair many breakfast parties himself, including one held in 1873 for English novelist Wilkie Collins, also attended by American literary giants of the day, William Cullen Bryant, Samuel Clemens (Mark Twain), John Greenleaf Whittier, and Henry Wadsworth Longfellow.

Although "[t]he varying merits as well as style of the different British writers were dispassionately discussed," remarked one scholar in 1822,[22] breakfast parties were, by and large, social events thoroughly enjoyed by their coterie of witty guests. "You may be sure, if you are invited to breakfast, there is something agreeable about you," wrote Harriet Beecher Stowe, of a conversation with her fellow partygoers. Her neighbor at the table, the charming Thomas Macaulay, agreed. "Depend upon it; if a man is a bore he never gets an invitation to breakfast." "Rather hard on the poor bores," lamented an eavesdropping lady.[23]

BREAKFAST IN THE KITCHEN AND THE BIRTH OF THE NOOK

By the end of the Middle Ages, the upper servants sometimes had breakfast in the pantry, even though every effort was made to stop the buttery and butler's pantry from becoming private eating and drinking places.[24] The butler's pantry was a small room typically located off the kitchen, a feature that came back into architectural fashion in the 19th and 20th centuries, but was already centuries old for grander houses. The butler's pantry, where the household's kitchen valuables such as silver and wine were stored and the buttery, where the candles and beer were kept, was a sort of breakfast parlor for the higher-ranking housekeepers and a place to enjoy a bit of time away from boorish scullery staff.

In Scotland, a feature of kitchens without pantries was the fabled porridge drawer. According to popular apocrypha, Scottish mothers would pour a week's supply of porridge into a tin-lined drawer in her Welsh dresser (an open-topped cabinet similar to a china hutch) on a Monday, then after the oatmeal had solidified, she would slice off portions called "caulders" for her husband's lunches all week, sometimes frying them, wrapping the slab of congealed oat-meal in paper. Their use, according to sources, seems to have died out some time at the end of the 19th century. Evidence for these drawers is anecdotally presented in numerous accounts of Scottish culture and cuisine, yet no written mention of them appears before the 20th century. Plenty of people have heard of older homes in the United Kingdom having an odd kitchen drawer with old, crusty bits of oatmeal hanging around the crevices, but no one seems to have seen one with their own eyes.

Just as the pantry began to fade from favor in the early 1900s, the breakfast nook began to appear in the new American Craftsman–style homes. By then, average houses were typically not large enough to dedicate an entire room to breakfast, and family sizes were shrinking, eliminating the need for so much space to begin with.[25] The cozy breakfast nook became everything to the housewife: It alleviated her reliance on domestic help, by now mostly gone from everywhere but the wealthiest homes in the South and New England. It allowed her to serve meals in the kitchen without embarrassment, and she was spared the hassle of shuttling dishes in and out of a stiff dining room that would just require additional cleaning in return. It was a comfortable corner where she could relax with a magazine between her tasks. One article in a 1922 issue of the *Ladies' Home Journal* summed things up astutely:

> With the passing of the servant the housewife evidently realizes that her kitchen has become her workshop and office, where a great deal of her time must be passed: it is, in many instances, the most important room in the house to her. With a dainty little breakfast nook here she is not ashamed to bring her more intimate guests to lunch in the kitchen. . . . [E]ating in the kitchen is no longer a mark of ill-breeding—a thing to be done secretly; it is openly boasted of now.[26]

By the 1920s, the breakfast nook was so popular that some new houses in-cluded them even if the economy was unnecessary; one 1922 Hollywood Hills realty ad featured a breakfast nook in addition to the fully stocked model kitchen and maid's room. Even men's magazines discussed the nook. One 1921 article in *Popular Mechanics* suggested that one may be built by "any man possessing a little mechanical ability, and at a cost of only a few dollars for lumber, and will save the housewife innumerable steps between dining room and kitchen."[27] One supposes the husband had a few ideas of what the housewife might do with all her saved energy.

By the 1940s, the breakfast nook was further pared down to the breakfast bar, which was an extension of the kitchen counter to which stools could be pulled up for casual eating. Now, the housewife's most hurried meal of the day was even more expeditious: she simply passed a plate of eggs or bowl of cereal directly from the kitchen counter to her husband and children without a single extra, time-wasting step. Convenience was a must under wartime conditions, and kitchen modernizations prominently featured both the space-saving breakfast bar and nook. For most households in the first decades of the 20th century, nooks and bars were nice enough, but the real breakthrough was electricity.

MODERN APPLIANCES

Coinciding with the advent of the convenient breakfast nook, widespread adoption of electricity was another nail in the coffin for the field of domestic work. A short while after the invention of electricity, average homes had refrigerators to keep their eggs and milk fresh, and electric ovens and stoves took the guesswork out of baking biscuits and frying bacon. "Electric cooking is now taking its place with electric lighting as an adjunct to the modern house," wrote a Princeton physics professor in 1895.[28] Humble housewife Maud Lucas Lancaster was an early adopter of electricity in the kitchen. There was just one catch to all the new-fangled gadgetry: No one knew how to use any of it. Though appliances would eventually become indispensible to housewives, they first had to be trained to cook with invisible electric power instead of tangible, familiar flame. Lancaster's 1911 *Electric Cooking, Heating, Cleaning, Etc: Being a Manual of Electricity in the Service of the Home* became a fundamental how-to guide for nervous housewives.[29]

Soon after the electrification of American kitchens, the latest breakthroughs in technology were being applied specifically to the morning meal, when busy housewives needed convenience the most. The little machines were kept right on the table, where they could entertain the family and advertise one's wealth in addition to eliminating trips back and forth to the kitchen. "Think of the fun one can have making toast at the breakfast table, each one buttering the crisp fresh pieces as they come from such a toaster, instead of getting red-faced and heated over the stove or even a gas range," tittered an article titled "Electricity in the House," in a 1913 issue of *American Homes and Gardens*.[30] The magazine's "Helps to the Housewife" column now had real "helps" to offer: the coffee percolator, the tabletop chafing dish and griddle for cooking bacon and eggs—all with the ease of flipping a switch. "Here is the cooking of a breakfast provided for, and all at the table. Here is work turned into more or less of a frolic. What a boon to the housewife when without a maid."[31]

What a boon, indeed. Long before space-age fantasies of domestic robotics would appear in pop culture, appliances became the housewife's "little electric servants," so dubbed a 1919 issue of *Edison Monthly:*

> Having made its first appearance on the breakfast table, bright and flawless in its shiny nickle [*sic*] splendor, [the toaster] is used almost constantly, like a brand new toy, by nearly every member of the family. . . . "How did we ever get along without it?" is the question that arises again and again.[32]

If toast was the emblem of a woman's household success, then the electric toaster was a true game changer; it was an equalizer. "Electric toast is the best breakfast food," said a 1923 article in *Electrical Merchandising.*[33] The first electric toasters became commercially available in 1909, but the Waters-Genter Company's Model 1-A-1 Toastmaster—the pioneer of familiar pop-up toasters found in every American household—would not hit markets until 1926, coinciding neatly with the introduction of pre-sliced Wonder bread to American households in 1925.[34]

In his 1990 essay "The Crux of Toast," semiotics professor Arthur Asa Berger calls white bread "middle class," but mechanized, pre-sliced white bread was apparently what electric toaster inventors had in mind all along. Though the appliance relies on such a product, Berger dismissed the modern electric toaster as an enabler of sub-par bread:

> Ultimately the toaster is an apology for the quality of our bread. It attempts, heroically, to transform the semisweet, characterless, "plastic" packaged bread that we have learned to love into something more palatable and more manageable. Perhaps our handling this bread and warming it up gives us a sense that the bread now has a human touch to it, is not an abstract, almost unreal product. The toaster represents a heroic attempt to redeem our packaged bread, to redeem the unredeemable. . . . Every piece of toast is a tragedy.[35]

"Tragedy" may be a bit hyperbolic. Toasting bread preserves it by removing some of the moisture, and makes it more palatable if the bread is stale (or, many will argue, even if it is fresh). Toasting bread improves its flavor by way of the Maillard reaction. The process, described by chemist Louis-Camille Maillard in 1912, results in the creation of hundreds of unique flavor compounds. Similar to caramelization, the Maillard reaction is also responsible for the superior flavor of grilled meats, fried potatoes, roasted coffee, maple syrup, and golden pancakes. Breakfast would scarcely be complete—or nearly as tasty—without it. And toast would hardly be as convenient without an electric toaster.

General Electric toaster, model D-12, from 1909 is considered the first commercially successful toaster in U.S. history. (PRNewsFoto/Grain Foods Foundation, Michael McKoveck)

Approximately 80 percent of American households today have a toaster, according to the nonprofit trade organization International Housewares Association. Toasters can even heat frozen waffles, in the event that the owner's household is not one of the roughly 50 percent of American homes that owns a waffle iron.[36]

The first electric waffle iron was invented in 1911 by American Thomas J. Steckbeck, four decades after Dutch-American inventor Cornelius Swartwout patented America's first stove-top waffle maker.[37] Steckbeck's electric model, funded by General Electric, included a built-in thermostat to prevent the waffles from burning. Before GE's release of the modern appliance, most home cooks did not bother attempting waffles. Despite their popularity, ten and a half pounds of hot iron were too much for the average layperson.

Those earliest irons, invented by the ancient Greeks for making their version of waffles called *obelios*, were long-handled plates to be held over a fire. By the 13th century, Europeans forged versions with the familiar honeycomb pattern.

Ornate versions were also forged in the Middle Ages, emblazoned with coats of arms, landscape illustrations, or religious icons. Today, electric irons may still be purchased that brand one's waffles with the face of Jesus. Also available are the visages of Hello Kitty and Mickey Mouse.

Electric appliances not only simplified breakfast, but they made some products consistent, and consistently better. Coffee particularly exemplified this. "It would be difficult to over-estimate the difference between coffee prepared in the ordinary way and when made in an electric percolator," assured Maud Lucas Lancaster.[38] Gone were the days of boiling coffee to a sludge and hoping for the best. Electric coffee makers also allowed cooks to use a third less coffee per pot, perhaps a trade-off when considering the initially high costs of appliances and electricity. Nonetheless, coffee makers continue to be a top-selling small appliance, with sales growth reported every year since their invention more than a century ago.

Prior to the percolator, coffee making was a rather complicated ordeal. One could simply boil finely ground coffee into a thick mud, as they did in Turkey, the Middle East, the Balkans, and the Caucasus. This worked well enough for several hundred years, but one had to sip carefully around the settled coffee grounds.

"The best method of preparing a beverage from coffee, or, as it is termed, *making coffee*, is a subject that has received a good deal of attention," understated 19th-century historian Robert Hewitt.[39] In his *Coffee: Its History, Cultivation and Uses*, Hewitt described several techniques for brewing coffee. He suggested mixing coffee with dissolved egg whites, hartshorn (deer antler) shavings, or isinglass made from eels' skins or dried fish bladder to "clear coffee rapidly." He explained the percolator invented in the 1700s by one Count Rumford of England, the fountain coffee maker, and the pneumatic filter. The American writer continued on the subject, patriotically noting that "Yankee ingenuity has not been idle in trying to solve the problem as to how this beverage can best be made," and after reviewing some 175 coffee maker patents produced by American inventors, he said, "we find some of the devices both curious and ingenious."[40]

Hewitt concluded his summary of coffee makers with his favorite method. Without naming it, he describes in meticulous detail the first coffeepot patented in the United States, a machine that, according to its modest 1825 patent, was merely "a mode for extracting the strength from coffee." Hewitt, however, rhapsodized the coffee from Lewis Martelley's machine: "[i]t is perfectly pure, and is poured from the coffee-pot as clear as amber, and resembling wine."[41] Martelley, despite creating what Hewitt deemed "the general economizer and only true method of preparing coffee," went on to die in obscurity.

Within the first half of the 20th century, nearly every analog kitchen device had an electric counterpart: pancake griddles, egg coddlers, and teapots were each made electronic, and so were a few items that perhaps tried to do too much at once. The three-in-one breakfast machine includes a coffee maker, a toaster, and a hotplate-style griddle to cook eggs and/or sausage on top. Though a few versions became available to consumers by the turn of the 21st century, they do not seem to have the wide-ranging appeal of single-task breakfast appliances. "Automatic Breakfast Machine Fails to Awake Interest," concluded the headline for a review in *Wired* magazine.[42] "The Perfect Appliance for Lonely Breakfasts," deemed another.[43]

Other modern contraptions intended to streamline the morning meal have come and gone, but most Americans simply prefer the familiar objects seen in kitchens for the past hundred or so years. Of the top ten most popular kitchen appliances on Amazon.com, nine are used for preparing breakfast: Three are blenders, two are juicers, two are coffee makers, one is a toaster oven, and the other is an electric kettle (the last one is a popcorn popper).

Of course, low-tech breakfast gadgets still abound. In the 20th century's teen years, the grapefruit spoon made eating the large citrus an easier task. Rather than having to supreme the fruit with a paring knife—an arduous and time-consuming task—the diner could slide the serrated tip of the spoon or the curved blade of the grapefruit knife into each cell and liberate the juicy segments from within the individual, bitter membranes. Though they were a novel invention sold primarily in fine gift stores, early 20th-century etiquette guides nonetheless insisted that "spoons of a special shape are given as a rule with the grapefruit or orange course."[44] Unless a specific spoon is offered for the purpose, a dessert spoon was to be used to eat breakfast cereal, but never a teaspoon, which was only for stirring tea or coffee. A century after the invention of cereal, most Americans still find that all they need to enjoy breakfast is a bowl and a spoon.

CONVENIENCE FOODS FOR WORKING MOTHERS

"The habit of eating some cereal for breakfast is happily becoming almost universal," wrote Christine Terhune Herrick.[45] With the rapidly growing variety of pre-made cereals available to American housewives in the late 19th century, she added, "there is no reason why any one should have occasion to complain of monotony." Herrick did not know that packaged breakfast cereals would also provide a great amount of relief to the increasing numbers of American mothers entering the workforce during World War I. Not only were women now expected to keep up their own homes without domestic help, but many of them were now employed helping with the war effort as well.

Despite nutritionists' increasing warnings of dyspepsia, processed and canned foods soared in popularity. As the United States moved past the second Industrial Revolution at the turn of the 20th century, modernization in the kitchen and the introduction of convenience foods transformed the way people ate breakfast in the home, as well as effecting social change for women outside of the home. Advertisers promised working women that their products could meet their needs, and as early as 1912, ads for Post Shredded Wheat offered working women relief from "The Strain and Stress of Life." With all that newly freed time in the morning, it is perhaps no coincidence that the American Women's Suffrage Movement gained momentum in the years following World War I.

Mothers who opted to stay at home needed ready-made and quick-to-prepare breakfast foods, too—not just to free up time for more creative pursuits, but, according to advertisers, because their children's lives utterly depended on it. Until the 1920s, child and infant mortality were a frequent, tragic part of family life. Early advertisers began to use scare tactics to pressure women to buy their products. Breakfast products like Ralston's Wheat Food were the only way for mothers to protect their children from certain death. Nestlé warned mothers of "The Dangerous Business of Being a Baby," promising that their clean, healthy products could save lives.

The 1920s and 1930s were a time of convenience and modernity in the kitchen, introducing many of the foods that modern Americans still associate with breakfast. Ballard's Oven Ready Buttermilk Biscuits (the first refrigerated, pre-made biscuit dough; later to be owned by Pillsbury), bottled fruit juices, and a variety of instant cereals and coffee that needed only to be mixed with hot water all entered American supermarkets during this time. A few years after freezers were stock items in American kitchens, so were Eggo frozen waffles. In fact, even in households with a waffle iron, toasters likely heated the morning waffles.

During World War II, women entered the workforce in unprecedented numbers, and ads for convenience foods showed greater acknowledgment of the fact, targeting working mothers more directly. However, the anxieties about female social roles had already been arising in the 1920s and 1930s, and women working outside the home during the war created further upheaval, even if it was "for the boys." Cooking persisted as a sidenote to solving marital problems caused by the shift in household power, and preparing a man's favorite foods was one way for a wife to placate her husband's wounded ego. Pancakes and syrup (as long as they were better than his mother's) were sure to fit the bill.

Postwar, American baby boomer households found an increased reliance on ready-made foods such as instant oatmeal, yogurt cups, and packaged breakfast cereals. Urged to leave her paid employment outside the home, pleasing and caring for her husband at breakfast was, once again, the highest priority for American wives, or at least as far as magazine writers and government officials were concerned. Convenience foods and modern appliances were great liberators to women who had gotten a taste of independent working life during the war, enabling them to simultaneously play Career Lady and keep hubby happy. Feminist Betty Friedan wrote in 1963 that appliances and ready-made foods allowed the postwar housewife to "save time that can be used in more creative ways."[46] However, for all her applause, Friedan did take offense to food companies targeting women's guilt for abandoning their children, calling marketers "manipulators."

Marketing directly to children was one such manipulative—if not also ingenious—strategy. Once television was mainstream, breakfast cereals could be advertised during Saturday morning cartoons, when kids were not only a captive audience, but one likely to be without adult supervision. Cartoon characters from children's television programming were used to cross-promote the cereals. In 1958, for example, Kellogg's Frosted Flakes mascot Tony the Tiger teamed up with Huckleberry Hound and Snagglepuss, characters from the animation company Hanna-Barbera.[47] In the 1940s, Cheerios featured Mickey Mouse on the box. To alleviate their guilt for not having time to cook a full breakfast, overworked mothers indulged Junior's shrill pleas for Sugar Smacks.

Because of links of increased sugar consumption to childhood obesity, the use of cartoons and cultural icons to advertise breakfast cereal has received much attention over the past forty years, resulting in a failed attempt by the U.S. Federal Trade Commission in the 1970s to ban the use of cartoons to target advertising to children. In 2009, a second wave of attempts to convince companies to voluntarily stop using cartoon characters to advertise unhealthy breakfast foods to children was, unsurprisingly, ineffective.

Cereal companies made other attempts to attract children, appealing to smaller appetites with pint-sized portions. In the early 1940s, Kellogg's began producing individual servings of kids' favorite breakfast cereals in variety packs, which ended fights in the grocery store by eliminating the crippling decision of which one cereal to buy. "'Choose-it-yourself' breakfasts like this one give everyone in the family (including Mom) more freedom," promised a 1956 Kellogg's advertisement, along with a note to "Modern Mothers" about the psychological importance of allowing children to make confidence-building decisions. Some ads ran with the notion, depicting the "Junior Executive alone with a decision," poring over which of the ten tiny boxes should be his breakfast.[48]

Better still, the small cereal boxes were packaged in a built-in bowl, designed to be easy for children and one less dish for Mom. And for extra fun, suggested the ads, the milk could be poured into the wax-lined Kel-Bowl-Pac and eaten right from the box. "Just take the box in both hands and break open the top along the perforated line as shown. That's all there is to it! A perfect portion every time!" Unfortunately, most children lacked the manual dexterity to seamlessly perform this task. The difficulty of opening the perforated front panel and slicing open the wax paper or plastic lining without spilling the cereal required the delicate touch of an advanced origami artist.

When it came to the choice between an instant breakfast of cold cereal straight from the box or a lavish feast of bacon, eggs, and freshly baked breakfast cakes, many Americans found happy middle ground using shortcut products like pancake or biscuit mix. By the 1920s, the now-commonplace "little electric servants" had lost much of their novelty and the new generation of housewives had the same old challenges for getting breakfast on the table: namely, the hassle of measuring flour and milk, cracking eggs, and standing over a stove to provide a hot breakfast. Now, instead of a maid to help in her kitchen, the American woman had Ann Pillsbury, Betty Crocker, and Aunt Jemima on her team.

Some products sidestepped promises of simplifying women's lives and audaciously claimed to be superior to home cooking. Cooking "from scratch" with Bisquick gave wives the upper hand over their mothers-in-law, against whom women had been pitted for culinary superiority and their husband's true affections. "Biscuits he will say are better than those his mother made," assured Bisquick in the 1930s.

Pancake and biscuit mixes were indeed a blessing to housewives—not just because they eliminated the tedium of measuring and sifting dry ingredients ("more freedom on Sunday," promised Betty Crocker), but because they offered expansive variety. One box of powdered mix could produce pancakes, biscuits, waffles, crepes, muffins, cinnamon rolls, or even croissants, if the cook was feeling adventurous. Most importantly, shortcut products still required a *bit* of cooking, allowing pensive housewives to save face and avoid the guilt that came with taking the easy way out with ready-made foods.

Once market researchers realized that some women were reticent to use convenience products, advertisers shifted tactics. High-volume, freeze-dried coffee became available after World War II, but one market study showed that housewives were reluctant to buy Nescafé instant coffee because they associated the product with laziness and shameful extravagance. When market researchers realized this, their advertising instead promoted thrift, and recommended letting the coffee "steep for a moment to bring out extra aroma and Nescafé's pure coffee deliciousness." A few years after the revealing study, Nescafé also created a coffee maker specifically for their product; of course, it was merely a warmer with a carafe into which hot water and instant coffee granules would be added, but it gave the illusion of real coffee, freshly brewed.

Decaffeinated instant Sanka was introduced in the 1930s. Sanka was originally marketed for people who wanted to drink coffee after dinner, but soon became the beverage of choice for anyone who wanted to avoid a case of the jitters. The bright-orange packaging of Sanka left such an impression on the American public that orange handles are still used on coffeepots to distinguish decaf from regular coffee. Until the mid-1980s, Sanka was chemically decaffeinated using dicholoromethane, a sweet-tasting solvent commonly used as a paint stripper.

Soon, other foods were made into scientifically processed versions under the guise of quality control. In the 1950s, this meant instant coffee and non-dairy creamer. For those tired of their cream going lumpy, Coffee-mate offered superior coffee whitening and an extended shelf life; Coffee-mate came with something else cream did not: a warning to "avoid use near an open flame."

Some convenience products were more affordable than their analog, offering additional incentive to shoppers. Orange drinks like Tang and Sunny Delight were formulated to be more affordable and shelf-stable than juice. Introduced to grocery stores in 1959, powdered Tang Instant Breakfast Drink was the kid's complement to Mom's instant coffee. It only contained 2 percent juice, but was nonetheless among the National Football League's Selected Official Training Foods for being "high nutrition, high energy." It had a stupendous twenty-three grams of sugar per two-tablespoon serving.

Even before convenience foods were available to housewives, expediency in the kitchen was a sought-after achievement. Cookbooks like *Quick Cooking: A Book of Culinary Heresies for the Busy Wives and Mothers of the Land* by Flora Haines Loughead assured the 19th-century housewife that "there is no waste in the kitchen so much to be deplored as wasted time."[49] Eighty years before feminist Betty Friedan wrote as much, Loughead wrote, rather audaciously for her era: "Whether the hours thus saved to the busy housewife shall be devoted to rest, self-improvement, to out-door recreation, to the training of her children, or to the discharge of other and more pressing cares, is left to her own decision."[50]

CHILDREN LEARN TO COOK

Thanks to convenience foods and packaged mixes, a freshly cooked, hot breakfast was still a possibility for American children, and did not rely on mother's attention. In the 1920s, advertisements for Aunt Jemima pancake mix appeared in *Boys' Life* magazine, but even earlier, Teco's corn- and rice-based self-rising mix assured boy scouts that the pancakes made from Teco and water were "good as those mother makes at home," all while conserving precious wheat to "serve the cause of freedom" during World War I.

Teaching culinary self-sufficiency to children began at breakfast. Even if a child was too young to cook his own pancakes, he could pour cereal and milk into a bowl and waddle, sleepy-headed and pajama-clad, to the television. He would not have to disturb his parents, who may be sleeping in on the weekend. By the 1920s, children were certainly capable of pouring milk over their own cereal, as Shredded Wheat proposed in a 1928 ad, with its image of a ruddy-cheeked boy cradling boxes of cereal under his arm with the tagline "Getting his own breakfast." As of the 1990s, approximately 80 percent of children prepared their own breakfasts—only snacks have a higher rate of child-selection and preparation.[51]

In 1948, one article noted that "nine out of ten women bring a box of corn flakes or their children's current favorite ready-to-eat cereal to the table. Mothers find the youngsters like to pour their own or use individual packages when available."[52] Serving the cereal box and empty bowl at the table instead of pouring the cereal in the kitchen and bringing the filled bowl to the table had, until then, been a novelty for housewives, and as was the case of eating in the kitchen's breakfast nook, the once uncouth habit was eagerly accepted into common custom.

For some mothers, letting children prepare their own breakfasts was not just a time-saver, but an intentional parenting decision. "Even very little children are happy when they think they are useful," wrote abolitionist and women's rights activist Lydia Maria Child in 1831. It is probably no coincidence that such a champion for women's rights should promote putting children to work when it may be of particular service to their long-suffering mothers. Preparing breakfast for a child who is able to help himself does not teach the child independence or life skills, yet many mothers—who would never tolerate a ten-year-old's request for help tying shoes, for example—continue to make breakfasts that children could easily accomplish on their own. Some mothers felt this did their children a disservice in the long run. "I fail my children if I treat them like guests in their own home," wrote one woman in a 1988 issue of *Working Mother* magazine.[53] This was particularly true in the latchkey-kid days of the 1980s, when both parents—or the primary caregiver, in the growing number of single-parent households—typically worked outside the home. Average children had to pull their own weight to contribute to the success of the household.

In the 1908 children's cookbook *When Mother Lets Us Cook*, the first recipe is for boiled eggs. A few pages in, scrambled eggs on toast are a foray into cooking for the more adept child. A good portion of the book is devoted to dishes commonly eaten for breakfast. Recipes for omelets, nest eggs, stewed fruits, and pancakes—among myriad others—suggest that the morning meal was typical for children to learn to cook. (The book's remaining recipes suggest that candy was the other meal particularly suited to children.)

Learning to cook breakfast was not just the job of girls. Meatloaf and cherry pie were never important for young men to master; on the contrary, breakfast was a meal that boys could cook without endangering their masculinity. A 1936 article in *The Delineator* titled "Come Into the Kitchen, Boys" beseeched young men to take to the stove. "The lad who cannot assemble an edible breakfast in 15 minutes . . . is unfitted for the responsibilities of matrimony or to pose as the head of a household."[54]

Ladd Plumley, author of numerous articles on camp cooking, wrote in a 1917 article "Boys and Cookery" that to be "a more efficient citizen" a man should be able to, among other things, "make coffee, bake a pan of biscuit, [and] conjure an omelet."[55] In the *American Cookery* article, Plumley reminisces about having learned to cook while watching his mother, "very likely bothering her to distraction, as she prepared breakfast." He concludes his rallying cry by telling

Boy Scouts cooking over a campfire, 1918. Courtesy of the Library of Congress.

American mothers that they "should take a little thought of the importance of teaching the small boy of the household how to make coffee and execute other juggleries with raw provisions."

While Plumley stressed the importance of cooking as a basic life skill, he admitted that there should be very few moments in a man's life when he would come to rely on the skill. Boys only really needed to know how to cook breakfast and one or two stand-by meals like steak or fried fish for emergencies or when camping.

MEN HELP

Where convenience foods and the skilled hands of children failed to fill the void, American men—perhaps wistful for their boyhood memories of campfire pancakes—stepped up to the plate. This phenomenon has been on the rise over the past few decades; in 1965, only 5 percent of men took the helm with any sort of regularity, but now nearly a third of meals prepared at home are done so by men. This trend has been a boon for many overworked mothers and has tipped the balance of household labor slightly closer toward center, but in the past half-century the meal most often prepared by fathers (besides the backyard barbecue) seems to have been breakfast.

Prewar, getting one's husband to help was anathema. Cooking one's own breakfast was for the poor sap who found himself between Mother and Wife. A 1920 issue of *Popular Science Monthly* offered that appliances were there to help. "With an electric percolator and a toaster you can get your breakfast."[56] The article continued, though, supporting the notion that men should not need to enjoy the cooking. "Don't like to cook your own breakfast? Neither do many married men." The rest of the article was filled with helpful suggestions for employing technology to find a wife so that the hapless bachelor may end his personal hell brought on by having to prepare his own breakfast.

Part of the problem with getting men into the kitchen, as identified by a 1927 article in *The Rotarian*, was that available recipe books (with the notable exception of preeminent French gastronome Brillat-Savarin) had primarily been written by and for women. Another male author called cookbooks "a lot of bunk anyway." In the 1921 *Ladies' Home Journal* article "What to Cook When the Wife Is Away," journalist Bozeman Bulger wrote of fumbling in the kitchen with a friend while his wife was on vacation.[57] Another friend, a confirmed bachelor named Ballou (for whom cooking was a "pet topic") came to save them, teaching them the secrets of how not to screw it up. The focus of the man's training was on breakfast dishes, and by the time the wife returned a week later, the author, now a master of breakfast cookery, was able to surprise her with a lovely breakfast of baked eggs and bacon.

This kind of helper-husband cooking was something of a fantasy for married women. In the fictionalized how-to guide *A Thousand Ways to Please a Husband* (1917), dreamboat husband Bob offers to turn the tables, and announces that he will prepare Sunday breakfast for his doting wife Bettina. She was positively tickled at the idea, and made a celebration of it, festooning a table on the front porch with linens and flowers, and cooing encouragement at Bob as he fumbled with frizzled beef and cream, toast, and a pot of coffee. After their "jolly and leisurely meal," Bob washed the dishes, proving that the book was not actually intended as a young bride's instruction manual, so much as pornography for housewives.

In the postwar era, cookbooks directed to men began to proliferate, largely focusing on "manly" foods like steak. If a man should need to make biscuits, insisted the aggressively masculine-named Brick Gordon in 1947, he could use a beer bottle instead of an effete rolling pin.[58] A pat of butter was for sissies; a "man-sized lump of butter" should be used to fry eggs. Gone were the days of a man being relegated to toast and coffee in the morning; now, a macho breakfast of bacon and fried eggs could be his, with or without a woman's help.

Only hobby or necessity cooking was typically done by men; daily cooking was still—make no mistake—women's work. Of the rare cooking that was undertaken by the head of the household, Saturday or Sunday breakfast was most traditional. Because it was the weekend, it still qualified as a special occasion, and therefore an acceptable time to cook; because the meal was still largely centered on hearty fare like eggs, salty meats, and stick-to-the-ribs pancakes, breakfast was safe for a man to cook without jeopardizing his heterosexuality.

During World War II, morale-boosting ads suggested that it was the little things that kept Americans afloat during tough times. One 1943 ad showed the fictional Mr. Potter carrying a breakfast tray to his wife, a nervous smile on his face. "'Mr. Potter's Sunday Morning Special' Scrambled eggs . . . coffee (a little spilled in the saucer) . . . toast (just a bit on the burned side). . . . It's just Mr. Potter's way of thanking Mrs. Potter for putting up with him all these years." Interestingly, this was an ad produced by the brewing industry, reminding those demoralized by rationing and wartime that beer was there to help. This public service announcement managed to still portray men as adorably, forgivably inept in the kitchen, but suggested that the reader think of the good that could come, if he could put his ego in check.

On the contrary, humorist Frank Sullivan found that cooking breakfast could bolster a man's ego. In his 1938 essay, "A Bachelor Looks at Breakfast," Sullivan declared that "[t]here is no reason why a man should not cook his own breakfast and a number of reasons why he should, one being that it is good for his ego. . . . I have been getting my own breakfast on Sunday mornings for the past three months, and as a result my ego is the size of a prize squash at a county fair."[59]

For fathers, cooking breakfast allowed men to maintain their heroic position in the family. "Breakfast has traditionally been Dad's domain," insisted men's cookbook author and manliness expert Bob Sloan, in his 2007 *Dad's Own Cookbook*. Advertisements reiterated that plenty of otherwise unhelpful dads excelled at the weekend breakfast. A 1962 ad for Aunt Jemima pancake mix showed one of "the dandiest dads" who makes pancakes on weekends wearing his wife's ruffled apron, leaning in for a hug and kiss from his angelic daughter.

Fathers typically focused their culinary efforts on novel foods that mothers did not have time to cook every morning; this festal (celebratory) versus ferial (everyday) cooking distinguished men's role as something worth celebrating.[60] It was not unusual for the man of the house to have a specialty that he prepared with some regularity, perfected by time and practice. "Even though weekend foodways as a whole may be characterized by a greater freedom of food choices, the male cook typically establishes sovereignty over a given weekend meal for which he always prepares the same foods," noted American folklore historian Thomas A. Adler in 1981.[61]

With fathers at the helm, mothers could rejoice for the morning off, and children delighted in eating pancakes and bacon instead of cold cereal or oatmeal. In 1964, preeminent chef and cookbook author James Beard wrote fondly of his own father's Sunday breakfasts, recalling that

> he had a favorite late Sunday breakfast menu, which he produced every week, save in winter, consisting of deliciously sauteed chicken served with a bacon-and-cream sauce made in the saute pan. With this dish there were generally hot biscuits, toasted crumpets, or just good toast. In winter the menu changed to sausage, smoked fish, or country ham. These expressions of my father's culinary skill were memorable indeed, and whenever friends stayed with us on weekends, they used to request his breakfast.[62]

In June 2012, men's magazine *Esquire* polled nineteen famous chefs on typical dishes their fathers had prepared when they were growing up. For roughly half of them, it was breakfast dishes like waffles with bacon bits or eggs cooked sunny-side-up that had left the most indelible impression.[63]

LIKE MOTHER USED TO MAKE

Though many Americans today have fond memories of the breakfasts prepared by their fathers on weekends, advertisers did not attempt to cultivate men as consumers. Most cooking has been traditionally performed by women, and those foods prepared by one's mother have long been held in the highest nostalgic esteem. In 1874, the catch-phrase "like mother used to make" was coined by American poet James Whitcomb Riley, in a dialectic poem about a man drinking a cup of coffee and being suddenly transported back to his mother's arm while she cooked breakfast.[64]

Despite a few feminist attempts to encourage women away from the stove, most wives and mothers would not dare. More than a century after domestic manuals first insisted on it, cookbooks for the housewife of the 1950s continued to advise women that they should be pretty, bright, and amiable while serving breakfast, or risk their husband turning his disappointment to the morning paper. Journalist and cookbook author Ida Bailey Allen wrote in 1952 that breakfast was the most important time for the housewife to be "pleasant and even-tempered," lest she ruin the entire day for her family. Allen offered explicit

Breakfast, 1962. (Copyright Bettmann/Corbis/AP Images)

direction on how the woman of the house might adjust her attitude, cheerfully suggesting that "if you will use your own good will and make up your mind to face the day without the feeling that the burden of the whole world is on your shoulders, before you know it, there will be a smile on your face, a light in your eyes and cheer in your voice to glamorize the whole family."[65] If that failed to do the trick, the housewife could always take amphetamines.[66]

Keeping her family happy was a top priority for housewives, but simply getting breakfast prepared in time to send the children off to school and her husband off to work was just as important. The quotidian breakfast had to be fast, but women could still show their affection with the products they chose for their families. Images of glowing mothers, lovingly preparing an array of warm foods for their tow-headed cherubs, dominated magazines and newspapers in the first half of the 20th century. The ads insisted that mothers use their products "because you love them so much"; in 1960, Quaker Oats assured mothers that the best start to the day was "a hug, a kiss and a hot oatmeal breakfast." Such ads—of which there were myriad—painted the image that a warm, comforting breakfast *was* a mother's love.

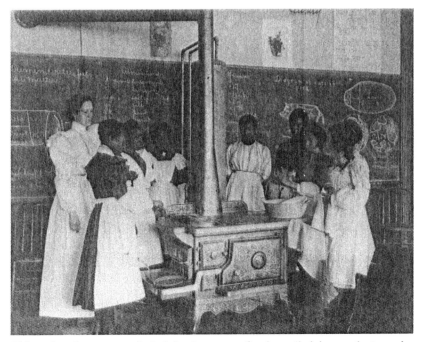

African American women in training to prepare for domestic jobs as private cooks, ca. 1899. Courtesy of the Library of Congress.

For a time, though, "Mother's home cooking" was something of a farce. From the Civil War until the Civil Rights Movement of the 1960s, many of the comfort foods enjoyed at breakfast were perfected not by "Mother," but by hired black cooks employed by private households. Cookbooks like *Dishes & Beverages of the Old South* (1913) by Martha McCulloch-Williams revealed a wistfulness for the antebellum foodways, and until the 1980s, advertisements for products such as Aunt Jemima's pancake mix, Mrs. Butterworth's maple syrup, and Cream of Wheat farina cereal continued to perpetuate this nostalgia for indentured servitude.

Many have criticized the fictitious Aunt Jemima for being a symbol of pervasive racism and classism in the United States; however, on pancake cookery, she was a subject matter expert, doling out advice to anxious white housewives apparently not yet accustomed to doing their own cooking. One 1953 advertorial featured the headline "Pancake Queen tells Mrs. America about her Newest Pancake Success"; Aunt Jemima, the wise and seasoned professional, could teach the "Queen of Homemakers" herself a thing or two about breakfast.

Elsewhere in the United States, traditional home cooking was informed not by the mother of the home, but by the food tradition of the disenfranchised classes. In Appalachia, home cooking was assimilated from the diets of indigenous people. Between the Daniel Boone days of the 18th century and the abject regional poverty of the 1950s, traditional breakfast foods like fried cornmeal mush, smoked meats, fried apples (after the 17th century), and cornbread with beans— foods largely learned from the Cherokee Indians—changed very little. Even prim Quakers, steadfast in their adherence to old English ways, adapted Native American foodstuffs such as hominy and tomatoes into their morning meal.

Other traditional home cooking was brought directly from one's homeland and interpreted through the American lens. *Chilaquiles, huevos rancheros,* and *migas,* favorite morning foods of the southwestern United States, were inspired by home cooks from Mexico. Aside from its use of blue corn rather than yellow, *chauquehue*—an old-fashioned New Mexican specialty—is indistinguishable from the fried corn mush prepared by native women of the Great Plains and the pioneer wives who learned from them. Apple dumplings, Dutch babies, and scrapple, traditional breakfasts of Amish country, were introduced by German immigrants and adapted to American ingredients. The sweet, fried dough fritters called *beignets,* the Creole accompaniment to chicory coffee, were brought to New Orleans by the French in the 18th century.

Traditional foods, it could be argued, are truly defined by a mother's cooking simply for the fact that culinary traditions are passed down from generation to generation by those who do the cooking. A mother's recipe for her child's favorite blueberry muffins will differ ever so slightly from her own mother's, using more nutmeg, say; her child's version, in turn, will reveal subtle variation based on differences in technique or ingredient quality.

HOLIDAYS AND SPECIAL OCCASIONS

The traditional breakfast foods of the past, thanks to the complications of modern life, have largely been transferred to weekends and special occasions. Postwar, pancakes or omelets may have been eaten on weekdays (at least some-times), but the daily full breakfasts of the 18th and 19th centuries were long gone without a staff of domestic workers to complete the task. However, on holidays and weekends, with everyone gathered together at home, it was pos-sible to have pancakes *and* omelets, and bacon and potatoes to boot; breakfast became part of a day's feasting.

Until the middle of the 20th century, breakfast on Sundays was a quick bite before church (if anything at all), which would be followed by a larger brunch. This could be a dish prepared on Saturday evening to be reheated the follow-ing morning, as suggested by M. Tarbox Colbrath in her 1882 *What to Get for Breakfast*. Colbrath, perhaps in defense of her book's purpose, recommended never skipping breakfast, especially not on church days. Hungry people, she ar-gued, did not make good parishioners. "Do not lessons from experience prove that an easy, nourishing, and readily digested breakfast is the right one for Sun-day?"[67] Her ideal Sunday breakfast, for both nourishment and ease of prepara-tion, was baked beef and beans, which she acknowledged was an affront at the "time honored" pork and beans for Sunday breakfast; she considered pork to be "the most indigestible of all meats, besides being unscriptural."[68] While wel-come among cowboys in western territories, her version would certainly have been disdained by Bostonians.

As the 20th century wore on, some church services began later on Sunday mornings to accommodate breakfast and increase attendance and the time people would be willing to spend in pews. Some churches recommended serv-ing breakfast to get parishioners in the doors as early as 7:00 a.m. In Jewish households, no bread was to be eaten before the Shabbat Kiddush (Saturday blessing), so families might enjoy a light nibble of fruit, cereal, or muffins before heading off to synagogue.

Because of this tendency to skip breakfast before religious services, Jewish holidays seem to not have any specific traditional breakfast foods associated with them, even though each of the holidays have their own traditional and ritual foods and many of these would indeed make fine breakfasts. None of the delectable fried doughnuts or fritters prepared for Hanukah were particularly intended for the morning meal, even though they would all be eagerly eaten for breakfast by *goyim*. Even latkes, the hash brown–esque potato pancakes, were not specifically for a Hanukah breakfast. It was not until the late 18th century that Germans began adding potatoes to pancakes, and around fifty years later for Jews of Eastern Europe; however, these were not necessarily prepared for Hanukah. *"Aunt Babette's" Cook Book* (1889), the first American Jewish cookbook written after the Reform of Judaism, does include a recipe for potato pancakes and advises the cook that "[i]n cold weather have all the breakfast plates heated."[69] Cold plates would certainly be an expected bother during Hanukah.

Colbrath had no suggestions for a special occasion such as Christmas, though the holiday breakfast is typically eaten at home, after the children have opened their presents. Until the turn of the 20th century, Christmas's celebratory meal was dinner; it took people some convincing that they could do away with the trouble of preparing an ornate dinner and opt instead for a relaxed breakfast with the family. In "A Christmas Breakfast," published in a 1906 issue of *American Motherhood* magazine, author Dr. Mary Wood-Allen told a story of a stressed-out mother planning the elaborate holiday dinner for her family.[70] Mrs. Wallace, the troubled housewife, was convinced by her children's teacher Miss Ingalls, who insisted that a Christmas *breakfast* was all the rage among her social circles, and Mrs. Wallace's young daughter added that if her teacher's chic city friends could have a Christmas breakfast, "it must be the 'swell' thing to do." After hemming and hawing, Mrs. Wallace decided "it would be something quite novel and original," and her simple breakfast was, naturally, an effortless success. "I am so glad you had a Christmas breakfast, mother," her son said, and Mrs. Wallace was declared the "sweetheart" of the holiday by all.[71]

While that tale might cloy a bit, it does paint an interesting portrait of early-20th-century America. Traditions were beginning to shift and evolve with the times, and this was exciting. Women's magazines began including articles on "Successful Plans for Christmas" that included breakfast. A special Christmas breakfast was one of *A Thousand Ways to Please a Husband* (naturally, dreamboat husband Bob was there to impress the family with his waffles). Appliance companies were eager to advertise that their breakfast wares were a perfect holiday gift for Mother, to be enjoyed right away. In 1938, the Kitchen-Aid electric coffee grinder was ready to "stimulate good spirits daily—from Christmas breakfast on."

Sometimes the Christmas breakfast was just a large collection of many dishes, or as much of anything as one could eat; one Appalachian recalled of his Depression-era childhood that "[t]hat's one day we got all the eggs we wanted."[72] There was also a greater focus on baking the types of breakfast breads and cakes that had largely disappeared from home kitchens by the 1910s. Coffee cakes, cinnamon rolls, and tender apple cake would be part of a leisurely Christmas breakfast, and persist as part of many family holiday traditions today.

Some breakfast treats are specific to certain holidays. In Pennsylvania, potato doughnuts called *Fastnacht kuchen* or "Shrove Tuesday cakes" are eaten on the day before Lent; this holiday is also known as Fat Tuesday (or Mardi Gras) for the tradition of eating fried foods. "Without fail, every year on Shrove Tuesday, or 'Fast Nacht,' the day before the beginning of Lent, these cakes were made," wrote Edith M. Thomas in her 1915 *Mary at the Farm*, a fictionalized account of the Pennsylvania Dutch based on her interviews of real people.[73] She noted the tradition of making Fastnacht kuchen (or just fastnacht) "it would have been a very important event, indeed, which would have prevented the baking of these toothsome delicacies on that day."[74]

In England, Shrove Tuesday is alternately known as Pancake Day. Because of the ritual fasting of Lent, the use of sugar, eggs, flour, butter, and other rich foodstuffs was restricted, and households cleared their cupboards of these ingredients by preparing pancakes. How shriving, or confessing one's sins in order to purify the soul, should come with a pancake feast is a mystery, but a long-standing one nonetheless; one 18th-century source supposed it came from "the Greek Church."[75] According to legend, the ringing of the shriving bell signaled parishioners that it was time to head toward the confession, but that one year these bells came early in the morning. A housewife, in the middle of making breakfast, ran out of her house with her pan still in her hand, flipping her pancake as she ran toward the church. For the past five and a half centuries, this story has been reenacted in a traditional pancake race, the oldest of which has been held in Olney, Buckinghamshire since 1445. Today, Pancake Day is celebrated as an actual race; runners must sprint 415 yards (379 meters) while flipping a pancake—clad in an apron and bonnet for historical authenticity, of course—before passing the finish line at the Church of Saint Peter and Saint Paul.

The day before Pancake Day is another high holy day centered on breakfast. The last meat day before Lent, Shrove Monday, is also known as Collopy Monday in reference to the tradition of eating thinly sliced meats. Though the thin flaps of meat have been called "collops" since the Elizabethan times, eating a breakfast of bacon with fried eggs on top has been part of the traditional Lenten preparations since the days of the Holy Roman Empire. This was partly because in medieval winters, all the meat available would have been salted, dried, and hung as bacon or ham. As was the case with the Pancake Day following Collopy Monday, finishing off the winter's stores before Lent would clear the larder, while the shroving would clear the conscience.

On Easter, all bets were off. Breakfast, as a meal, was never so symbolic—or literal—than when it broke a fast. During Lent, a wealthier 16th-century family (specifically, the gluttonous Earl of Northumberland and his wife) would have gotten by on salt fish, herrings, or sprats for breakfast, instead of the customary half a chine of mutton or a chine of beef; during Easter, they could have their chine, and a calf's head to boot. In Cheshire, one custom was for two sheriffs to shoot bows and arrows into the sky before a calf's head and bacon breakfast feast as part of a "loving assemblye" partaken by the mayor, alderman, and members of the better-off general public. This tradition was so strictly enforced that in 1670, the sheriffs were fined £10 for not keeping the Easter calf's head feast.

Symbolic foods like breads were draped across the breakfast table to remind diners that Lent was over. Eggs, as Christine Terhune Herrick put it in 1900, "are a *sine qua non*."[76] She helpfully suggested a simple affair, taking advantage of hot cross buns left over from Good Friday and serving the Easter eggs devilled. This simple eggs and hot cross buns breakfast is also taken by Queen Elizabeth II today.

The *Original Buckeye Cookbook and Practical Housekeeping* (1905) suggests sturdier fare for Easter Sunday: broiled sirloin steak, French rolls, potatoes, radishes, boiled eggs, and waffles with honey. It was considered "very correct" in the early 20th century to close breakfast parties with waffles and honey or syrup instead of an ice, and if there were ever a time to be very correct, it was Easter. Other authors insisted that Easter breakfast, like all breakfasts, required planning and a table sufficiently resplendent to show off the breakfast parlor. "Blossoms and Easter eggs for breakfast are absolute necessities to observe the day properly," insisted one contributor to *Table Talk* magazine in 1904, who recommended potting violets or forcing daffodil bulbs into bloom weeks in advance of the holiday breakfast to ensure that the flowers are ready for their spotlight.[77]

The Polish tradition called święconka, or "the blessing of the Easter basket," dates back to at least medieval Christianity, but likely has pagan roots. An ornate basket of meats, eggs, cakes, and breads is prepared and brought to church to be blessed on Holy Saturday (the day before Easter). On Easter morning, following a daybreak mass, people rush home and gorge on the basket's foods that had been banned during Lent. The tradition was brought to America as early as the 17th century, with the first Jamestown colonists and is, for many Polish Americans, one of the last vestiges of their culture that survives in the United States.

Mother's Day was enacted as a legal holiday in 1914, but it was not until the 1940s that it went from a solemn, dignified holiday venerating the women who have given birth, to one where mothers could get something they really needed: breakfast in bed (or brunch, if she also got to sleep in). This breakfast is traditionally fumbled together by the children of the house, with guidance from their father. Over the past century, the holiday has celebrated mothers' innumerable efforts in domesticity by rewarding them with one morning meal; ironically, the holiday was originally conceived to celebrate women's political efforts outside of the home—the very efforts that eventually brought women the daily conveniences they really needed, like instant oatmeal and electric toasters.[78]

Even more ironically, many mid-century advertisements suggested giving mothers breakfast appliances as Mother's Day gifts, to help her through her drudgery the other 364 days of the year. In 1940, Sunbeam supposed their automatic Coffeemaster made a perfect gift for Mother's Day, because, as the ads touted, it allowed women to "simply put in the water, flip a switch, and go about [her] other duties *in peace*."

THE MORNING AFTER

"Many a man who glibly opens wine at night, cooked his own breakfast that morning on an alcohol lamp," wrote American architect and humorist Herman Lee Meader in 1903.[79] If a man had too much to drink the night before, Meader subtly warned, his chances for breakfast in bed may have been blown. Conversely, if things had gone well, a bachelor might be cooking two breakfasts instead of one. He had better be ready to follow through on his line, "how do you like your eggs?"

Of all the reasons for a man to learn to cook breakfast and for it to be socially acceptable for him to do so, impressing a sexual partner may have been fairly high on the list. Preeminent food writer M. F. K. Fisher wrote in a 1948 article for *Gourmet Magazine* that "[a bachelor's] approach to gastronomy is basically sexual, since few of them under seventy-nine will bother to produce a good meal unless it is for a pretty woman."[80] If a bachelor had sealed the deal, it was even more important that he could scramble some eggs. "Cookbooks for men occasionally designated breakfast as a bachelor's post-coital activity, which would of course bolster gender norms," wrote gender studies professor Jessamyn Neuhaus.[81] If a man was a good morning cook, a woman may forgive a less-than-stellar sexual performance. "Make a great breakfast and she'll boast to her friends when she gets together for the official review," hoped cookbook author Rocky Fino in his 2005 *Will Cook for Sex*.[82]

Sexuality and food have classically gone hand in hand. As early as the 1930s, showing two people eating breakfast together was used metaphorically in movies to reveal that the couple had shared an evening of carnal pleasure. A request to eat breakfast together could be a coy invitation to stay the night; if a guest had been invited to the bedroom, *not* staying for breakfast signaled that the event had either been unimpressive to the houseguest (who had perhaps sneaked out in the middle of the night) or that the event had not been intended to foster emotional intimacy. Whether one ate breakfast in one's own home or in someone else's was largely a matter of circumstance, of personal taste, or of luck.

BREAKFAST OUT

Although lunch is the meal most commonly eaten outside of the home, more than two-thirds of Americans eat the morning meal on the go. Breakfast has been eaten in stagecoaches and trains, while waiting for the bus, or while sitting in one's car in rush-hour traffic; it has been eaten in hotels and restaurants, and in cafeterias at school and on corporate campuses. Because of the rush of the morning, breakfast suffers the most from cut corners, if it is not cut entirely.

The American tradition of eating breakfast on the go started with the Mayflower. Of course, plenty of Native Americans ate pemmican and dried meat during their morning hunts and traveling work parties for several millennia before the arrival of Europeans. For two centuries, people traveling via boat to the New World suffered from the effects of poor rations, though the maggots infesting their hardtack biscuits and oatmeal at least provided a bit of much-needed protein. By the second half of the 20th century, some breakfast foods were designed specifically for portability and ease of eating while on the move, eventually culminating in the advent of vitamin-enriched breakfast shakes in a can, fortified cereal bars, and fruit-flavored yogurts packaged in a tube that could be injected directly down one's throat.

For those immigrants and pioneers who continued their travels to the American West, the day began with a hearty breakfast cooked on the wagon trail. Most morning meals differed little from the day's other meals; coffee, beans, cornbread, and bacon featured prominently. For those who made it all the way to California, lucky miners might find themselves skipping the beans and instead sitting down to a Hangtown fry.

The mid-19th century witnessed the rise of the cowboy cook. These rugged settlers not only survived, but flourished in the wild West. Cowboys changed the American breakfast landscape forever with their fervent embrace of country-fried steak, beans, and biscuits baked in a cast-iron skillet over an open flame, washed down with thick, molasses-sweetened coffee.

Women, for the first time, were not banished to the kitchens; as a matter of fact, on the wagon trail, they no longer had kitchens to which to be banished. Once a family or community settled land, women helped harvest, homestead, and run businesses alongside men. They enjoyed the freedom of eating in restaurants, where they would not be supervised by escorts, and could enjoy foods they did not have to cook themselves.

When people are traveling for work or pleasure—or for conquest, as has frequently been the case—their gastronomic hand is often forced. The breakfast choices one typically makes can be most revealing while traveling abroad. Personality largely dictates the types of breakfasts people choose when away from home: Some xenophobes take their breakfast preferences with them wherever they travel; others mix the food influences from different places that they have encountered, resulting in such cultural amalgams as kedgeree. Some are true culinary adventurers, willing to try anything new—even a bowl of spicy tripe stew.

Starting in the 1870s, the continental breakfast of finer hotels was created to address people's needs not only for comforting familiarity, but for simplicity. A hotel or restaurant that provides a variety of breads, fruits, and hot foods will please most people who cannot prepare a home-cooked breakfast or do not have time for a feast of stewed kidneys and waffles. Hotels outside the United States often provide the same continental breakfast with the addition of foods more appealing to their own culture; for example, a Tokyo hotel might serve green tea, miso soup, and grilled fish in addition to Western-style coffee, fruit, and croissants.

In the mid-1920s, the "lunch car" officially became known as a "diner" because the small, mobile restaurants were increasingly serving breakfast foods in addition to the midday pie and sandwiches. The explosion in diners post–World War II helped spur this trend by serving breakfast foods all day, catering to the needs of graveyard-shift factory workers at first, but later to the needs of late-night revelers in need of the nostalgic comfort that can only be provided by a stack of buttermilk pancakes and a bottomless cup of coffee.

In the 1940s, doughnut shops became the first fast-food establishments that served breakfast foods. Fast-food breakfasts made their real ascent in the 1970s, with the introduction of Jack in the Box's Breakfast Jack in 1971 and the McDonald's Egg McMuffin one year later. Driven by coffee sales, gas stations and convenience stores followed suit, and with promises of microwavable breakfast burritos and prepackaged bagel sandwiches, weary morning travelers flocked to these inexpensive options.

Children, too, benefited from an affordable approach to morning dining. At the turn of the 20th century, public schools in the United States and abroad began to identify the necessity of breakfast in ensuring the adequate health and academic performance of children, and as a result, many schools began providing breakfast to their students. The School Breakfast Program, a spinoff of President Lyndon B. Johnson's Child Nutrition Act of 1966, later responded to pressures to provide for the needs of the growing number of working-class, dual-income families. As a result, millions of low-income and at-risk children across America eat a federally subsidized breakfast at school.

Though people do sometimes go out for breakfast to while away a lazy weekend morning, most breakfasts are eaten outside the home to save time in the matutinal hurry or while commuting, or because they are simply away from home.

ABROAD

In 1828, an emigrant named James Parks wrote a letter to his parents, warning them of (among other things) the food on the sailing ship bringing him and his wife from Sussex, England, to Albany, New York. Complaining of "tea that was not half tea; oatmeal [that was] half ground pease," Parks became one of America's earliest disgruntled breakfast customers.[1] Parks's timing was rather unfortunate; by the 1850s luxury steamer ships cut the trip to the United States to only twelve days, instead of the four months to a year that it had taken emigrants between the 1770s and the 1840s. The victuals on these swanky steamer ships were measurably better than the dried beef and stale crackers of old.

In the Shamrock Society of New York's helpful manual *Emigration to America: Hints to Emigrants from Europe, Who Intend to Make a Permanent Residence in the United States* (1817), those planning a relocation to the United States are given the proverbial heads-up; "First of all, he should regulate his diet, and be temperate in the quantity of his food."[2] He is instructed to follow the example of the American laborer, who consumes little in the way of rich food or strong drink. The European laborer who "receives meat or fish and coffee at breakfast" (in addition to meat at the other two meals), the Shamrock Society warned, "insensibly falls into a state of too great repletion, which exposes him to the worst kind of fever during the heats of summer and autumn."[3] Considering the high cost of relocating to America and the low wages of the average laborer, it is somewhat unlikely that overconsumption of meat was much of a problem for most immigrants.

Immigrants brought their own foodways with them, or the best approximations of them. When foods did change, it tended to be additive, through consumption of new foods or by including new ingredients into familiar foods. Studies of modern American immigration show that breakfast foods tend to shift first, presumably because the meal holds the least amount of cultural significance for most people.[4] Indeed, a meal that is typically eaten quickly, on the go, or skipped entirely is one that could adapt most readily.

The colonists from England had adopted American foodstuffs into their diet out of necessity, but later by choice. The Native American trinity of beans, corn, and squash—also known as the three sisters—found its way into English breakfast dishes. Cornmeal stood in for wheat and oatmeal in the porridges, breads, and pancakes from the Old World, and later, potatoes, tomatoes, and other nightshades would become indispensable and integral parts of the Anglo-American breakfast.

In the mid-19th century, the wave of emigration from Germany and other parts of northern Europe brought to the Midwest a variety of foods that easily fit into the American breakfast landscape. The Pennsylvania Dutch created meat dishes like *pon haus* or scrapple to make best use of pork scraps left over after butchering, incorporating New World cornmeal into the traditional German recipes that used rye and other darker grains less available in America.

Nineteenth-century cookbooks began to reflect the growing "melting pot" cultural blend; *La Creole Cuisine*, written in 1885 by internationally renowned writer and Greek immigrant Lafcadio Hearn, revealed the multicultural influences on American cooking. The book features such breakfast recipes as stewed Irish potatoes, Indian cakes and corn oysters influenced by Native Americans, and a variety of more traditional English recipes like veal hash with poached eggs; he also noted that adaptation of foreign recipes was not set in stone. "'Dripped' coffee is the French mode, but many make it in the old-time way by boiling. It is a matter of personal taste, not to be interfered with in this 'land of the free.'"[5]

In the days before widespread overland travel, some people embarked on ships to take them from one part of the United States to another, but the accommodations were scarcely much better than those offered from the old country to America, nor was the trip much faster. H. C. Bailey, a Methodist evangelist who sailed from New Orleans to San Francisco in 1853 recalled the conditions soberly:

We were wet, bedraggled and almost half-famished, waiting on deck for breakfast, wondering what it would be and how it would be served. We could see no tables, no signs of approaching breakfast, until about eight o'clock, when a number of pint tin cups and a barrel of crackers were brought out.

Two passengers, who were acting as stewards for their passage, served out the coffee. Every one took a cup of coffee and some sugar and helped himself to the crackers. This constituted our breakfast.[6]

FRONTIER COOKING

In the 1840s, Americans were confident that they were on the precipice of greatness. Though the Midwest was largely settled by Germans, Swedes, and Poles, most pioneers farther west were old-stock Americans looking for new opportunities, driven by duty to their god and their country. "Frontier cookery combined and transcended the histories of origin and emigration," wrote American history author Cathy Luchetti in *Home on the Range: A Culinary History of the American West* (1993).[7]

American author Laura Ingalls Wilder wrote of her pioneer childhood in her 1935 *Little House on the Prairie*. Her family traveled through the Midwest in the late 19th century, pulling up stakes and resettling on new lands several times during Wilder's early life. Recalling a season spent headed west through the Indian Territory (toward what is now near Independence, Kansas), Wilder wrote that one morning she and her sister Mary "sat on the clean grass and ate pancakes and bacon and molasses from the tin plates in their laps."[8] Another day, "Laura and Mary were up next morning earlier than the sun. They ate their breakfast of cornmeal mush with prairie-hen gravy, and hurried to help Ma wash the dishes."[9] Breakfast would be cooked and eaten before sunup so that the wagon could be on its way at daybreak; afterward, they loaded up the wagon, hitched their horses, and continued on their way through the roadless grassland.

The food people brought west was largely dictated by the constraints of space and practicality; dried goods like beans, flour, and coffee, and sides of bacon stored in barrels of salt, were breakfast staples. Food was rationed carefully, and breakfast often consisted of dinner from the night prior. Biscuits, coffee, and salt pork were regular entries in written accounts of a typical morning on the Oregon Trail. Some people brought dairy cows along for milk, and oxen were specifically brought because their lumbering gait churned the cream into butter by the sway of the wagon alone.

TRAINS AND COACHES

As the century wore on, people with means found it much simpler to travel west by stagecoach. This did not necessarily mean the accommodations were much more elegant than those of a wagon hitched to a yoke of oxen. Englishwoman Frances Milton Trollope wrote of her travels (among other scathing facts about antebellum America) that the stagecoaches did not have set times for stopping at stations for meals, and "these necessary interludes, therefore, being generally impromptu, were abominably bad."[10]

Mark Twain, in his typical fashion, wrote eloquently of the breakfast he was served at a stagecoach station house in *Roughing It* (1872). The station-keeper served him "a disk of last week's bread, of the shape and size of an old-time cheese, and carved some slabs from it which were as good as Nicholson pavement, and tenderer."[11] Twain's dining mates were also treated to "condemned army bacon which the United States would not feed to its soldiers in the forts. . . . We may have found this condemned army bacon further out on the plains than the section I am locating it in, but we found it—there is no gainsaying that."[12] Lastly, the station-keeper poured them "a beverage which he called 'slum gullion,' and it is hard to think he was not inspired when he named it. It really pretended to be tea, but there was too much dish-rag, and sand, and old bacon-rind in it to deceive the intelligent traveler."[13] A slang dictionary from 1874 defined "slumgullion" as "any cheap, nasty, washy beverage," which, according to Twain's account of the brew, seems a fairly accurate assessment.[14]

Most startling to Twain, though, was the breakfast conversation shared with the other tough customers of the trip. "Its western freshness and novelty startled me, at first, and interested me; but it presently grew monotonous, and lost its charm," he remembered.[15] Though he could not recall specifically what was said, he was fairly certain it was "too strong for print." It is unsurprising that Twain should find such colorful people on his journey. Many of those frequenting station houses at the time would have been men accustomed to living and traveling alone or with other men. Trappers, miners, and mailmen working for the Pony Express were not well known for their ability to mix with polite company.

Trappers subsisted almost entirely on game—mostly meat from animals they trapped for fur. Small furbearers like raccoon, opossum, rabbit, and squirrel were all on the breakfast menu. "We had raccoon for breakfast, dinner and supper, with no vegetables; and upon extra occasions, we had cakes fried in raccoon oil," wrote one 19th-century pioneer.[16] Legendary trapper "Kit" Carson, it was told, made a breakfast of the beavers from his traps. Daniel Boone "killed a buffalo and [was] thought to have a good breakfast." The intrepid woodsman killed it when, in a bison stampede, he hid behind a tree and "punched the terrified beasts with his rifle barrel as they rushed past."[17]

Nonetheless, some traveling by coach found the food to their liking. Journalist Samuel Bowles wrote of eating dried peaches, canned fruits and vegetables, bacon, hot biscuits, and green tea and coffee. Although he wrote in *Across the Continent* (1865) that "[e]ach meal was the same; breakfast, dinner and supper were undistinguishable save by the hour," he also mentioned enjoying "canned chicken and oysters off tin plates, and drinking our coffee with the brownest of sugar and the most concentrated of milk" at a camp in Julesburg, Colorado and a "sumptuous breakfast" before heading off among the Mormons at the Great Salt Lake.[18]

Captain Sir Richard Francis Burton, a surly British adventurer and geographer, rarely missed an opportunity to criticize the food he encountered while traveling along the Pony Express route in 1860. In Nebraska, he found "a breakfast composed of various abominations, especially cakes of flour and grease, molasses and dirt, disposed in the pretty equal parts."[19] Farther west along the route, Burton found more disappointment in a station run by Germans, further souring his disposition. "For a breakfast cooked in the usual manner, coffee boiled down to tannin (ever the first operation), meat subjected to half sod, half stew, and, lastly, bread raised with sour milk corrected with soda, and so baked that the taste of the flour is ever prominent, we paid these German rascals 75 cents," he glowered.[20] Remarkably, that was not even the worst thing he had to write about his experience:

> Our breakfast was prepared in the usual prairie style. First the coffee—three parts burnt beans, which had been duly ground to a fine powder and exposed to the air, lest the aroma should prove too strong for us—was placed on the stove to simmer till every noxious principle was duly extracted from it. Then the rusty bacon, cut into thick slices, was thrown into the fry-pan: here the gridiron is unknown, and if known would be little appreciated, because it wastes the "drippings," which form with the staff of life a luxurious sop. Thirdly, antelope steak, cut off a corpse suspended for the benefit of flies outside, was placed to stew within influence of the bacon's aroma. Lastly came the bread, which of course should have been "cooked" first.[21]

While camping near the Snake River in the 1860s, journalist Samuel Bowles ached for the simpler breakfasts of home. "There was a yearning for something delicate for the Sunday morning breakfast,—a bit of cream toast, or a soft egg, and some milk-ameliorated coffee; but . . . we had to take our victual and drink 'straight,'—plain ham and bread and butter and black coffee,—or go without."[22] Bowles later wrote of traveling on the new Transcontinental Railroad, built between 1863 and 1869.

Before the advent of the dining car, rail travelers had to wait for a meal stop, hurriedly detrain with all of the other passengers in a sea of hungry bodies, jam into the station restaurant (creating a fair amount of pandemonium in the process), inhale their breakfast, and then rush back onto the train before it departed. It is no wonder (though perhaps a bit unfair) that foreigners repeatedly remarked on the speed with which Americans consumed their breakfasts. People would have been most hungry at breakfast, after a night of travel. English author Walter Thornbury described in 1873 the scene in Buffalo, New York:

> The train slackened and stopped and out poured the hungry swarms. Five gongs of five opposition breakfast places banged and thundered for our custom. In a minute I was seated with some thirty other hungry souls stowing away white piles of hominy, pink shavings of corned beef, and bowls of stewed oysters, while a Negro boy waved a plum brush of wild turkey feathers over my head to keep off the greedy flies.[23]

Dining cars offered train meals on long distance trips even before the Transcontinental Railroad, but the food was typically nothing to write home about; rancid meat, cold beans, and weak coffee were the best most trains had to offer. The B&O Railroad offered more elegant foods inspired by hotel menus and prepared by real chefs, but this was only available to first-class passengers. It was not until the Civil War that food was systematically prepared on trains. As competition among railroads intensified, the quality of food offered on "refectory cars" increased substantially.

In the 1870s, one who could afford to travel on the precursor to a dining car, the hotel car, could get an á la carte breakfast of "[f]ive different kinds of bread, four sorts of cold meat, six hot dishes, to say nothing of eggs cooked in seven different ways, and all the seasonable vegetables and fruits, . . . a variety from which the most dainty eater might easily find something to tickle his palate, and the ravenous to satisfy his appetite," raved one author.[24] "To breakfast, dine, and sup in this style while the train is speeding along at the rate of nearly thirty miles an hour, is a sensation of which the novelty is not greater than the comfort."[25] The author noted with a hint of Schadenfreude that "[a]n additional zest is given to the good things by the thought that the passengers in the other cars must rush out when the refreshment station is reached, and hastily swallow an ill-cooked meal."[26]

Illustration of passengers eating in a Pullman Palace dining car used on the Pacific Railroad, 1869. Courtesy of the Library of Congress.

In the 1870s, the railroad, for the first time, equalized the classes. "A working-class immigrant could learn from a ten-cent pamphlet the same rules of etiquette that an African American woman read as part of her education at normal school or that a white middle-class woman read in a beautifully bound etiquette manual," wrote Amy Richter in her 2005 *Home on the Rails: Women, the Railroad, and the Rise of Public Domesticity.* Now present in another part of a man's world, women civilized the rails; they brought a bit of home to the "world on wheels." For young women wanting to head west (and who were not particularly suited to a life as a teacher, cowgirl, or prostitute), hotel and restaurant work were their ticket.

Restaurateur Fred Harvey capitalized on this idea with his Harvey Girls, who brought "civilized dining" to the railway depots of the American West, particularly those along the Santa Fe Railway, which had no dining service. The Harvey Girls' neat uniforms and good morals—a sight for sore eyes for many rugged travelers of the era—were celebrated for their feminine decency and Victorian virtue. Soon, women and families traveling abroad began to flock to these establishments, too, rather than brave the unpredictability of a restaurant staffed and patronized only by unrefined western men.

COMMUTING

Rail passenger use declined dramatically between 1920 and 1934 because of the rise of the automobile. Service improvements and new, diesel-powered stream-liners, such as the gleaming Pioneer Zephyr (also known as the Silver Streak for its record-breaking speeds) reignited popular imagination in the 1930s, but the heyday of quality dining-car fare had passed. High-speed commuter rails did not offer breakfast; many, in fact, did not allow food or drink at all.

Although the horseless carriage had been invented in 1769, in the 1920s, American industrialist Henry Ford's affordable automobile changed every-thing. Americans loved the freedom of coming and going at whim, and did ev-erything in their cars. Eating while driving was an expeditious, if dangerous, way to save time, whether this was on long road trips or on the way to work. A 1914 issue of *Popular Mechanics* showed an "adjustable dining table for mo-tor cars" that simplified eating behind the wheel.[27] The 1939 *Rotarian* article "So You'll Drive" (written by Paul W. Kearney, author of the book *Highway Homicide,* among other works on driving safety) recommends starting a long trip with a moderate breakfast. While traveling by car, Kearney offers that his wife "likes orange juice and milk. I like malted milk with an egg, or orange juice with an egg." [28]

As the national highway system grew in the 1930s and 1940s, restaurants began to pop up near road exits, promising drivers a fast breakfast before they headed out for the day. In the 1940s, drive-in restaurants allowed customers to stay behind the wheel with service to their window. Some drive-ins featured breakfast on their menus as early as the 1950s, but eventually drivers realized that if they could stay in their cars to eat, they ought to be able to drive while they were at it.

Coincidentally, drive-in efficiency was not what restaurant owners hoped for, and in the late 1940s, the first drive-through restaurants (or "drive-throughs"), sought to solve that problem with the use of two-way radios instead of "carhop" waitstaff. In 1971, the first breakfast sandwich was available in a drive-through when fast-food chain Jack in the Box released the "Breakfast Jack."[29] That same year, the restaurant added its signature clown to the top of its speaker box menu board, greeting (and sometimes terrifying) drive-through guests too busy to eat inside.

The dangers of eating while driving have been well established; it is also evidently a hazard to have breakfast while seated in the passenger side. In 1992, seventy-nine-year-old Stella Liebeck of Albuquerque, New Mexico, was sitting in the passenger seat when her grandson drove his car through a McDonald's drive-through window. Liebeck ordered a cup of coffee, served in a Styrofoam cup, and her grandson pulled his car forward and stopped for his grandmother to add sugar and cream to her coffee. Liebeck placed the cup between her knees and when she attempted to remove the plastic lid from the cup, she splashed hot coffee all over her lap. The coffee, estimated to have been between 180 and 190 degrees Fahrenheit, caused third-degree burns all over the senior citizen's thighs and groin and hospitalized her for eight days. After McDonald's refused to pay Liebeck's $11,000 hospital bill, she took them to court, where a jury awarded her $200,000 to cover medical expenses and $2.7 million in punitive damages.[30] The lawsuit spawned a firestorm of national debate about personal responsibility, common sense, and the American penchant for frivolous litigation—all because of a hot cup of drive-through coffee.

Perhaps if Liebeck had been on a bicycle, she might have been spared her pain and suffering; McDonald's does not allow bikes in their drive-through; nor does coffee giant Starbucks. This has proven quite the hassle for the thousands of Americans who commute to work by bicycle. In Portland, Oregon, bicycle commuting is more than ten times the national average; a rate of 6.3 percent compared to 0.6 percent nationally, according to 2011 Census Bureau data.[31] Thanks to the public (and highly publicized) efforts of one Portland-based biking mother, Pacific Northwest fast-food restaurant Burgerville not only opened their drive-through to bicycles, but added bike lanes to many of their drive-throughs, making it the first restaurant chain in the country where one may bike up for a sausage and egg English muffin.[32]

HOTELS

American public houses were originally conceived as a means of "prevention and discouraging of vagabonds" and for the "restraint of vagrants," as dictated by provisions to colonial laws in the 1680s.[33] Homelessness was, for all intents and purposes, illegal, especially for immigrants; hotels gave the huddled masses a place to stay out of sight of the upper classes.

By the late 18th century, many inns included breakfast with the price of lodging. Some taverns also provided lodging. One Sunday in 1789, while he was touring Connecticut, General George Washington discovered that the locals discouraged travel on the Sabbath. This minor detail required him to stay at Perkins Tavern, "which, by the bye," said the first U.S. president, "is not a good one."[34] Superior Court Judge Harry Toulmin, an immigrant from England (mentioned in chapter 2 as having been delighted with "apple-pye" for breakfast), remarked in one of his letters that "[a]t American inns, all the gentlemen in the house breakfast and dine together."[35]

In some less-extravagant inns, guests often did more than breakfast and dine together; they often all slept in the same room, sometimes in the same bed. Even in these pared-down lodgings, however, the breakfasts were typically ample and varied, consisting of fish and meats, bread and butter, eggs, coffee, and tea. One critic nonetheless found tavern dining off-putting, shuddering over "the horrors of the kitchen of an American inn, with its darkness and negroes, and dirt."[36]

Early boomtown mining camps of the mid-19th century were so remote from major transportation routes that most foodstuffs arrived already rancid or infested with vermin. Worms and weevils were sifted from flour before cooks could make their daily griddlecakes; tinned butter arrived brown and putrid. Between the 1860s and 1870s, the gold boom drove the expansion of nicer accommodations; the number of hotels in San Francisco alone quadrupled, and by 1876, there were more than seventy places where a fellow could spend his earnings on a plush room and a hearty breakfast. Some hotels, like the Beaumont in Ouray, Colorado, was so luxurious that it was listed in the 1894–1895 edition of *Where to Stop: A Guide to the Best Hotels in the World*—the Fodor's of the Wild West.

In many 19th-century hotels, breakfast was still included with the price of the room. During the 1890s, journalist Richard Harding Davis called Delmonico's a place "where you can get a very good breakfast for $17"—the weekly rate for a room (around $425 today).[37] Most hotels operated under the so-called American plan, with the price of meals built into the flat rate. At the Astor House, a luxury hotel that opened in New York in 1836, the breakfasts astonished foreign visitors, as did the speed with which Americans ate their food—a habit they developed to comply with rigid train schedules. It was normal to serve buckwheat, rye, or corn pancakes, ham and eggs, sausages, oysters, fish, chicken, steak, pork, several kinds of biscuits and breads, as well as chocolate, coffee, and tea. In keeping with the social rules of the time, these regular, flat-rate meals, called "ordinaries," were served in separate dining rooms for ladies and gentlemen.

Many finer 19th-century hotels began the day with a breakfast buffet for their guests. Before then, breakfasts were generally so ponderous that what would be considered a buffet-sized array by today's standards would have just been an expectation in the 1890s. After Kellogg's and Post began mass-marketing cold breakfast cereal at the turn of the 20th century, lavish breakfasts fell out of everyday enjoyment, relegating the ten-course extravaganza to the odd holiday weekend. To deter freeloaders, some hotels offered paying guests a meal voucher that would grant admission to the breakfast buffet.

The buffet was not always all about the food. One dictionary of household furnishings mentioned the buffet as a piece of furniture, albeit one specifically suited to the morning meal. That particular treatise on cabinetry noted that "a buffet may, with some propriety, be restored to modern use, and prove ornamental to a breakfast room."[38] In this case, the buffet is a sort of china hutch, though in 18th-century France, persons of distinction often had an entire room called a buffet to hold their vases and fountains. Coincidentally, in nicer English homes, vases and china were stored in the butler's pantry, the favorite place for household help to take breakfast in privacy.

Earlier, the buffet more typically referred to the long table upon which an array of foods would be displayed for self-service, but before the century was over, "buffet" indicated the food itself. On a related note, the word "banquet" comes from the same word as "banquette"—the name for the bench in a breakfast nook. Though the word "banquette" actually comes from the Italian *banchetto*, meaning a small bench, later, a banquet came to mean a large, celebratory feast. "Banquet" and "buffet" may be used interchangeably by modern hotels to describe their abundant breakfast offerings, the variety of which rivals the Victorian era's.

Boarding Houses and the B&B

Starting in the 1600s, some people with larger houses opened their homes up to boarders for a nominal fee. The "board" in "room and board" came from the 16th-century use of a plank across one's lap for eating, before dining tables were commonplace in humbler homes. Hence, it was the food, not the lodging, that distinguished a boarding house. In most cases, this meant breakfast. Boarders would typically share some washing duties, as well as eating breakfast and sometimes dinner at a communal table with other guests at designated mealtimes. In the Western frontier, guests might be in charge of their own breakfast and lunch, with supper provided instead.

English travel writer Frances Milton Trollope noted in 1832 that if one wanted to eat in the morning, a boarding house guest "must rise exactly in time to reach the boarding-table at the hour appointed for breakfast, or she will get a stiff bow from the lady president, cold coffee, and no egg. I have been sometimes greatly amused upon these occasions."[39]

Boarding houses, while common to most American cities, were rare in London, explained *London of To-Day: An Illustrated Handbook* (1890). "The boarding-house of Boston or New York is a popular institution, frequented by all sorts and conditions of men and women." Unlike their American counterparts, the London boarding house, the handbook noted, was "chiefly a home for cultivated waifs, and one need not be afraid to declare that the cultivated waif is often the sweetest and most companionable person to be found in this unhappy planet."[40]

By the late 19th century, it was relatively rare for a boarding house to provide only the bed and breakfast and not supper. In one *Lippincott's Magazine* article, "Young America in Old England," three Americans traveling in London find themselves growing faint with hunger, and inquired about their dinner. Their house host, James, patiently explained, "Lor', miss, we don't furnish dinner here! This is a bed and breakfast place." The young women were perplexed at the notion, and continued their demands for dinner. When James suggested that guests typically go out for dinner, the women were indignant. "Go out? Where? To a horrid restaurant?" "We never makes it our business to inquire where our guests gets their dinners, miss," replied James, biting his lip from telling the women where they really ought to go.[41]

The bed and breakfast, affectionately known as a B&B, is now often treated as a cozy, romantic alternative to a hotel, but it is really no different from a boarding house that serves only breakfast instead of supper. These days, the destiny of many historic houses has been to become a bed and breakfast. This is even true of the home where, in 1892, Lizzie Borden was famously said to have murdered her father and stepmother with a hatchet.[42] Today, the historic Borden home offers eight rooms for overnight guests, including Lizzie's childhood bedroom, and guests are treated to the same breakfast enjoyed by Miss Borden's parents on the morning they were murdered: bananas, johnnycakes, sugar cookies, and coffee.[43]

RESTAURANTS

In *Simple Directions for the Waitress or Parlor Maid* (1917), domestic science expert Caroline Reed Wadhams advised that "[a]s breakfast is the most irregular and hurried of the meals, the waitress should have her wits about her to see that each person has what is needed at the time wanted."[44] Originally even home servers were called waitresses, but much of the advice from these early handbooks applied to restaurant staff as aptly as to domestic workers. The work of a breakfast waitress, it would appear, was just as demanding and thankless a century ago as it is today.

"Overtip breakfast waitresses," implored H. Jackson Brown in his *Life's Little Instruction Book* (1995). In an interview, Brown elaborated on his suggestion, "[t]hey're unsung heroes. I've never gone in a restaurant, no matter how early, when there wasn't a waitress. That means she had to get up earlier than I did—and fifteen percent of the minimal amount you pay for breakfast isn't enough for her."[45] Since breakfast is the least expensive of all meals, that fifteen percent amounted to very little.

American waitresses, breakfast or otherwise, did not always earn a gratuity. The first restaurants, the *thermopolia* of ancient Rome, were staffed by slaves, and this was a fairly consistent trend all the way until 18th-century France, when restaurants as we think of them today first opened. French cooking was popular after the American Revolutionary War, when France proved a worthy ally to the newly independent United States. Best yet, they knew how to cook. Like most Democrats, third U.S. president Thomas Jefferson had a real affinity for French cooking, a trait he acquired while serving as an ambassador to France in the late 1700s. He so adored *cuisine Française* that he brought his slave James Hemings to Paris to apprentice with French chefs.

The New York restaurant Delmonico's was one of the earliest American dining establishments to serve breakfast. Their 76 Broad Street location had previously been the site of a hotel owned by a Frenchman named Joseph Collet, a friend of the gastronome (and Jefferson contemporary) Jean Anthelme Brillat-Savarin—the man famous for, among other things, the quotation "tell me what you eat, and I will tell you what you are," commonly misquoted as "you are what you eat." Seven years before the Delmonico brothers bought out Collet, in 1827, Collet had set the stage for French restaurants in New York when he advertised the breakfast finery at his Commercial Coffee House: "Coffee, Chocolate, Soups of every description, Veal Cutlets, Mutton Chops, Partridges, Pheasants, Chickens, Beef a la Mode, Hogs Feet, Oysters, and every dish that constitutes either a breakfast, dinner, or supper."

After Delmonico's acquired the restaurant and hotel, they became famous for their breakfasts; they were the apex of metropolitan sophistication, and proper hosts knew that to really impress a party, one should throw it at Delmonico's. Politicians, high-ranking military officials, and movie starlets alike frequented the Delmonico's breakfast table.

In 1866, a breakfast banquet was held by the American Church Missionary and Evangelical Knowledge Societies in the Delmonico's banquet hall. Though the twelve-course breakfast was described in resplendent detail, the *American Quarterly Church Review* had an unfortunate announcement to make regarding the affair. "It is, in some respects, a nauseous subject," they warned dourly. "There is the odor of a feverish sick-room about it; the stench of a sore disease." With interest piqued, the reader must have continued anxiously. After listing each menu item and naming all six bishops in attendance, the *Church Review* declared that "a Breakfast at Delmonico's, on such an occasion, by those professedly intent on the special work of a suffering, crucified Saviour, in such a day of worldliness, and rebuke, and blasphemy as this, was an outrage on Christian propriety."[46] Unfortunately, it seems that the party had forgotten to include a sermon with its breakfast; the Evangelical Societies were more interested in the breakfasts than evangelizing.

Coffeehouses

In the 1830s, coffeehouses and oyster bars were the first restaurants to operate on a more casual "come and get it" schedule rather than one with set mealtimes, signaled by the sounding of a gong or bell. The timing for this explosion in casual restaurants could not have been better; in 19th-century New York City, many working-class apartments were built without kitchens. This architectural omission continued well into the 20th century, with some apartment buildings designed with the intention that tenants—presumably bachelors—would eat at the house restaurant instead of cooking. And there were other reasons for people to eat breakfast out; for example, before the advent of the electric waffle iron, many people did not bother with cooking them at home. Instead, they were left to professional cooks with the skill and upper body strength to wield heavy, long-handled irons over a fire.

Before its association with literary Beat scene, the coffeehouse was the setting for European politicos. The political breakfast parties of France and Great Britain caught on in the United States in the 1830s, providing intellectual stimulation over the morning pastries and coffee. Discussions of the abolition of slavery, the Whigs, and other current events commonly occurred in coffeehouses, and breakfast was there to fuel the revolutionary discourse. "An American sometimes speaks of his political traditions, meaning that his father was of the same party with himself; but there is no place where opinion differs so widely as at an American breakfast table," commented war journalist George Alfred Townsend.[47]

Author Harriet Beecher Stowe was fond of the breakfast parties she attended with British abolitionists Thomas Babington Macaulay and Henry Hallam, while traveling to England in the early 1850s. She enjoyed witty repartee on the subjects of architecture, literature, and religion, including a conversation with Robert H. Inglis, an English politician known for being of "high tory and high church." Beecher Stowe was too polite to mention whether she actually enjoyed that part of the conversation; considering Inglis's bigoted views on Jews and Buddhists, it may be safe to assume she did not.

Inglis's narrow views on the scope of House of Commons Library (which he chaired, having been a member for fourteen years) were overturned by Prime Minister Sir Robert Peel in 1850. In 1846, Peel had become famous for repealing the Corn Laws—trade laws that controlled the price of cereal to the detriment of the UK's working poor. This repeal kicked off Prime Minister John Gladstone's repeal of the duties on butter and eggs, and the end of sugar duties came in 1874 at the hands of Benjamin Disraeli, a novelist who moonlighted as a Prime Minister. Peel, Disraeli, and Gladstone—three men who bitterly loathed each other—formed an unlikely Prime Minister super-group in liberating the breakfast table from tyrannical taxation.

Rustic Western Dining

Outside the shiny megalopolis of the east coast of the United States, restaurants were booming as well. In the American West, train stations and coach stops served meals to hungry travelers. The food served in country taverns was usually nothing to write home about (though plenty, nonetheless, did), but once in a while the hospitality and effort shown to provide a good breakfast was worth honorable mention. A Scotsman named John Melish was working on mapping the western United States for Thomas Jefferson when he stopped into a backwoods inn in Coshocton, Ohio. The hostess began making Melish's breakfast by wringing the necks of two chickens; embarrassed by her effort, Melish wrote in 1811, he asked her for a simple boiled egg, bread, and tea to save her trouble and himself a bit of time:

> "Shall I fry some ham for you along with the eggs?" said she. "No," said I, "not a bit." "Well, will you take a little stewed pork?" "No." "Shall I make some fritters for you?" "No." "Preserve me, what, what will you take, then?" "A little bread, and tea, and an egg." "Well, you're the most extraordinary man that I ever saw; but I can't set down a table that way." I saw that I was only to lose time by contesting the matter farther; so I allowed her to follow her own plan as to the cooking, assuring her that I would take mine as to eating. She detained me about half an hour, and at last placed upon the table a profusion of ham, eggs, fritters, bread, butter, and some excellent tea. All the time I was at breakfast, she kept pressing me to eat; but I kept my own council, and touched none of the dishes, except the bread, tea, and an egg. She affected great surprize [sic], and when I paid her the ordinary fare, a quarter of a dollar, she said it was hardly worth any thing. I mention this circumstance to show the kind hospitality of the landlady, and the good living enjoyed by the backwoods people.[48]

Farther west, many restaurants were sometimes little more than a tent with a sign reading "home baking." In the 1850s, these rustic dining rooms catered to the needs of hungry miners, loggers, and railroad workers, but many restaurateurs were happy to capitalize on the fast fortunes of those men who had struck gold. In Placerville, California—formerly nicknamed Hangtown—the best way to celebrate hitting pay dirt was by ordering a Hangtown fry. As the story goes, a miner, flush with new money, came into the Cary House Hotel restaurant demanding the most expensive breakfast on the menu. The omelet of eggs, bacon, and fried oysters cost him six or seven dollars, or the equivalent of $175 today. Eventually, the specialty breakfast spread from the gold mine camps of the Sierra Foothills to the Pacific coast, becoming a popular way for gentlemen to flaunt cash all the way from San Francisco to Seattle. If a gentleman were feeling particularly prosperous, he might have his Hangtown fry "with cheesecake," meaning his omelet came with a prostitute.

Breakfast Diners

By the 1920s, eating out had become a national pastime for Americans, and restaurants catering specifically to the breakfast crowd began to open across the United States. The Creole Donut and Waffle Shop in Ocean City, New Jersey, was, before the 1927 fire, a popular place to eat "Downyflake doughnuts" and "Southern waffles" with a hot cup of coffee.

In the 1930s and 1940s, Harlem dance halls like the Savoy and the Radium Club hosted "breakfast dances" at 4:00 or 5:00 a.m. on Sunday morning to cater to those late-night revelers who had been going since the night before. By the 1950s, the concept had spread to other areas like Kansas City, Miami, and Reno, with the help of jazz great Count Basie. It is uncertain whether the breakfast was intended for the customers or the musicians who kept them entertained all night, but the fried chicken and waffles, ham and eggs, and hot coffee were welcome sights after a night of dancing and drinking.

Outside the all-night jazz club hullaballoo, twenty-four-hour diners were growing in number alongside the factories that operated around the clock. Twenty-four-hour restaurants were "a new war baby," dubbed a 1943 issue of *American Restaurant* magazine. These diners and cafeterias were typically sited near factories to serve those who worked long hours at any of the three shifts, but with an eye to those working the overnight period nicknamed the "graveyard shift." One complaint of the war, offered *Popular Mechanics* magazine in 1942, was that in order to keep America's war machine well oiled, "[m]illions of us will have to go on the night shift. This means breakfast around 3 p.m.

or 11 p.m."[19] Grocery stores began operating on a twenty-four-hour schedule to accommodate the "swing shift wives" stuck with matching their husbands' unorthodox work schedule, but some wives had their own shifts to work. The twenty-four-hour diners made sure everyone had a hot breakfast before (and after) their shift.

After the war, many factories continued running all night, and so did the diners. In the 1950s, a spate of American waffle and pancake chains opened their doors within a few years of each other: the Original Pancake House and Denny's in 1953, International House of Pancakes in 1958, and the Bob Evans chain opened the first of its restaurants in 1962, though Mr. Evans had been running a successful breakfast diner and sausage company since the late 1940s. Although plenty of restaurants served breakfast before the 1950s, it was the type of postwar, middle-class consumerism that drove them to specialize in breakfast—and steaks, frequently—and to serve it all day long. The ability to get breakfast any time of day was one way for Americans to achieve a perceived better way of life.

Breakfast restaurants developed their own specialties, including the everpresent home fries. According to the fictional character Roast Beef from the

Waffle Shop, ca. 1950. Courtesy of the Library of Congress.

American web-based comic Achewood (written by Saveur contributor Chris Onstad), home fries from restaurants present certain challenges, aside from the fact that if they are served in a restaurant, they are technically no longer "home" fries. Among the "Major Problems of Restaurant Home Fries" is that some breakfast establishments fail to achieve proper crispness on the edges of the potatoes.

> I have even seen home fries where the potatoes were somehow chewy. Once you make a potato chewy you are doing things so wrong that you would be better off just not touching the potato at all, and instead giving it to the customer so that he could take it home and try to make sense of it himself.[50]

After the 1940s, drivers could fill up two ways at truck stops before hitting the road, at any hour; typically a fueling station was positioned along with a twenty-four-hour diner. Most truck-stop diners had menus that reflected the nocturnal dining habits of truck drivers. Hearty meals that could pass for either breakfast or dinner abounded: chicken-fried steak with biscuits and gravy, omelets, or steak and eggs are all common fare. "Ham and lye hominy [grits] in red-eye gravy is a specialty at truck-stop diners in Louisiana. Drivers order it not because it is good, but because, through years of trial, they know they can eat it and survive," wrote reporter Elliott Chaze in a 1962 piece for *LIFE* called "Lethal Legend of Truck-Stop Food." After testing twenty different truck stops, Chaze called truck-stop food "continental cuisine with an awful difference" (a notable one being that cold raccoon casserole was offered in diners of the Deep South) but admitted that trying truck-stop food was one of those things that "one must do as a matter of principle." Most, however, do it as a matter of necessity—truck drivers are wont to eat breakfast wherever they can fit a sixty-foot trailer.

Fast food

Pre-workday fast-food breakfasts are nothing new; they did not even originate in the 20th century. Victorian journalist Henry Mayhew described in *London Labour and the London Poor* (1851) the thousands of costermongers (street vendors) who walked into London in the pre-dawn hours and stopped at various coffee sellers' carts or "early breakfast stalls" along the way to buy their breakfast—"a couple of herrings, or a bit of bacon, or whatnot," perhaps a sausage or an egg sandwiched in a bread roll called a bap. After swallowing the coffee or tea and returning the mug, a stall owner could then continue on to their own stall or wagon, eating as they went.[51]

Sir Walter Scott wrote of having a "lusty breakfast of bread and ale"; due to the recent overpopulation (and resulting squalor) in Scotland, this was said by Scottish caricaturist John Kay in 1838 to have "latterly consisted of a half-penny bap and a very small modicum of beer." The bap, dating back to early 16th-century England, is the preferred vehicle for a bacon and egg breakfast sandwich.

The fast-food breakfast may have been an English invention, but some may argue that Americans perfected it. The Wichita, Kansas–based hamburger chain White Castle had experimented with fried egg sandwiches during World War II, but discontinued them after the end of wartime meat rations. The first wave of fast-food restaurants to stick to breakfast was spawned by postwar doughnut shops like Winchell's Donut House in a sunny Los Angeles suburb in 1948, and Dunkin' Donuts in Quincy, Massachusetts, in 1950. Coffee and doughnuts became the quickest way for commuters (and cops) to stay the morning hunger until lunchtime.

Unlike other breakfast items, the breakfast sandwich was ideal for the drive-through: it could be wrapped tightly in paper and eaten with one hand. Jack in the Box's Breakfast Jack and Eggs Benedict sandwiches were introduced in 1971 (the same year as their clown-headed drive-through speaker box), setting the stage for the drive-through breakfast sandwich. The Egg McMuffin—a varia-tion on Jack in the Box's Eggs Benedict sandwich—was created in late 1971 by McDonald's franchisee Herb Peterson. After McDonald's founder Ray Kroc ate two of them in one sitting, the first Egg McMuffin was officially added to the menu in Belleville, New Jersey, in 1972. In 1975, McDonald's opened its first drive-through, just in time for the Egg McMuffin to go national, launching the second wave of fast-food breakfasts. Today, breakfast comprises 15 percent of McDonald's sales, and nearly every fast-food chain in the country offers a breakfast menu.[52]

Cafeterias and Automats

Even faster than fast food (and similarly lacking wait staff) were the self-serve cafeterias and automats. The concept for the cafeteria was based on the Swedish smörgåsbords observed by entrepreneur John Kruger, who opened the first caf-eteria by name in Chicago in 1893. Visibility of the kitchen assured customers that sanitary conditions were being maintained; this was a high priority during the hygiene craze of the late 19th century. At the same time, the national res-taurant chain called Child's Restaurants was innovating the self-service format by introducing trays and the "tray line" to the dining room. In 1905, a cafeteria cleverly named The Cafeteria opened in Los Angeles with catchy slogans such as "Food That Can Be Seen" and "No Tips." For many diners, the freedom of coming and going when one wanted and not having to tip a waiter was worth the trouble of walking one's own food to the table.

Through their promise of cheap food and escapism, cafeterias reached their zenith during World War II. They served as a momentary respite from restrictive food rations, offering people a chance to leave the depressing isolation of their homes and relive the experience of eating out at a time when no one could really afford it. After the war, with the rise of diners and fast food, most cafeterias closed, but Texas-based Luby's Cafeteria opened their doors in 1947 and still offers a breakfast buffet on weekends.

For those wanting even less human contact for their meal, there were the automats. Consisting of little more than a row of vending machines surrounding a seating area, the first automats were built in 1901 in Philadelphia based on plans from Sweden and parts from Germany. Unlike modern vending machines, automats provided hot food, which was prepared by cooks eerily concealed behind the machine's façade, who would slide the cooked food into a metal slot to be opened by the customer with the turn of a knob. The hot meal was waiting behind a small glass door, for only a few nickels.

Offering coffee and a muffin for a dime, the best-known automats were those run by the Horn & Hardart company in Philadelphia and New York. Being enclosed and unstaffed, the Times Square location quickly became prime cruising habitat for gay New Yorkers in the late 1920s.[53] It was also where touchy malcontent Ezekiel Volsky, the twenty-one-year-old protagonist of Charles Reznikov's *By the Waters of Manhattan* (1937) took his breakfast. Eager to "be out under that strange sky before it was day," Ezekiel fished around in his pockets for change, and found a few nickels and a forgotten dime.

> He would not have to go home for breakfast; and this taste of freedom was so dear to him, he made up his mind to husband every cent he could to be free.
>
> He reached the Automat where he had had coffee the afternoon before. Now a row of compartments showed halves of melons, gaudy reddish yellows, and at the steam table were strips of bacon, dark against a huge dish of scrambled eggs. He had the coffee and the modest yellow of three corn muffins, and was satisfied.[54]

In this brief interlude, Ezekiel's selection of the modest corn muffins is symbolic of his identity as a working-class Jewish immigrant, while experiencing the gleam of the big city through the automat. In this one scene, Reznikov captures the appeal that these humble breakfast establishments had for many people; by serving comfort foods from behind a tiny glass door, automats were simultaneously familiar and novel. Like the cafeteria, automats were largely rendered obsolete by the drive-through fast-food restaurant, and by 1991, the last Horn & Hardart automat closed forever.

EATING ON THE JOB

Before the automat and cafeteria found their way onto today's corporate campus, most people had to either bring food from home or wait for it to come to them. Even earlier, many found themselves traveling far from home to find work; the chuck wagon brought breakfast to those whose work took them afield rather than to new urban centers.

Chuck Wagons and Camp Cooking

During the mass westward expansion that followed the Civil War, cattlemen would often spend months away from a home base, driving cattle into vast

Cowboys eating breakfast, with chuck wagon, ca.1880–1910. Courtesy of the Library of Congress.

rangelands. One cattle rancher known as the "father of the Texas panhandle," Charles "Charlie" Goodnight sought to feed cowboys driving cattle from Texas to New Mexico and invented the chuck wagon in 1866. Goodnight modified an old Army Studebaker wagon by adding a "chuck box" to hold the victuals; the lid of the wide box served as a countertop, and a water barrel and bag of firewood were attached to the sides of the wagon. The meals-on-wheels device was named for the 17th-century word "chuck" pertaining to a piece of meat, not its inventor; the 19th-century colloquial use of "chuck" described any cowboy food, as well as a cheaper cut of beef between the neck and shoulder.

American artist Ross Santee wrote of early 20th-century chuck-wagon breakfasts in his 1928 *Cowboy*, noting that "[t]he meals never varied much. We had steak an' eggs or salt pork for breakfast, hot bakin' powder biscuits, frijole beans an' lick [molasses]."[55] Other chuck-wagon breakfasts could include fried bacon, strong coffee without milk or sugar, and corn dodgers—small, hard corn cakes baked in the ashes of a fire. Later recipes would call for the dodgers to be sweetened with sugar and fried in a special griddle, but these were not the stoic dodgers of the rugged cowboy.

Cowboys prepared food unabashed by the social rules that dictated cooking to be women's work. The rare women on the ranching frontier were confounded—if not a little enticed—by the hearty men who could cook just as expertly as they could, and perhaps teach them a thing or two. One ranch wife wrote of her recent marriage to a "real cowboy." Upon waking from their honeymoon in the stark reality of their sudden lives together, her new husband asked for his breakfast. "You should be so thankful I married you that you'd be glad to cook breakfast every morning." His bride was unimpressed. "What the hell do you think I married *you* for?" she quipped.[56]

This spunky ranch wife had a point. In camp, cooking was a man's domain. Though the expectations may have been relatively low, some men nonetheless turned a camp breakfast into an opportunity to show off. In *The Young People's Cookbook* (1925), "Uncle John" has appointed himself not the camp cook, but the camp *chef*. "'Some one has said that the "three B's," beans, bacon and bread are the essentials of camp fare,' said Uncle John, 'and it is probably true enough. But in camp as elsewhere, variety is not only greatly appreciated, but it adds a special piquancy—for it is often so little expected.'" All it took, Uncle John surmised, was a bit of "gumption and ingenuity."[57]

This theme was echoed by magazines and books directed at boys and men from the early to mid-20th century, particularly if they used specific products. Aunt Jemima pancake mix, it was purported, allowed boys to make pancakes "as good as Mother makes," by just adding water. (The hapless boy scout may not have realized that Mother was, in fact, making the exact same pancakes with the same mix.) In the 1920s, to corner the camp scout market, Aunt Jemima began producing pancake mix in individual packages to stay dry while camping. Furthermore, it was a teaching tool for "[h]ow to make a new scout a good cook . . . *in ten minutes!*" Unfortunately, most young men would not care to hone their skill outside the campsite.

Mess Halls

The use of "mess" to describe food dates back to the 13th century. The Old French *mes*, meaning a "portion of food" was drawn from the Latin verb *mittere*, meaning "to send" and "to put"; hence, the original meaning is "a course of a meal put on the table." By the 15th century, "mess" referred to a group of people eating together, and this use persists to describe military dining halls, though in the latter half of the 19th century, it referred to the dining tents of cowboys, loggers, and miners as well.

Often just a tent with an assembly of tables, the mess hall was where workers took meals at designated times. On the ranch, men would climb out of their bunks before daybreak, light a fire to take the morning chill off of the bunkhouse, and amble down to the mess hall to silently eat a breakfast of steaks and sausages, ham and eggs, fresh cornbread or biscuits, and hot, black coffee. By sunup, all ranch hands would have left the breakfast table and begun their day's chores.

In logging camp mess halls, the food was just as substantial as in any other camp where laborers come to break bread. In 1887, one wool weaver made his way to a Maine logging camp to do a bit of business, and reported on what he observed in a mess hall at the camp in the woods. "The regular bill of fare in a logging camp is as follows: breakfast: beans, hot biscuit without butter, tea without milk or sugar, fried pork, and fried potatoes. . . . I will leave it to my readers to imagine the odor that pervaded in that cabin, with over forty men in there."[58]

Until the 20th century, soldiers ate most of the same breakfast foods as lumberjacks and cowboys: beans, salt pork, and coffee. During the American Civil War, however, the lines that were drawn by slavery were also reflected in the foods eaten by the soldiers. Confederate soldiers could eat "hog 'n hominy" and corn dodgers made with cornmeal sifted for vermin prior to baking; often the dodgers were baked directly in the ashes of the fire, earning them the moniker "ashcakes." The soldiers of the Union Army might breakfast on biscuits and fried cod cakes made from dried salt cod.

More likely, however, northern Civil War soldiers ate hardtack. This dense, firm biscuit was designed for longevity rather than palatability. The high salt content made it unattractive to mice and cockroaches, but not to weevils. Weevil larvae positively adored hardtack, leading the biscuits to be repugnantly known as "worm castles." By crushing the hardtack with the barrel of a rifle and mixing with water, one could make a firm dough that could be fried in the lard rendered from a bit of fatback, a dish called "skillygalee"; these could be buttered or crumbled into coffee. Soldiers could make a hot breakfast cereal of "bully soup" by boiling powdered hardtack with cornmeal, water, ginger, and a little wine. Unlike soldiers from other wars, Civil War fighters took almost all of their meals in the field, rather than in a mess hall. In many units, soldiers pooled their resources and had their rations collectively prepared by a hired cook, similar to a chuck-wagon cook, who may or may not have been successful in finding appetizing new ways to prepare hardtack.

During the war, inflation led many to consider other options for breakfast. In 1861, bacon sold for 12 cents per pound; by the end of the war four years later, it cost $11–13 per pound.[59] In the South, food items were far more difficult to come by than in the North, driving prices to ridiculous heights. By 1865, coffee, tea, sugar, and milk could not be had for any price. Without hot coffee in the morning, one supposes the Rebels had no more fight left in them; the victory went to the North that year.

During World War I, every effort was made to provide soldiers with a better diet, beginning with breakfast. Unfortunately, the quality did not always match the quantity. One soldier wrote to his sweetheart in 1917 of the breakfast provisions at Fort Slocum, in New York Harbor:

> It was some meal. First corn flakes and milk and you know I like milk so [I] took a lot. It didn't look much like Jersey milk and certainly did not taste like it. At first I thought we must be late [and] someone put out dish-water in the pail by mistake. I found out later that it was plain water with just enough condensed milk in it to make the right color. The rest of the breakfast was pretty good until we came to the last course, get that—two hard boiled eggs. They looked as if they had been picked up from under the roost.[60]

During World War I, evangelical Christian group the Salvation Army sent young women to France to give American enlisted men a much-needed taste of home. Dubbed "Doughnut Girls," these Salvationists made coffee and doughnuts for the doughboys, rain or shine, using kitchens and stoves cobbled together from cans and scraps of metal. In 1938, the Salvation Army instituted National Donut Day to honor the Doughnut Girls who crossed enemy lines.

Goading the soldiers with the cheery slogan, "Doughnuts will win the war!" the American Red Cross's Donut Dollies cooked on World War II battlefields, as well. Perhaps the most famous among these was First Lady Eleanor Roosevelt, who doled out coffee and doughnuts during a USO tour of Europe. When Mrs. Roosevelt was chatting with GIs, she came upon a crew of cooks preparing breakfast and wondered aloud why the cook was slapping dough against his chest. "Isn't that a funny way to make pancakes?" she asked. "That's nothing," he replied. "You ought to see how we make donuts."[61]

In 1941, the Institutional Department at Kellogg's had developed its eponymous Kel-Bowl-Pac to meet the needs of the military. Capitalizing on the war, one 1944 advertisement called the tiny cereal boxes "a perfect dish for times like these," but it later became a popular way to serve cereal to children at summer camps, recreation centers, and schools.

Military Rations

"Billy ate a good breakfast from cans," wrote American author Kurt Vonnegut in his monumental war novel *Slaughterhouse Five* (1969), and Vonnegut was right. Somewhere between freshly baked doughnuts and maggot-riddled hardtack lay the typical fare of a soldier. There were the ubiquitous pots of beans, for instance. Army cookbooks like *Camp Fires and Camp Cooking, or Culinary Hints for the Soldier* (1862) recommended beans served with chopped, fried onions and a sprinkle of vinegar, noting that "[i]n this way they make a first-rate dish for breakfast or supper with bread and coffee."[62] More commonly, however, soldiers subsisted on canned, military-issued rations ("rats").

During the American Revolutionary War, provisions for the Continental Army were somewhat privatized, largely provided by sutlers—food merchants who followed the troops. Since the early days of the Continental Army, with its heavy reliance on salted meats and dried goods, A-rations were considered essential to soldier welfare and morale. These were fresh foods served in the mess hall that could be prepared on-site or shipped in from another facility. Modern versions of the A-ration, colloquially called a "bag nasty," might contain breakfast sandwiches and individually packaged bowls of cereal—a throwback to Kellogg's World War II–era Kel-Bowl-Pac. B-rations were made from canned foods that do not require refrigeration, but were similarly prepared in mess halls by military cooks. C-rations were canned, ready-to-eat meals intended for field consumption. The ration's "B"-unit—breakfast—served to GIs during World War II consisted of biscuits, hard candy, coffee, and a meat and vegetable hash. C-rats were eventually replaced by the MRE (Meal, Ready to Eat, called "Mr. E"—"mystery" for short) in 1981.

During World War II, GIs were given Field Ration, Type K—better known as K-rations—which allotted their day's three meals. As opposed to A-rations, which contained fresh foods such as fruit and milk, and B-rations, which were preserved foods prepared in mess kitchens for large groups of people, K-rations were not only prepared from preserved foods, but were individually packaged for soldiers to consume in the field in case of emergency. Breakfast K-rations typically included a can of chopped ham and eggs or veal loaf, a package of biscuits, a dried fruit bar or cereal bar, halazone water-purification tablets, a four-pack of brand-name cigarettes, candy-coated chewing gum, instant coffee, and sugar (granulated, cubed, or compressed).

Aside from their generally unappetizing flavor, military rations had a reputation for their tendency to cause gas and constipation simultaneously, earning rations a variety of colorful nicknames. Some mess halls served officers "knee pads" with "400W"—sturdy pancakes made with C-ration mix and maple syrup as thick as the eponymous engine oil. The ubiquitous creamed, chipped beef on toast, affectionately known during World War II and beyond as "shit on a shingle" (or "same old stuff" in polite company; S.O.S. for short) was a favorite breakfast and emblematic of the military experience. Of all the foods eaten while serving one's country, it was this breakfast classic—perhaps this food alone—for which veterans waxed nostalgic after returning home from the battlegrounds.

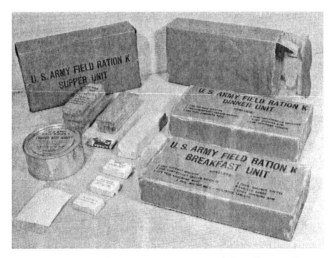

World War II K rations, 1943. Courtesy of the Library of Congress.

Breakfasts were also the fuel for a more civilized type of battle. At the end of the 19th century, Theodore Roosevelt and the "political boss" of the Republican party, New York Senator Tom Platt, had a series of morning meetings while fighting over the New York governorship. "One of the things that particularly grieved the theoretical idealists and the chronic objectors was the fact that Roosevelt used on occasion to take breakfast with Senator Platt," wrote biographer Harold Howland in 1904.[63] Reformers criticized Roosevelt for visiting Senator Platt at his hotel for breakfast, fearing that the governor could not enjoy breakfast with the senator without taking orders from him; on the contrary, wrote Howland, "when Roosevelt breakfasted with Platt, it generally meant that he was trying to reconcile the Senator to something he was going to do which the worthy boss did not like."[64] Roosevelt, who became governor (and later the president of the United States) later wrote of his visits with Platt that "[a] series of breakfasts was always the prelude to some active warfare."[65]

BREAKFAST IN SPACE

While orbiting the Earth in 1962, astronaut John Glenn ate the first meal in outer space: applesauce from an aluminum squeeze tube. During his four-hour, fifty-five-minute flight, he had other various food cubes and semi-liquids. Scientists were not even sure food could be swallowed or digested in microgravity, but this soon became the least of their worries. Breakfast, it turned out, was a notoriously difficult meal.

The first problem was that astronauts, like ordinary Americans, all liked something different in the morning; some took black coffee and toast, while others craved bacon, eggs, and a stack of pancakes with butter and syrup. The second problem came down to the particulars of packaging and preparing foods that people typically ate for breakfast. If the National Aeronautics and Space Administration (NASA) could get humans into space, however, they could certainly dehydrate an egg.

The Space Food Systems Laboratory had the technology to master the art of dehydrating eggs into yellow Styrofoam pellets, and scrambled eggs became one of the first breakfast foods of the space program. Unfortunately, the Space Food Systems Laboratory did not have the technology to trick astronauts into liking the foods. Many astronauts, some of whom were on active duty in various branches of the military, refused even to try the eggs, because the dehydrated and rehydrated eggs reminded them of those served back at the base.[66] While eating scrambled eggs in space, the third problem with space food presented itself when bits of egg began to float off plates and drift into the air, sticking to walls, air vents, hair, and floors.

Some breakfast foods were a natural fit for outer space. Although it is popularly thought to have been invented for the space program, the powdered, orange-flavored breakfast drink Tang had already been developed for public use in 1957. Sales were poor until astronauts drank it on the *Gemini* flight in 1965. After tasting the various food cubes on *Mercury*, Glenn requested it. Other foods presented a greater challenge. Bacon was a necessity with scrambled eggs, but cooking it on a spacecraft was impossible. Instead, *Gemini* astronauts ate bacon bars made from cooked, crumbled bacon pressed into chewy bars. Toast was another challenge because in microgravity, crumbs would get into everything—especially nasal passages, as it unfortunately happens. Single-bite toast cubes were introduced on *Gemini*, but these were more like salad croutons and were not quickly embraced by astronauts.

Astronauts, especially the first ones, were men with basic tastes, and for whom a classic steak and eggs fit the bill. On the morning of May 6, 1961, astronaut Alan Shepard was no different; he enjoyed a bacon-wrapped filet mignon and scrambled eggs, then stepped into *Freedom 7* and became the first American in space. Shepard's meal had been designed to keep him sated and to digest slowly, but after that day, his manly, high-protein breakfast became the official lucky meal for astronauts to eat pre-launch.

On April 12, 1981, the day of the first orbital shuttle flight, NASA's mission control developed its own food tradition. NASA test director Norm Carlson brought in a pot of beans and a pan of cornbread; the launch was successful, and the beans and cornbread—traditional breakfast of those original American pioneers—was devoured. Thirty years later, the cry "beans are go!" still signals a successful launch, celebrated with beans and cornbread made using Carlson's original recipe.[67]

EATING AT SCHOOL

"To drive children into school in order to fill their heads when they have nothing in their stomachs is like pouring water into a sieve; unless you stay the vacuum in the stomach the knowledge will not remain in the head," insisted American journalist Albert Shaw in 1891.[68] The School Fund Societies began in Paris in 1867 to address this very concern, and by 1890, a free breakfast program had been instituted in Birmingham, England, providing children with "a substantial hunk of bread and a cup of warm milk."[69] Prior to that, numerous children were sent off to school without a meal. Even worse, English antiquary Thomas Fosbroke wrote in 1819, was that in 18th-century Gloucester, "[a]fter tobacco came into use, the children carried pipes in the satchels with their books, which their mothers took care to fill, that it might serve instead of breakfast."[70]

It was readily recognized in Europe that starving children cannot learn, and the provision of free breakfasts spread through the continent between the 1860s and 1920s. A breakfast requiring no preparation had been a part of the morning of Norwegian schoolchildren since the late 1920s. Known as the "Oslo breakfast," it consisted of rye-biscuit, brown bread, butter or margarine fortified with vitamins, whey cheese, and cod liver oil paste, 1/3 liter of milk, raw carrot, apple, and half an orange.

As early as 1905, charitable religious organizations began offering free breakfasts in churches to needy schoolchildren. It became the clarion cry of those writing on the nutritional and educational needs of children that Birmingham's program should be applied in America. The country's first free breakfast program for destitute children was offered by Philadelphia businessmen in 1930, but they ran out of money for the program two years later.[71] Finally, in 1966, the national School Breakfast Program (SBP), an offshoot of the 1966 Child Nutrition Act, was established as a two-year pilot project designed to provide categorical grants to assist schools serving breakfasts to children that qualified as "nutritionally needy" based on their family's income.[72] In 1975, the program received permanent Congressional authorization, after the evident success of a very different free breakfast program.

Among the most significant political achievements of the Black Panther Party was their Free Breakfast for School Children, also known as the Free Children's Breakfast Program, which reached its peak in 1969 and 1970. It was the Free Children's Breakfast Program that led the Director of the Federal Bureau of Investigation (FBI), J. Edgar Hoover, to declare that "the Black Panther Party, without question, represents the greatest threat to internal security of the country."[73] In the 2002 documentary "Hoover and the F.B.I.," film director Roger Guenveur Smith speculated that it was not the militant action of the Black Panthers that was most menacing to the American government; rather, "the Free Children's Breakfast Program engendered a certain following on the Black community's part, a certain respect on the Black community's part. I mean, nobody can argue with free grits."[74]

The Free Children's Breakfast Program, first set up in a church kitchen in Oakland, California, in 1968, was set in place not only to provide nutrition to at-risk youths, but to teach African-American school children about Black history, much in the way that Hebrew school educates Jewish children about the

Black Panther Free Breakfast for School Children Program, 1969. (Copyright Bettmann/Corbis/AP Images)

heritage of the Jewish people; however, the FBI criticized the program as propagandist. Nonetheless, thousands of children benefited daily from the nutritional breakfasts of eggs, bacon, grits, toast, and orange juice. This was considered by many to be the type of radical, direct social action that truly helped the Black community, in a time when hunger was a demoralizing reality for innumerable urban families. Full bellies and full minds, it was posited, was the first step in escaping oppression.[75]

In College

When young adults are left to their own culinary devices—sometimes for the first time in their lives—calamity has often ensued. Without Mother to provide balanced meals, a diet newly centered on fast food causes the much-maligned weight gain known as the "freshman fifteen." Upon waking, many college students reach for such crudities as cold leftover pizza or cup o' noodles from a Styrofoam cup (if they eat anything at all), but the nutritional landscape of the college breakfast was not always so bleak.

At Oxford in the 1890s, students were treated to breakfasts of "dove-tart and spread eagle."[76] In *The Adventures of Mr. Verdant Green: An Oxford Freshman* (1893), the protagonist is roused from his bed by the promise of these foods, but not before wondering aloud just what those foods were. His colleague Mr. Bouncer, incredulous at Green's ignorance, explains:

> Why a dove-tart is what mortals call a pigeon-pie. I ain't much in Tennyson's line, but it strikes me that dove-tarts are more poetical than the other thing; spread-eagle is a barn-door fowl smashed out flat, and made jolly with mushroom sauce, and no end of good things. I don't know how they squash it, but I should say that they sit upon it; I daresay, if we were to inquire, we should find that they kept a fat feller on purpose. But you just come, and try how it eats.[77]

Green enjoyed his spatchcocked chicken so much that he considered bribing the cook for the recipe to give to his mother.

When college breakfasts were bad, it was typically the student housing that was to blame, not the school's dining hall. In *Around the Tea-Table* (1798), clergyman Thomas De Witt Talmage blows the whistle on the conditions endured by his seminary students at Yale or Princeton. "The damage begins in the college boarding-house. The theological student has generally small means, and he must go to a cheap boarding-house."[78] Maligned as they are today, the 19th-century dormitories were too ritzy for the humble theologian. Unfortunately, boarding-house food left even more to be desired. Talmage describes the moribund breakfast offerings of the typical seminary boarding house in poetic detail:

> A frail piece of sausage trying to swim across a river of gravy on the breakfast-plate, but drowned at last, "the linked sweetness long drawn out" of flies in the molasses cup, the gristle of a tough ox, and measly biscuit, and buckwheat cakes tough as the cook's apron, and old peas in which the bugs lost their life before they had time to escape from the saucepan, and stale cucumbers cut up into small slices of *cholera morbus*. . . . Many of our best young men in preparation for the ministry are going through this martyrdom.[79]

Later writers on the subject of college diet supposed that the problem was not just financial, but temporal. "His chief lack is a lack of time," explained American educator Charles Franklin Thwing.[80] In his *If I Were a College Student* (1902), one student described having eaten a "simple" breakfast of doughnuts and bologna. "Such a simple breakfast is not one best fitted for the college boy or girl," Thwing lectured. In Thwing's later books, he offered five pointers for students: Get enough sleep; exercise; eat plenty of simple food (but not too much); don't worry; and have fun. "In a word, be a good animal."[81]

College breakfast, when taken at all, was on the run. American educator and essayist William Lyon Phelps wrote in "Eating Breakfast" (1930) of Yale undergraduates that "the streets were filled with undergraduates sprinting to chapel."[82] A lady in Phelps's company was shocked to see that the boys were running across campus with their tongues hanging out. "I set her right at once," wrote Phelps. "Those are not tongues, those are griddle cakes!"[83]

PRISON

Though Charles Thwing did not extrapolate that those who disregarded his life-coach advice were necessarily bad animals, it may be agreed that bad animals commit crimes, and consequently, do not enjoy good breakfasts. There is some evidence that those who skip breakfast are more likely to commit violent crimes. Domestic terrorist Timothy McVeigh ate a cold spaghetti MRE for breakfast on the morning he bombed the Alfred P. Murrah Federal Building in Oklahoma City on April 19, 1995, killing 168 people.[84] Perhaps if he had been more of a pancakes and omelets fellow he would have had second thoughts.

Studies show that self-control is linked to blood glucose levels, which are lowest in the morning before eating breakfast.[85] Skipping breakfast, it may then be logically surmised, could have wide-ranging implications in social behavior. "Numerous self-control behaviors fit this pattern, including controlling attention, regulating emotions, quitting smoking, coping with stress, resisting impulsivity, and refraining from criminal and aggressive behavior," wrote one researcher.[86] This may explain why so many criminals are from a lower socioeconomic bracket; they are too poor to eat breakfast every day, or working parents are not available to prepare it.

For some truly bad animals, breakfast may have been the last meal. Though it has not been the typical choice of those facing the garrotter, breakfast was served as the last meal of more than one death row inmate on execution day. On the morning of February 25, 1879, English murderer Charles Peace, subject of a Sir Arthur Conan Doyle Sherlock Holmes novel, requested a breakfast of eggs and a large amount of salty bacon before being sent to the gallows.[87] The bacon was not quite to his liking ("this is bloody rotten," were his words), and after his salty meal, he made an additional request for a glass of water. His request was denied.[88]

Infamous serial killer, rapist, and necrophile Ted Bundy declined a special last meal, and was instead offered a steak (medium-rare), eggs (over-easy), hash browns, toast with butter and jelly, milk, juice, and coffee. He refused to eat it.[89] Steak and eggs is considered the "traditional" last meal offered if none is specified by the inmate; it is also the traditional meal of astronauts before launch, and the customary breakfast eaten by soldiers headed for battle since World War II.[90] Breakfast is the first meal and the last meal.

SOCIAL GATHERINGS AND CELEBRATIONS

Breakfast serves an important function for another group of people facing imminent death: the elderly. Meeting at any of the hundreds of local breakfast clubs across the United States offers a chance for the otherwise isolated geriatrics to reconnect with friends and colleagues for a low-priced or free meal. Rotary clubs across the country have hosted weekly breakfast club meetings for about a century; Rotarians, like the attendees of political breakfast parties of the 19th century, enjoyed a bit of social discourse with their bacon and eggs. Interestingly, although morning meetings tend to favor the early-rising elderly, breakfast club attendees have historically been around ten years younger than the Rotary average.

Starting after the Civil War, the National Grange of the Order of Patrons of Husbandry was formed to promote the economic and political well-being of the community and agriculture. In sparsely populated rural communities, the Grange Hall is still the center of the town's social activity. Grange breakfasts provide connection to one's neighbors, even if those neighbors live several miles away. For a few dollars, members eat their fill of pancakes, sausages, and potatoes, and have a lively chat about the price of corn.

Pancake banquets—not including those on Shrove Tuesday—have been held since at least the 19th century. Pancake benefits were hosted by churches and ladies' auxiliaries to raise money for good causes and to show appreciation for veterans, among other things. One benefit held by the "My America" League after World War I was attended by glamorous film stars Crystal Herne, Margaret Dale, and Virginia Fox Brooks, to honor the boys who marched home from the Great War.[91] The curative powers of pancakes were evidently even more potent than the beautiful celebrities; the twenty flapjacks consumed by one sailor helped alleviate his post-traumatic stress disorder, noted a 1919 *McClure's* article. The brooding sailor "hinted at a dark sorrow in his life, which he did admit later in the day, had been mitigated a good deal by the pancakes."[92]

Except for the Mother's Day breakfast in bed prepared by the children of the family, celebratory breakfasts typically take place away from home. In actuality, Mother's Day is the busiest day of the year for the restaurant industry. Celebratory or not, Bloody Marys, mimosas, and other breakfast cocktails are more typically consumed while dining out.

Wedding Breakfast

An ancient Greek superstition told that if a crow appeared at a wedding breakfast, a divorce would be unavoidable, unless all present cried out with one accord, "Maiden, scare away that crow!"[93] Inversely, unless a bride and groom wanted trouble from the water fairies, they should use the same finger-bowl during their wedding breakfast.[94] Regardless, before the Reformation in the 16th century, the wedding service was a Mass and the bride and groom would have been fasting before the wedding; therefore, the first meal following the ceremony was necessarily a breakfast. By the 19th century, even cookbook author Isabella Beeton lamented that "[t]he orthodox wedding breakfast seems likely to become a thing of the past so much has it been superseded by the wedding tea that now takes its place at afternoon weddings."[95] Nonetheless, Mrs. Beeton had hope yet for society; "Still," she wrote, "there are many who prefer the old-fashioned breakfast which, like the *dejeuner* of the French people, comes at the time of day when people can enjoy a meal."[96] She goes on to provide a couple of seasonal menu options, which would seem vast and heavy by today's standards, but which were rather par for the Victorian course.

Stateside, the tradition held into the first quarter of the 20th century, but as weddings became more casual than a Holy Communion, the breakfast became a luncheon, and then a reception. The meal often exhibited qualities of both a breakfast and a luncheon. A wedding breakfast, wrote preeminent domestic expert Marion Harland in 1905, may consist of grapefruit with a Maraschino cherry, then an oyster or clam course, then a light soup, a fish course, lamb chops or roast chicken with potatoes, and finally a dessert with coffee. Champagne was *de rigueur*. Harland provides a final etiquette tip for the newlywed celebrating her church nuptials. "The breakfast over, the bride slips away quietly, to change her dress for the wedding journey."[97] After such a breakfast, it was presumably into a muumuu.

Peyote Breakfast

A ceremonial breakfast plays an important role in the peyote rituals of indigenous people of North America, predominantly in tribes from central Mexico north to the Great Plains. The ritual did not spread to the tribes of the United States until the second half of the 19th century, though some Apache embraced it much earlier.[98] The peyote ritual purportedly enables its participants to commune with their dead ancestors, and acts as a catalyst for contemplative prayer and invocation for the recovery of the sick.

The ceremony, which dates back to pre-Columbian Mexico, centers on consumption of the hallucinogenic peyote cactus (*Lephophora williamsii*) and communal overnight meditation in a tipi. When the first daylight appears, the morning-star song was sung, and the breakfast ceremony began. The water carrier women passed around sacramental foods—water, maize, fruit, meat—in a clockwise direction, and after the ritual meal was consumed, the ceremony was concluded with the meat song. Traditional foods included pemmican of venison, suet, and dried fruit; pounded, dried maize; cornmeal mush; and water.[99] The meat and maize of the peyote cult in the United States is likely derived from the venison and dried corn in the Huichol peyote rites of west-central Mexico. The fruits and other sweets were eaten to counteract the peyote's bitterness.

In accounts of peyote ceremonies of the 20th century, the peyote breakfast could include any number of surprisingly nontraditional foods to represent the water, maize, fruit, and meat: cherries in Jell-O, broken peppermint stick candy, soda crackers, Cracker Jacks (a brand of packaged candied popcorn), sweetened Cream of Wheat (a brand of wheat farina cereal, usually served as a porridge), canned fruit cocktail, or canned corned beef.[100] It is perhaps a commentary on the current state of Indian affairs that ancient, sacred traditions have become filtered through lenses of poverty and American convenience.

A second breakfast is typically served following the Native American church services that conclude the ritual. This is a typical American breakfast of eggs, toast, hash browns, and coffee, served well after sunrise.

When executed properly, the morning meal is certainly worthy of veneration and a place in holy ceremony. It is no wonder it has been celebrated in the arts for centuries.

BREAKFAST IN THE
ARTS AND MEDIA

As a part of daily life, breakfast was as worthy a subject for the arts as any other subject, and certainly as worthy as any other meal. Though there have never been any operas or plays written about breakfast, some filmmakers have a penchant for placing critical scenes at the breakfast table. Just as the 17th century was truly the golden age of breakfast in Europe, it was also known as the Golden Age of Dutch painting, and this was never more evident than in the Dutch still life paintings known as breakfast pieces.

In Kurt Vonnegut's 1973 *Breakfast of Champions or, Goodbye Blue Monday*, the waitress mutters the titular Wheaties breakfast cereal slogan whenever serving a customer a martini. In this novel (which is actually not at all about breakfast), Vonnegut names his narrator Philboyd Studge, a nod to a short story by Edwardian satirist Saki, "Filboid Studge, the Story of a Mouse That Helped." The humorous "Filboid Studge" is a story about the use of clever advertising to create fervor for an unpopular, unpalatable breakfast cereal (and not at all about a mouse), but more importantly, it is a thinly veiled poke at the Clean Living movement of the same era.

The 1961 romantic comedy *Breakfast at Tiffany's* turned Audrey Hepburn—a pretty actress with a slim, boyish figure—into an American icon of classic beauty. The film opens with a scene of Hepburn's character, a café society girl named Holly Golightly, wearing a Givenchy gown and large sunglasses, gazing into the window of the Tiffany & Co. jewelry store, sipping coffee and eating a Danish. Conversely, the 1985 John Hughes film, *The Breakfast Club*, while also iconic, has no scene featuring the morning meal at all. The film's title comes from the nickname invented by students and staff for detention at New Trier

High School, the school attended by the son of one of John Hughes's friends; in turn, "The Breakfast Club" at that school likely took its name from the title of American radio's longest-running network entertainment show, broadcast from Chicago from 1933 to 1968.[1]

LITERATURE

Written works have discussed breakfast for centuries, for millennia even. In the 8th century BCE, Homer included a breakfast scene in *The Odyssey*.[2] Charlotte Brontë's protagonist Jane Eyre nearly gags on a bite of burned porridge. In P. G. Wodehouse's 1916 *Jeeves Takes Charge*, Jeeves the valet takes charge of, among other things, his employer's hangover, with a concoction of egg yolk, Worcestershire sauce, cinnamon oil, cognac, and other mystery ingredients. Novelist Anthony Trollope wrote numerous works with detailed breakfast scenes; he even gauges writing prowess with the morning meal in his 1883 autobiography, by describing how he was able to write 2,500 words before dressing for breakfast each day.[3]

Just as it did in high society, in 19th-century literature, breakfast enjoyed the spotlight. Sir Walter Scott's first foray into prose fiction, *Waverley* (1814), presents a resplendent breakfast scene, clearly depicting the superlative Scottish breakfast: "The table [was] loaded with warm bread, both of flour, oatmeal, and barleymeal, in the shape of loaves, cakes, biscuits, and other varieties, together with eggs, reindeer ham, mutton and beef ditto, smoked salmon, and marmalade."[4]

In Thomas Love Peacock's 1831 *Crotchet Castle*, the vigorous middle-aged clergyman Reverend Doctor Folliott details his breakfast preferences: "Chocolate, coffee, tea, cream, eggs, ham, tongue, cold fowl, all these are good, and bespeak good knowledge in him who sets them forth: but the touchstone is fish."[5] The divine then took his seat at the breakfast table with his dining mates, and composes his spirits "by the gentle sedative of a large cup of tea, the demulcent of a well-buttered muffin, and the tonic of a small lobster."[6] The good reverend then compliments his tablemate's country for its talent with a fish breakfast.

In his classic *Moby-Dick* (1851), American author Herman Melville devotes chapter five, "Breakfast," to a humorous scene around a breakfast table.[7] The men of the whaling ship *Pequod* are at port for the night; with the cry "Grub, ho!" the landlord of the Spouter Inn announces breakfast the following morning. Upon entering, a wandering sailor called Ishmael (the narrator) expects breakfast to be jovial, with the men swapping boisterous whaling stories, but instead the scene is rife with nervous tension as the fearless seafarers sit in awkward silence, seemingly intimidated by the polite breakfast table.

One of the *Pequod*'s whalers, the mysterious harpooner Queequeg, brings his harpoon to breakfast so that he can use it to reach across the table and spear foods; here, bringing the weapon to the table is not a faux pas, but an odd sign of his gentility. Queequeg forgoes the polite-society coffee and rolls for rare beefsteak; this is an obvious nod to the character's cannibal roots, but also a metaphor for the swarthy, tattooed harpooner's raw masculinity and primal power. Using this breakfast scene in *Moby-Dick*, Melville effectively juxtaposes the familiar with the exotic, flipping social norms in order to endear the "savage" Queequeg to the reader, while making an astute commentary on cultural perspective.

Nathaniel Hawthorne wrote in his gothic novel, *The House of the Seven Gables* (1851), that "[l]ife, within doors, has few pleasanter prospects than a neatly arranged and well-provisioned breakfast-table."[8] The protagonist Hepzibah Pyncheon, a middle-aged socialite who has since fallen into destitution, wants to impress a houseguest with a home-cooked breakfast. The only problem is that Hepzibah is inept in the kitchen, requiring her to recruit help from her charming cousin Phoebe.

By joining forces, the two Pyncheon women prepared a wonderful breakfast of broiled mackerel, the aroma of which "arose like incense from the shrine of a barbarian idol" and buttery Indian cakes, of a "hue befitting the rustic altars of the innocent and golden age,—or, so brightly yellow were they, resembling some of the bread which was changed to glistening gold when Midas tried to eat it."[9] To wash down the meal, Mocha coffee with a fragrance sweet enough that it "might have gratified the nostrils of a tutelary Lar."[10] That the coffee was deemed fit for ancient Roman guardian deities is a testament to the care Hepzibah had taken in selecting each bean.

Hepzibah had set her prettiest damask linens on her dainty breakfast table, had used her finest china, silver creamer, and crested spoon, and Phoebe set out a glass pitcher of roses and flowering pear branches (signaling the breakfast was in the spring). The breakfast table "looked worthy to be the scene and centre of one of the cheerfullest of parties," bringing a tear to Hepzibah's eyes.[11] She had gone to so much trouble because she was expecting a special guest: her brother Clifford, who had spent thirty years behind bars, falsely imprisoned for murder.

In *The House of Seven Gables*, Hawthorne has used breakfast to illustrate the departure from the strains of daily life; it is a time when the "material delights" may be "fully enjoyed," implying that during breakfast one may feed the spiritual as well as the physical self.[12] As the breakfast scene continues, the now elderly Clifford, having spent half his life deprived of such splendor and beauty, comes to the breakfast table, attempting to grapple with the scene before him. As he voraciously eats his breakfast, his ability to appreciate these pleasures is reawakened; the reader witnesses the homecoming of the human being whom Clifford once was, glimpsing a "flickering taper-gleam in his eyeballs" that "betokened that his spiritual part had returned."[13]

Instead of being portrayed in the same sparkling, spirituality-renewing sunshine as American written works, the American breakfast table often came under scrutiny when described by English authors. Some criticized the quality of the foods or the sloppy preparation of it, while others claimed true concern for American health, such as English travel writer Harriet Martineau, who, like many of the American Clean Living Movement proponents, was appalled at the American habit of eating hot bread and a variety of pork products at breakfast. (To be fair, this excess was trotted out for Martineau's benefit while she was a guest in a wealthy Southern home, and was not indicative of the way all Americans lived.)

Cookbook author and domestic expert Marion Harland wrote several novels in addition to her 1870 *Common Sense in the Household*. In *At Last* (also published in 1870), Harland portrays Mrs. Sutton, a comely fifty-year-old widow, dressed for the breakfast table in the same cheerful attire that housewives' manuals advised women to don in order to please their husbands. "She looked fresh and bright as the early September day, with her sunny face and in her daintily-neat attire," and breakfast is mentioned several other times in the book, as "always pleasant."[14] This is consistent with the way Harland wrote about breakfast in her domestic guides, and her domestic expertise was evident in the way she wrote about cooking in her novels.

American authors of the domestic or "sentimental" novels of the early to mid-19th century often wrote cookbooks and domestic manuals as well, paving the way for a generation of authors, including Hawthorne, to espouse breakfast with the literary portrayal of American life. The themes of kitchen management and cookery became central in the scientific kitchen movement and novels alike, domestic or not. Didactic fiction as a genre targeted toward female audiences persisted into the 20th century with works like *A Thousand Ways to Please a Husband* (1917).[15] Books that encouraged young women to embrace the "romance of cookery and housekeeping" were generally preferable to titillating light fiction or worse, dime novels, which were considered by some experts to promote hysteria, physical evils, and precocious development.[16]

At the turn of the 20th century, after proponents of the Jacksonian era's Clean Living Movement brought breakfast cereals to the forefront, written descriptions of the breakfast table began to lose their glow. The natural next step in the evolution of the literary breakfast was satire. In 1911, English author Saki (nom de plume of H. H. Munro) followed suit and wrote the short story "Filboid Studge, the Story of a Mouse that Helped."[17]

A struggling artist named Mark Spayley is in love with Leonore, the daughter of Duncan Dullamy, a businessman who is secretly having trouble selling his breakfast cereal, Pipenta, even after sinking a fortune into advertising. Dullamy, a "man of phantom wealth," is eager to marry off his daughter before he completely goes broke, so he cuts Mark a deal: Make a successful advertisement for Pipenta and he can marry Leonore. Mark is astonished, and accepts.

The breakfast food was renamed to Filboid Studge ("It wants a better name," Mark had decided), and the new ad campaign was released three weeks later. Rather than depicting children growing big and strong from eating the cereal, it showed what could happen if one did *not* eat the cereal: They might just die and go to Hell. The advertisement, depicting Society ladies, politicians, celebrities—all of the leading men and women of the day, "smiling still from force of habit, but with the fearsome smiling rage of baffled effort"—rendered into Lost Souls, sentenced to eternal damnation. "The poster bore no fulsome allusions to the merits of the new breakfast food, but a single grim statement ran in bold letters along its base: 'They cannot buy it now.'"[18]

Mark Spayley had caught on to the notion that people would do things from a sense of duty, rather than desire. No one would have eaten the cereal out of pleasure, but housewives were driven in hordes to buy out grocery stores because *they must*.

> Once the womenfolk discovered that it was thoroughly unpalatable, their zeal in forcing it on their households knew no bounds. "You haven't eaten your Filboid Studge!" would be screamed at the appetiteless clerk as he turned wearily from the breakfast-table, and his evening meal would be prefaced by a warmed-up mess which would be explained as "your Filboid Studge that you didn't eat this morning."[19]

The commentary on the religious and dietary zealotry of Sylvester Graham and John Harvey Kellogg—Seventh Day Adventists who advocated health reform, temperance, and sexual abstinence—is hard to miss. Saki's portrayal of a world in which Filboid Studge reigned supreme was a witty warning of what dystopia awaited America if "[t]hose strange fanatics who ostentatiously mortify themselves, inwardly and outwardly, with health biscuits and health garments" were left in charge.[20] In the end, Dullamy regained his wealth by selling out before a new, even more unpalatable cereal could be brought to market, or,

God forbid, that "tasty and appetizing" foods would make a comeback and "the Puritan austerity of the moment might be banished from domestic cookery."[21]

The introduction to Saki's collection of short stories *The Chronicles of Clovis* (which included "Filboid Studge") was written by A. A. Milne, an essayist who would go on to write beloved children's book *Winnie the Pooh* in 1926.[22] While American authors were beginning to step away from the breakfast table as the warm center of the home and symbol of civility, English authors like Milne were still holding the morning meal in high esteem. In fact, breakfast was so beloved by English writers that morning meals were mentioned both frequently and laudably in the first half of the 20th century.

Like many English and northern Europeans, the hobbit's feeding schedule consists of six meals, three of which occur before lunch: breakfast, second breakfast, and elevenses, as portrayed in the Middle-earth stories by Oxford English professor J. R. R. Tolkien. In Tolkien's inaugural *The Hobbit, or There and Back Again* (1937), protagonist Bilbo Baggins is sitting down to a second breakfast (having finished his breakfast and opened up his doors for a bit of fresh air and sunshine), when in walked the wizard Gandalf, scolding Bilbo for being late for a meeting. "and here you are having breakfast, or whatever you call it, at half past ten!"[23] Bilbo reluctantly leaves his second breakfast half-finished and races out the door without cleaning up.

Bilbo spends much of his adventure bemoaning the lack of a sufficient breakfast (not to mention second breakfast or elevenses). The only real morning feast is consumed by Gandalf: "Two whole loaves (with masses of butter and honey and clotted cream) and at least a quart of mead," which he finishes off by sending out satisfied curls of silver smoke from his delicious pipe of breakfast tobacco.[24]

It may have been Tolkien's intimate knowledge of early Germanic folklore that inspired his inclusion of second breakfast (*zweites Frühstück*) in his works. Germans, like the English, revered the other morning meals. In Bavaria and Poland, special dishes are made exclusively for second breakfast. In Thomas Mann's 1924 *The Magic Mountain* (*Der Zauberberg*), widely considered one of the most influential works of 20th-century German literature, frequent and detailed references are made to second breakfasts. Bread started breakfast, and "extra-strong coffee"; on Sundays, it might be "warm rolls and smoked beef, washed down by a glass of old port."[25] For second breakfast, beer is served along with "cold cuts on toast."

English writers more commonly included descriptions of elevenses than second breakfasts, though first breakfasts were certainly up for discussion as well.

In *Winnie the Pooh*, the titular bear and his aptly named friend Piglet are having a chat about the morning.

> "When you wake up in the morning, Pooh," said Piglet at last, "what's the first thing you say to yourself?" "What's for breakfast?" said Pooh. "What do you say, Piglet?" "I say, I wonder what's going to happen exciting today?" said Piglet. Pooh nodded thoughtfully. "It's the same thing," he said.[26]

Similar to Bilbo Baggins, Pooh is almost singularly focused on obtaining his next meal. Later in the morning after breakfast, as mentioned in *House at Pooh Corner* (1928), Pooh liked another "little smackerel of something." "I generally have a small something about now—about this time in the morning," he said to his friend Owl.[27] For elevenses—the midmorning snack after second breakfast but before lunch—Winnie-the-Pooh preferred honey on bread with a mouthful of condensed milk. There are several other mentions in the books about Pooh noticing the time on the clock and suggesting that it might be nice to have a little something to eat. Another literary bear named Paddington (from Michael Bond's 1958 *A Bear Called Paddington*) often took elevenses at the antique shop on Portobello Road, run by his friend Mr. Gruber. Mr. Gruber had a sticky bun and hot chocolate for his elevenses, sharing with Paddington that "there's nothing like a chat over a bun and cocoa."[28] Paddington, who liked all three, agreed.

Later works of fiction waxed no less rhapsodic over the morning meal, even when breakfast had little to do with a scene than to restore peace and order to a chaotic dystopia. In Thomas Pynchon's *Gravity's Rainbow* (1973), "Now there grows among all the rooms, replacing the night's old smoke, alcohol and sweat, the fragile, musaceous odour of Breakfast, permeating, surprising, more than the color of winter sunlight."[29] Pertaining to the plant genus *Musa* (which includes bananas and plantains), the breakfast that character Pirate Prentice cooks with his friends included banana waffles, banana croissants, banana kreplach, and banana jam, and in a large crock he has bananas fermented with honey and Muscat raisins to make banana mead. The smell of the banana breakfast fills the room by "weaving its molecules" into the party's very DNA, imbuing the warm room with life, when outside lay a bitter ice field with rockets screaming overhead.

PAINTING AND DRAWING

Some of the earliest nonreligious painting of the Middle Ages was of still lifes, and by the 15th century, many of these were of foods. Leonardo da Vinci was among the first to break from religious subjects in the late 15th century, with his studies of bowls of fruit, but scenes of the breakfast table would wait until the meal was more widely accepted socially.

Dutch Breakfast Paintings

The Dutch Golden Age of painting was exemplified by still lifes. In the early 17th century, Flemish Baroque artist Clara Peeters won acclaim for her portrayals of flowers and fruits arranged together, in scenes that would later become known as *ontbijtje*, or "breakfast pieces."

Unlike the metaphorically obtuse imagery depicted in funerary works called Vanitas, wherein skulls and rotting fruit predominate, *ontbijtje* give the viewer a subtle peek into the daily lives of the 17th-century Dutch. While Vanitas paintings are rife with obvious symbols indicating the fleeting nature of life in this world, breakfast pieces have no hidden meanings. In the first half of the 1600s, the simple peasant's breakfasts of bread with herring or cheese and a mug of beer as painted by artists like Pieter Claesz come in contrast to Floris Gerritsz van Schooten's platters of pies and fresh fruits, or Jacob van Hulsdonck's hams with fat cheeses and goblets of wine that one might have found in a wealthier household, but these depictions are not really intended as a social commentary; they are simply pleasant paintings of the breakfast table. Cheese, butter, beer, and bread were all commonly eaten for breakfast by the Dutch in the 17th century, and this is reflected in the ubiquity of these foods in paintings of the era.

A few items of food near the corner of the table typify the Dutch breakfast pieces. Though the paintings were a literal presentation of delicacies that the upper class might enjoy, they were also a rather overt religious reminder to avoid gluttony—particularly by including images of the bread and wine of the Holy Communion and the early Christian symbol of the fish. It is an interesting coincidence that these were also the foods typically eaten by Europe's working class, to whom the Church had long showed leniency toward the taboo of eating breakfast.

Dutch still lifes reached their climax by the late 1630s, when the *ontbijtje*, or "little breakfasts," became *banketje*, or "little banquets." Willem Claeszoon Heda's and Pieter Claesz's later-17th-century depictions of the table, while lushly detailed and ornate, were often bawdy scenes of embellished goblets; silver bowls carelessly tipped over and wine carafes with their lids left up; aphrodisiac oysters and lemons with curled peels hanging off the table's edge; crumpled white table linens wadded up like lingerie.

The popularity of breakfast pieces soon spread from the Netherlands (particularly Haarlem) to Flanders and Germany, and also to Spain and France. The other Europeans added their own touches to the breakfast pieces; German painter Georg Flegel added a bit of animal portraiture to his still lifes by including insects and birds, as seen in his *Still Life with Fish* (1637), which features the simple breakfast of a dish of sprats, a carafe of wine, and a fly crawling across a loaf of bread.

Portraits

Though they mostly painted still lifes, Dutch painters of the 17th century also included breakfast in their portraits; these images of eating or drinking were known as *tronies*. Whereas other *ontbijtje* painters tended to focus more on the "still" than the "life," Pieter Cornelisz van Slingelandt's *Breakfast of a Young Man* in the late 1600s brings a joviality and animation to the breakfast foods. The herring on the young man's plate is carved up, ready for eating; his knife stuck into the table. His brown bread—a sign that the subject is working class— is nestled on the tablecloth next to the blue and white china plate—a sign that the subject was wealthy. His jacket and vest are unbuttoned at the bottom to allow his full stomach a bit of breathing room, as he eyes a full glass of beer with a jocular smirk on his face.[30]

In the 17th century, men and women in Dutch portraits were often shown cooking foods—a working-class pursuit. Jan Steen's *The Old Pancake Seller* (1664), Gerrit Dou's *The Pancake Seller* (1650–1655) and Rembrandt's *Pancake Woman* (1635) all portray this profession in a positive light, with busy cooks and smiling patrons, eager for their hotcakes. The pancake seller was painted repeatedly, by numerous artists, for several centuries. Italian contemporary painter Pietro Longhi painted a woman selling pancakes in the mid-18th century; in the mid-19th century, Alexis van Hamme painted a scene more relative to Belgians in *The Waffle Seller*. By the 19th century, the focus of portraiture seems to have shifted to softer subjects, particularly of those in the newly formed middle class. American illustrator Edmund Ashe's 1894 drawing *A Bachelor's Breakfast* is a sad glimpse into the lives of those men unsuited to marriage. It depicts a middle-aged man frowning over his pan of popping popcorn, while children gawk at him pityingly through a window.

In his 1868 *Breakfast in the Studio (The Black Jacket)*, Eduoard Manet nods back to the golden age of Dutch still lifes by including lemon peels curling salaciously off the table's edge, but toward the end of the 19th century, breakfast

Edmond Ashe's "A Bachelor's Breakfast," 1894. Courtesy of the Library of Congress.

scenes had long begun to pull away from the ostentatious table draped in expensive shellfish, citrus fruits, and silver platters. Impressionist art prominently featured the home, with the mistress of the house at the glowing center of quiet family life. Sometimes domestic help was pictured in the background, carrying on the mundane task of carrying coffee cups away from the table. This was reflective of an ideal not realized by most people, but was consistent with written descriptions of breakfast tables in more well-off households. Since most artists were typically quite poor themselves, these portrayals of luxury may have been akin to the habit of jazz musicians of the 1930s and 1940s singing about food during the Depression; they were using art to fantasize about things they lacked in their own lives.

French Impressionist Pierre-Auguste Renoir was from a working-class family, but his paintings were typically of the upper classes (though this likely had more to do with the fact that it was the wealthy who commissioned paintings than Renoir's fascination with them). *Breakfast at Berneval* (1898) depicts typical middle-class life: mother setting the breakfast table as her child gazes up at her, a young man casually reading a book in the foreground. A year earlier, American painter Mary Cassatt completed *Breakfast in Bed*; the portrayal of a bright-eyed toddler in bed with her stirring mother echoed other Impressionist themes of breakfast being a quiet meal with the family. Though his work was decidedly less rosy, in 1883 Henri de Toulouse-Lautrec nonetheless painted his mother at breakfast as well. Instead of cooing into the face of a child or gazing softly across her table, however, Mrs. Toulouse-Lautrec was seated solemnly in front of a cup of tea, with downward gaze.

Some artists of the era depicted breakfast without the family. Guillaume van Strydonck's *Breakfast at Blankenberge* (1890), shows a group of gentlemen seated in the breakfast parlor, enjoying coffee and rolls—probably discussing the important current events in politics and literature. This was one of the few portraits of the breakfast table that do not feature a woman.

After the turn of the 20th century, breakfast scenes in paintings began to lose their romantic undertones, but nonetheless portrayed a reality that at least some Americans were living. American Impressionist William McGregor Paxton painted two different women having a quiet moment alone in the morning. In *The Breakfast* (1911), a woman is twisted in her chair like a pouting child, staring at the floor, having lost the battle for her husband's attention to the morning paper. Her alone-time is not her choosing. In *The Morning Paper* (1913), a woman—perhaps the same one—enjoys a bedside cup of coffee with a newspaper of her own.

Beloved 20th-century portraitist Norman Rockwell painted two different scenes of the American breakfast table, both of which, coincidentally, are a humorous peek into the private lives of unhappily married couples. In *The Breakfast Table* (1930), for instance, a childless couple is having a quiet breakfast; the husband is buried in his newspaper as the deserted wife sitting across from him stares off into space. As captured eloquently by Rockwell (and William McGregor Paxton), it would appear that the warnings of domestic guides were true: A wife had better be cheery and interesting in the morning or she stands to lose her husband to the sports section.

Two decades later, Rockwell painted a different couple at the breakfast table; this time, husband and wife each have their own newspaper . . . and their own opinions about the headlines. In *Breakfast Table Political Argument* (1948), the morning's lively debate appears to have become as heated as the toaster on the table; the pretty young wife, a Harry Truman supporter, has her arms crossed defensively across her chest and her lip firmly out, while her ranting husband points insistently at a photo of Republican candidate Thomas Dewey. The posturing of the couple was perhaps Rockwell's commentary on the difference between the political parties, one that some may suggest remains today. A toddler beneath the table is crying—a metaphor for the American people during election season, weary of the bickering.

Food was a common subject of Pop artists of the 1960s. American painter Wayne Thiebaud was most famous for his cakes, but his etchings *Bacon & Eggs* (1964) and the nearly identical *Breakfast* (1995) reveal his fascination with the standardization of morning meal in the diner setting. The only differences between these two works is the changed placement of a small ramekin of ketchup; the silverware wrapped loosely versus unwrapped; and the diagonally cut versus whole toast. The stark similarity between the two pieces hearkens back to breakfast menus from chain restaurants like Denny's or International House of Pancakes; order bacon and eggs at a Denny's in Tulsa, Oklahoma, and it will be the very same plate of food one receives in Columbus, Ohio. Or perhaps Thiebaud was simply pointing out that in thirty years, the only thing that has changed about breakfast, evidently, is the location of ketchup on the table (which is to say, the more things change, the more they stay the same).

The theme of sameness was repeated by other artists in the Pop movement. One notable example of using repetition to make a statement was Andy Warhol. Though he was more famous for his soup cans, Warhol drew inspiration from Corn Flakes shipping cartons in 1971, when he created a collection of boxes that look more or less identical to what one might see in a bulk grocery buying club. In what may only be described as the ultimate meta-Pop, Warhol was later photographed by American artist Bobby Grossman holding a German box of Kellogg's Corn Flakes onto which Velvet Underground singer Lou Reed had been superimposed.[31] The mind reels to consider what abstinence advocate John Harvey Kellogg would have thought; Lou Reed is openly bisexual.

PHOTOGRAPHY

Besides Andy Warhol, Grossman photographed a number of other Pop icons for his 1978–1979 "Cornflake" series.[32] Grossman took some of the most emblematic photos of the 1970s and 1980s cultural scene in New York City, but the Cornflake series is particularly effective at humanizing super-human celebrities like Talking Heads front man David Byrne and Blondie singer Debbie Harry. The absurd image of an abrasive, rebellious punk rock musician grinning innocently over a bowl of corn flakes is perfectly consistent with the rest of the humorous jabs that Pop art makes at popular culture.

Many other famous people have been photographed eating breakfast. Elvis Presley was photographed at the breakfast table in 1958 (with an unopened Kel-Bowl-Pak of Corn Flakes, coincidentally); the Beatles were photographed numerous times in the 1960s, enjoying a bit of toast and tea or a doughnut.[33] In a 1952 issue of *Pageant Magazine*, Marilyn Monroe was shown in bed, draped provocatively in her bedsheets, cracking raw eggs into a glass of milk.[34] Seeing celebrities eating (or drinking) breakfast has a way of bringing them down to the level of everyday people, which makes these photos all the more appealing to the unfamous masses.

Photographer Jon Huck captured the humble, mundane sensibility of breakfast by shooting a hundred of his friends with their morning meals.[35] Huck's "Breakfast" series (2007) conveys a voyeuristic character; because people tend to eat the same thing for breakfast every day, and it is frequently eaten alone, breakfast bears a much more ritualistic and private nature than lunch or dinner. This may be behind the fact that some of the people captured by Huck resemble their breakfasts. A bald man photographed with his hard-boiled egg is one obvious example, as are the mousy dishwater-blonde with a bowl of oatmeal, or the serious, dark-eyed man shot with his cup of black coffee.

Huck's photographs also encourage the viewer to make personal judgments about the subjects based on their breakfast choices. The apples-almond-wheatgrass combo belongs on the breakfast table of whom one may assume to be a health fanatic; the viewer might find that this assumption is substantiated by the subject's bright eyes and self-contented smirk. A man with adventurous facial hair has made a similarly undaunted breakfast choice: ham with poached eggs doused in hot sauce. One gaunt, slack-jawed woman stares slightly off-camera, photographed with only a roasted sweet potato. One might conclude that she has an eating disorder, or is a vegan.

CINEMA

Everyone who has eaten at a restaurant has experienced the annoyance of being told that some desired item is unavailable, but never is this more unbearable than first thing in the morning. Restaurant breakfasts can make or break one's day, and they can make or break a film. Breakfast scenes in movies establish normalcy from which to deviate; they celebrate life's calm, quotidian moments; they demonstrate a character's true colors. To say that breakfast is the most important meal of the day may be trite, but its role in film is grossly underestimated.

Due to the urgency of the morning, or perhaps to the fact that one does not always present one's most polite, patient self in the morning, frustration is a recurring theme in theatrical breakfast scenes. In the diner scene of the 1970 cinematic classic *Five Easy Pieces*, Bobby (played eloquently by a young Jack Nicholson) orders a "plain omelet, no potatoes, tomatoes instead, a cup of coffee and wheat toast."[36] Stymied by the restaurant's "no substitutions" policy, he is forced to engage in a verbal fencing match with the waitress to attempt to get exactly what he wants on his plate. Desperate to get wheat toast (not available as a side order), Bobby thinks he has delivered his *coup de grace* by ordering a chicken salad sandwich, but asking the waitress to hold the mayo, the lettuce and the chicken. "Hold the *chicken*?" The waitress is incredulous. Bobby utters the famous line from the film, "I want you to hold it between your knees." Needless to say, he did not get his toast; he is instead asked to leave the establishment. The scene powerfully illustrates the generational conflict that characterized the late 1960s while humorously demonstrating the daily, minor irritations one may experience over breakfast.

Another movie took the exasperation with customer service a step further. In the famous "Whammy Burger" scene in the crime drama *Falling Down* (1993), William "D-Fens" Foster, played by actor Michael Douglas, experiences the crushing disappointment of coming to the fast food restaurant for a ham and cheese "womlet," only to find that the restaurant had stopped serving breakfast a mere four minutes earlier.[37] The scene, in which tightly wound D-Fens says "I want breakfast," only to be told that they were no longer serving it, is the breaking point in D-Fens' psyche; he calmly reaches into his bag and pulls out a semi-automatic handgun, fires shots into the ceiling, and proceeds to hold the patrons of the restaurant hostage while he waits for his food. This scene provides a fascinating social commentary on whether the customer truly is always right, while, again, illustrating the tenuous thread that holds people together before they have had something to eat in the morning.

Writer and director Quentin Tarantino seems to have a keen interest in breakfast; several of his films use breakfast scenes to mark pivotal moments. In *Reservoir Dogs* (1992), eight ruthless criminals with colorful pseudonyms are eating breakfast before heading out to a planned diamond heist.[38] At the end of the meal, one of the men, Mr. Pink, refuses to pitch in a dollar to tip the waitress on the grounds that he is anti-tipping. "I don't believe in it," he states firmly. (Mr. Pink, played by Steve Buscemi, would have loved cafeteria dining.) He defends his position: "I don't tip because society says I have to. Alright, I tip when somebody really deserves a tip. If they put forth an effort, I'll give them something extra. But I mean, this tipping automatically, that's for the birds. As far as I'm concerned they're just doing their job."[39] The conversation quickly devolves into a philosophical debate about why society does not deem fast food employees "tip-worthy," whereas waitresses in a restaurant or diner are to receive a gratuity. Mr. Orange, convinced by Mr. Pink's argument, requests his dollar back. The rest of the men defend the waitress and her profession.

Tarantino's 1994 *Pulp Fiction* has not one, but *three* scenes that take place at breakfast; the film is bookended with the same breakfast diner scene.[40] The second, known as "The Big Kahuna Burger scene" is the audience's first exposure to the wry Old Testament sensibility of Jules Winnfield (Samuel L. Jackson), who declares, "hamburgers: the cornerstone of any nutritional breakfast!" before reciting Ezekiel 25:17 and unloading the clip of his 9mm into the recipient of his sermon. Another scene uses Pop Tarts hopping out of a toaster to cue Butch Coolidge (Bruce Willis) to empty a machine gun into his would-be assassin—a man who had evidently helped himself to Coolidge's kitchen cabinets. The film's epilogue, as mentioned, takes place in the breakfast diner where Winnfield, having experienced an epiphany, reveals his greater destiny; this significant moment of character development is staged at breakfast.[41]

Older films provide an entertaining glimpse into the social mores of the past. In *The Public Enemy* (1931), Tom (James Cagney) is angry with Kitty (Mae Clark) for "giving him lip"; she had rebuffed his request for a stiff drink for breakfast, so he smashed a halved grapefruit into her face and stormed off.[42] In a later interview, the film's director William Wellman said he added the grapefruit to the quarrel because when he and his wife got into fights, she would stonewall him with emotionless silence. Mrs. Wellman always had a grapefruit for breakfast, and Mr. Wellman had often fantasized about shoving the grapefruit into her face just to get a reaction out of her and to see her express some emotion.[43] Fortunately for his wife, Wellman was able to work out some of these fantasies by enacting them in his film instead of at his own breakfast table. Societal expectations of married women of the era may have spoiled Wellman on the notion that a cheerful housewife at the breakfast table should be a given.

During the early years of cinema, breakfast was sometimes used as a clever device to signify that lovemaking had occurred, particularly since strict censorship dictated that nothing resembling sex could be shown on screen.[44] In *Gone with the Wind* (1939), Southern belle Scarlett O'Hara (Vivien Leigh) is carried

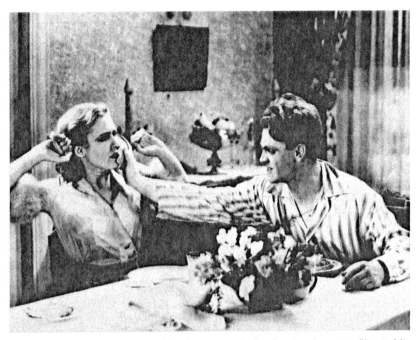

James Cagney smashes a grapefruit into Mae Clark's face in the 1931 film *Public Enemy*. (AP Photo/Warner Bros.)

up the stairs kicking by Rhett Butler (Clark Gable) after a late-night fight in the library.[45] Censors were insistent that the scene not portray anything resembling a rape, but this was perhaps moot; as the following scene fades in, Scarlett is stretching, sighing, and smiling coyly with a breakfast tray next to her bed.

Other early movies featured couples moving awkwardly through the motions of their breakfast as they become accustomed to each other's company outside the bedroom. In the 1945 film *The Clock*, the newlywed Alice (Judy Garland) silently pours the first cup of coffee for her husband Joe (Robert Walker) in their honeymoon suite; it is the first morning of her married life and unsure of how he takes his coffee, reads his face to get it right: one level—not heaping—teaspoon of sugar, a little cream.[46]

In another postwar film, *Winter Meeting* (1948) neither of the "morning after" scenes are particularly warm.[47] Susan Grieve (played by the irascible Bette Davis) and Slick Novak (Jim Davis) are cloistered in her tiny kitchen as they fumble together breakfast. In the second of these breakfast scenes, Susan is noticeably lighter in spirits. She happily brings a tray of breakfast up to Slick to enjoy in bed and he eats it hungrily, passionately, giving the viewer a notion of what their lovemaking had been like. Sadly, however, it was for naught. Slick eventually confessed to Susan that he was headed for priesthood. Their trysts and breakfasts were apparently not enough to sway him from the cloth.

TELEVISION

Breakfast scenes were seldom used in a sexual context in early television programs, primarily because the vast majority of early television centered on the nuclear family and moral high ground, and censorship was strong. At the turn of the 21st century, the show *Sex and the City* frequently used breakfast scenes to provide the backdrop for a group of four women to rehash their evening's escapades, but breakfast scenes have more traditionally been symbolic of family life—of American virtue and trustworthiness.

In its two seasons, the surreal television series *Twin Peaks* (1990–1991) included numerous breakfast scenes. (Coincidentally, "Breakfast" series photographer Jon Huck was the sound engineer for the 1992 prequel film, *Twin Peaks: Fire Walk With Me.*) Many of the dozens of Twin Peaks coffee-drinking scenes took place in the fictional Double R Diner, but the most famous breakfast scene takes place at the diner in the Great Northern Hotel where agent Dale Cooper (Kyle MacLachlan) was staying while investigating a murder.[48] Agent Cooper, a proponent of strong, black coffee, pulls the waitress aside to inform her of his approval of the java she poured. "This is—excuse me—a *damn* fine cup of coffee." He orders his eggs "over hard" ("I know, don't tell me—'hard on the arteries,' but old habits die hard—just about as hard as I want those eggs"); his bacon "super crispy—almost burned"; and after seeing the perfect specimen of early 1990s beauty walk in (played by the raven-haired Sherilyn Fenn), Cooper requests grapefruit juice, with the drawled condition, "just as long as they're freshly squeezed."[49] Here, breakfast is used to portray Agent Cooper's simplicity: He likes breakfast foods, coffee, and beautiful women.

A character's love of breakfast is also used to signify honest, American values. In the modern sitcom *Parks and Recreation*, mustachioed man's man Ron Swanson (Nick Offerman) is a lot like Agent Cooper. "I'm a simple man," says Swanson. "I like pretty, dark-haired women and breakfast food."[50] He has a poster of bacon and eggs prominently displayed on the wall of his office. Waffles are also the favorite food of his co-worker, Leslie Knope (Amy Poehler), a character defined by her scruples.

In the 1950s, with the increased American practice of eating in front of the television, some networks began designing programs specifically for viewing at the breakfast table. Morning shows, called "breakfast television" in Australia, New Zealand, and the UK, began in 1952 with the *Today* show, on the U.S. television network National Broadcasting Company (NBC). NBC already had a monopoly on morning programming with its radio variety show called *The Breakfast Club*, which had been running since 1933. *The Breakfast Club* was divided into four fifteen-minute segments that host Don McNeill called "Calls to Breakfast," covering informally discussed current events interspersed with music and comedy acts. Attempts to transition the program to television in the early 1950s failed.[51]

From 1945 to 1963, another radio variety show, *Breakfast with Dorothy and Dick* allowed twenty million listeners to drop in on Broadway columnist Dorothy Kilgallen and her actor-producer husband Richard Kollmar while they chatted about New York society gossip and nightclub goings-on over their Park Avenue breakfast table.[52] Their two children, Dickie and Jill, made appearances, as did their butler Julius, who prepared their breakfasts. The husband-and-wife breakfast radio show was a subgenre started by the "earlier" Ed and Pegeen Fitzgerald in 1938; the Fitzgeralds' show ended in 1942 when they changed networks. When Dorothy and Dick filled the Fitzgeralds' breakfast timeslot with their own show, a well-publicized rivalry ensued. The "Mr. Brains" and "Mrs. Beauty," team on *Tex and Jinx* (1946–1959) was the third major husband-and-wife breakfast show of the era, but Yale grad Tex McCrary and fashion model Jinx Falkenburg took the dreadfully dull high road and refused to get involved in the fray. They did not even pretend to eat breakfast while discussing current events.[53]

Morning news programs in the 1950s did not experience the same reach as newspapers, despite repeated attempts by numerous networks, and morning programs typically did not survive the transition from radio to television. Eventually the networks hit pay dirt, when early morning time slots became home to children's programming like the nationally broadcast *Captain Kangaroo*, which ran from 1955 to 1984, or local programs like Portland, Oregon's *Ramblin' Rod*, which ran from 1964 to 1997.[54] Hal Smith, best known for his role as town drunk Otis Campbell on *The Andy Griffith Show*, hosted a morning children's show called *The Pancake Man*, which was sponsored by the International House of Pancakes.[55] Each show consisted of a selection of jokes or skits performed by an amiable host, sandwiched between the real meat: cartoons.

Children and Cereal

Since its advent in the 1920s, television programs have been used to sell products, and cereal companies have long profited from cross-promotional efforts.

Cereal ads have featured child actors, actors from popular kids' shows, and cartoon characters. A 1950s ad for Kellogg's Frosted Flakes featured *Superman*'s George Reeves as Clark Kent, with children saying "Superman says Sugar-Frosted Flakes are the best!"[56] The cartoon squirrel and moose team *Rocky and Bullwinkle* was sponsored by General Mills eight months after the show's pilot aired, and the characters began popping up in advertisements for Trix, Cheerios, and Cocoa Puffs cereals almost immediately. In the 1950s, Post secured a deal with Looney Tunes, using cartoon characters Bugs Bunny and Daffy Duck in its Sugar Crisp ads, and the cartoon *The Flintstones* (1960–1966) inspired the creation of Post's Pebbles cereal in 1971, making it the oldest cereal brand to be based on a television character or series.

Starting in the early 1980s, films inspired cereal branding as well. Family movies like *E.T.*, *Star Wars*, *Gremlins*, and *Ghostbusters* all capitalized on cross-promotion in the 1980s, typically with some combination of sweetened Os and dehydrated marshmallows in the shape of characters. Taglines came straight from the movies: "Who ya gonna crunch?" asked Ralston's Ghostbusters cereal commercial; Kellogg's C-3POs were "a crunchy new force at breakfast."[57] In 1990, *Bill and Ted's Excellent Adventure* resulted in "a most excellent part of this complete breakfast." E.T.'s branding team cleverly triangulated marketing efforts with cereal maker General Mills and with the chocolate company Hershey; the E- and T-shaped cereal was chocolate and peanut butter-flavored—like E.T.'s favorite candy, Reese's Pieces. Cereal manufacturers offered free movie tickets with the purchase of cereal.

Video games, too, hopped on the cereal bandwagon: *Donkey Kong Jr.* had its own cereal, and commercials for the cereal "power pellets" launched by *Pac-Man* gave eight-year-old actor Christian Bale his first role. In 1988, *Super Mario Bros* was teamed with *Legend of Zelda* in the same box; Ralston's Nintendo Cereal System was divided into two slots so that the cereal could be mixed or poured separately. Today, the Nintendo Cereal System is highly sought-after by collectors of video game memorabilia; in 2012, an unopened box sold for upwards of $200 on eBay.[58]

Kids were often instructed in TV commercials to look out for "specially marked boxes" to find prizes. Kellogg's had begun offering "cereal premium prizes" in 1909, with the mail-order *Funny Jungleland Moving Pictures Book* available for ten cents with the purchase of two boxes of Corn Flakes.[59] Cereal companies encouraged kids toward endless pleading and other grocery store tactical warfare with their mothers, with the promise of flip books, kites, magnets, matchbox cars, Jackson 5 LPs (built right in to the cereal box packaging), mini-terrariums, and even video games, such as the 1996 *Chex Quest*.[60]

Criticism of the onslaught of marketing directed at children has largely focused on sugar-laden cereals because of the use of toys and cartoons to lure kids in. "Fun has always been an element of food marketing aimed at children," wrote Susan Linn, in her 2005 *Consuming Kids: Protecting Our Children from the Onslaught of Marketing & Advertising.*[61] According to one 1995 study for the *Archives of Pediatrics and Adolescent Medicine*, 16 percent of children's total viewing time consisted of commercial advertising; 47.8 percent of these commercials related to foods; and 84.6 percent of advertised cereals were high in sugar.[62] Numerous other studies substantiated the claim that the least healthy cereals were the ones most aggressively marketed toward children as young as two years old; even while increasing the overall nutritional content of their cereals, the companies ramped up advertising of the least nutritional products.[63] During Saturday morning cartoons, 27 percent of all ads are for breakfast cereal, and an astonishing 90 percent of commercials are for fatty or sugary foods.[64] The Children's Television Act of 1990, while well intentioned, did nothing to address the health effects of advertising sugar-laden cereals to youngsters.

Cross-promotion on cereal boxes was not always limited to sugary cereals. Nutritionally benign Wheaties began its association with sports in 1933 with a billboard on the wall at the minor league baseball field Nicollet Park in Minneapolis, Minnesota. Knox Reeves, the founder of the Minneapolis-based advertising agency that bore his name, was asked to write an ad for the billboard, and after a few moments, jotted down a sketch of a Wheaties box with the slogan, "Wheaties—The Breakfast of Champions."[65] In 1934, Lou Gehrig became the first athlete featured on the box; two years later, Jesse Owens became the first black athlete to appear on the box. Through the 1930s, Wheaties baseball broadcasts swept the nation, and athlete testimonials about the cereal became a key part of the broadcast package. Baseball legends Joe DiMaggio and Babe Ruth were early endorsers of the product. By 2012, nearly 500 athletes would grace the Wheaties box. Early advertisements for Wheaties did target young radio listeners with the fictional "Jack Armstrong," but when adult consumption of the product began to drop in the 1950s, Wheaties began associating itself with children's programming like *The Lone Ranger* and *The Mickey Mouse Club*. By the late 1950s, Wheaties realigned itself with sports and physical fitness.

MUSIC

During the widespread food shortages during the Great Depression of the 1930s and 1940s, songs about food were cornucopian. Jazz greats like Fats

Waller and Louis Jordan widely acknowledged the escapism provided by songs with food themes by writing dozens of them. Blues musician Bo Carter was particularly adept at using food as bawdy innuendo in the early 1930s, as evidenced by songs like "Banana in Your Fruit Basket" and "Your Biscuits Are Big Enough for Me."

Songs about food preparation were generally evocative of affection, especially a woman's. "My baby loves bacon, and that's what I'm making," sang the original funny girl Fanny Brice in her 1930 "Cooking Breakfast for the One I Love."[66] This tribute to preparing breakfast is an apt reflection of the idealized housewife in the 1920s and 1930s. The other lyrics point to morning cheeriness and the unbridled joy that comes from preparing her husband's breakfast, noting that her "happy hour" is when she is granted the time to cook while he is having his morning ablutions.[67]

British chanteuse Dusty Springfield sang about the morning after a tryst with a cheating man in her 1969 hit "Breakfast in Bed." The lyrics are a classic plea of the "other woman," begging another woman's husband to stay a little longer, to enjoy breakfast in bed, before heading home to his wife.[68] English band Supertramp sang about the American Dream in their 1979 "Breakfast in America." Their lyrics use breakfast foods to depict a charming naïveté in the song's teenaged protagonist, who muses that Americans are all so wealthy that they can eat kippers for breakfast every day.[69]

On their 1970 album *Atom Heart Mother*, progressive rock band Pink Floyd used a three-part instrumental song called "Alan's Psychedelic Breakfast" to describe a morning in the life of their roadie Alan Styles.[70] They performed the song live only four times; a slightly reworked version was performed in 1970 at Sheffield City Hall in Sheffield, England, with the band members cooking onstage, pausing between pieces to eat and drink their breakfast.

During the opening of the section called Rise and Shine, Styles can be heard muttering to himself, deciding what to have as he begins to prepare his breakfast. He mumbles a narrative of his matutinal preferences. He likes scrambled eggs, bacon, sausages, tomatoes, toast, and coffee. He remembers that he likes marmalade and adds porridge, admitting that he really likes all cereals. At the end of this section, the whistling sound of a teakettle can be heard as the music stops.[71]

As the next section of the song, Sunny Side Up, begins, Styles continues, describing breakfasts he had eaten while abroad as Pink Floyd's roadie, including "microbiotic stuff" in Los Angeles, while pouring himself a cup of tea, the kettle having just stopped whistling as he removed in from the burner.[72] He can be heard adding a bit of milk to his cup, stirring, and drinking his tea in three eager gulps. He pours himself a bowl of cereal, the light tinkling and unmistakable snap, crackle, and pop of Rice Krispies. He grunts and snorts "amph" as he shovels in spoonsful, chewing with his mouth open. The crackling of Rice Krispies segues fluently into the sound of frying bacon, roiling in hot fat as the song glides effortlessly into the third section, known as Morning Glory. The thirteen-minute-long song transforms the mundane experience of a bachelor consuming his breakfast alone into something remarkably poignant—an act of raw, human sensuality.

Other musicians have used meals as a way to relate to an audience. Between the songs of his 1976 live-recorded album *Nighthawks at the Diner*, American songwriter Tom Waits warmed up the crowd with sultry piano and sparkling, vaudeville-style banter about the meals he had had during his epicurean adventures in the greater Los Angeles area. In "Intro to Eggs & Sausage," he recalled having had a veal cutlet so tough that it tried to beat up his cup of coffee, but, lamentably, the coffee was too weak to defend itself.[73] From here, Waits seamlessly launches into "Eggs & Sausage," wherein he reminisces about visiting a late-night cafe that served breakfast at all hours. The waitress recited the menu, a litany of breakfast foods.[74] These breakfast diner foods had been burned into his memory—they are the chorus to the song—along with the pain of having been "86ed" (diner lingo for "canceled") by the woman he loved.

MAGAZINES AND NEWSPAPERS

In the 19th century, newspapers, magazines, and journals sometimes featured investigative articles about breakfasts, such as the 1870 essay "Dainty Bread," published in Charles Dickens's *All the Year Round*.[75] "Dainty Bread" provides a humorously thorough discourse on the respective qualities of English muffins, hot cross buns, pancakes, and other "stuffy, puffy aids to indigestion." There's even mention of Sally Lunn cake, a specialty of Bath, England, that migrated with early America colonists. "Whether Sally Lunn still makes teacakes, we do not know," ponders Dickens, "but such cakes are certainly among the kinds of dainty bread which have a curious history, if we only choose to ferret it out."[76]

Breakfast made headlines in the *New York Times*, when it reprinted an 1876 article from the London-based *Pall Mall Gazette*. The tersely titled "Breakfast" railed against the English habit of eating immediately upon rising, and especially on such heavy fare as beefsteaks washed down with tea. "In the first place the stomach is not prepared at that early hour for the rude exercise to which we condemn it, while in the second place the mixture of tea or coffee and meat is objectionable for two reasons."[77] The author continues by explaining that, according to "Science," tannic acid renders meat absolutely indigestible, a fact that had yet to be substantiated by any of the thousands of Victorians happily breakfasting on mutton steaks and tea with milk on both sides of the pond.

In the late 19th century, there were certainly plenty of Clean Living–era articles being published about the dangers of eating meat for breakfast, but that certainly did not stop anyone from having their bacon and eating it too. Anti-Victorian novelist Samuel Butler (who made no bones about his feelings on the difference between literature and journalism) wrote in his *Note-Books* (1880) of the sheer joys of bacon, despite the indignation of the low-income family hosting him while he was abroad. He was a bachelor cooking bacon for breakfast, and they were a family of four grown daughters, who could not afford meat, for breakfast or otherwise. "I used to feel very uncomfortable, very small and quite aware how low it was of me to have bacon for breakfast and no daughters instead of daughters and no bacon. But when I consulted the oracles of heaven about it, I was always told to stick to my bacon and not to make a fool of myself."[78]

As the 19th century wound down, magazines like the *Godey's Lady's Book* and *Ladies' Home Journal* ran more stories about breakfast rooms and nooks in American craftsman-style homes, and the breakfast table changed synergistically: Families began eating the morning meal in the kitchen instead of a formal dining room, which in turn spawned a revolution of breakfast appliances that could be used at the kitchen table, which could be advertised in ladies' magazines along with the spate of new, convenient breakfast foods being rapidly developed.

During food rations of World War I, eggless and meatless breakfasts were apparently on the minds of many. "Bacon has taken the wings of money and soared out of sight," wrote a columnist for the Pittsburgh Press on November 29, 1918; "and now while Biddy hen shivers on her roost and refuses to lay, our breakfast standby, eggs, follows after bacon—and the morning meal is left lonely and forlorn."[79] Because of the bitterly seasonal nature of egg-laying, even those with backyard chickens would be skipping omelets on that particular day of wartime rationing. (Interestingly, the war had ended two weeks prior to that article's publication.)

Rationing continued to make headlines even after World War II ended. In October of 1947, during widespread grain shortages in Europe, President Harry S. Truman called on Americans to abstain from meat on Tuesdays and from poultry and eggs on Thursdays, with the intention of reducing the amount of grain used for livestock feed. This had wide-reaching effects on breakfast for Americans, which rippled through the news media. Newspapers published

Truman's personal breakfast menus to help things along: prunes, oatmeal, toast, and coffee one day, perhaps a bit of tomato juice added another day.[80] One paper noted that White House housekeeper Mary Sharpe had completely omitted breakfast from her menus. The public was not impressed, as evidenced by newspaper headlines such as "Eggless Breakfast Plan Off to Poor Start Over Nation" and "Public Observance [of] Meatless, Eggless Days Very Spotty."[81] On meatless Tuesdays, people ate more eggs for breakfast to compensate for the lack of meat, and on Thursdays, restaurants and home cooks served more bacon and sausage to make up for the lack of eggs. For most people, though, the meatless and eggless days helped cement cereal's prominent place on the breakfast table.

Housekeeping magazines from the 1820s typically featured cooking advice and recipes, but magazines devoted entirely to cooking came later. In 1896, culinary reformer Janet McKenzie Hill founded the *Boston Cooking School Magazine* (renamed *American Cookery* in 1915). One short story in an 1898 issue discussed the latest fad of skipping breakfast. "Previous to my marriage I had been advised by physicians not to eat breakfast, and in fact I considered myself a shining example of the success of that new hygienic fad," said newly-wed Thaddeus in "Hygienic Honeymoon."[82] Unfortunately, his new bride was on the no-supper diet, so between the two of them, they were quite thin, and equally miserable. Eventually they decided to quit the silly diets, and lived happily ever after.

In the early 1920s, *American Cookery* included tips on decorating a charming breakfast room or how to make a "cozy corner" out of a built-in breakfast nook in the kitchen; there were sample menus for each week and witty quips about how to plan for fresh rolls in the morning. A housewife following these helpful hints was guaranteed the applause of an appreciative family. *American Cookery* was the end-all and be-all of cooking magazines until 1941, when two publishers, Ralph Warner Reinhold and Earle R. MacAusland, launched *Gourmet Magazine*.

Although *American Cookery* had been successfully bringing Americans cooking tips for four decades, the dowdy newsprint, small pages, and narrow focus was no match for glossy, cosmopolitan *Gourmet*. And *Gourmet* had real writers penning their articles, not just cooking-school teachers; noted culinary memoirist M. F. K. Fisher had already published several well-received books before writing for *Gourmet*. She wrote romantically of living alone in a tiny Hollywood walk-up, with only a hotplate to cook from, subsisting fairly entirely on scrambled eggs: "I grew deliberately fastidious about eggs and butter: the biggest, brownest eggs were none too good, nor could any butter be too clover-fresh and sweet."[83]

Fisher also wrote in her typically effervescent way about teaching children (and often, their parents) to overcome pickiness and other cultural prejudice in a 1958 article called "Consider the End." Fisher and her daughters were hosting two young American boys in a remote farm town in southern France. The boys were distraught at having to survive without breakfast cereal, presenting a germane teachable moment to Fisher. She considered it an important step in a child's journey toward self-sufficiency.

> If, for instance, he has been exposed, in relaxed pleasant company, to the somewhat brutal fact that not all children his age find breakfast cereal essential to their becoming football heroes or even bullfighters, he may astonish his mentors by facing without a whimper some slices of good fresh bread, a pat of sweet butter, and a jar of honey. A jug of milk is good with that.[84]

The bread they ate, which was delivered twice weekly, grew staler by the day, but they had good cheese. The boys adapted to their new breakfast with aplomb. "After a week of affronted misery without their packaged morning comfort, the boys began to get up when the sun rose, break off a rough piece of the drying bread and cut themselves a good slab of the cheese, and walk past the well for a beaker of sweet cool water. . . . Then they began to realize that bread and cheese and pure water are fine, for breakfast or any time."[85] Fisher figured out that breakfast was as apt a place as any to reeducate a person about adaptability.

"The British breakfast, I swear on my honor as a scholar, is without a peer on this globe's crust," wrote Robert P. T. Coffin in "British Breakfast," a 1948 article published in *Gourmet*.[86] Coffin, a Rhodes Scholar with graduate degrees from Princeton and Oxford and a prodigal son of the Boston Brahmin, had plenty of honor at stake. After taking a few paragraphs to bash French cooking, Coffin waxed beatific about the joys of the fatty meats that can only come from animals grazing on velvet British grasses, among sufficient fogs and dews. "The British breakfast! The never failing British art of making the most and best of things blossoms sweet in this gift to civilization."[87] He gushed about the splendor of having an entire room for dining on breakfast, about English kippers "as dry and neat as a golden butterfly."[88] Coffin was a frequent contributor to *Gourmet* well into the 1950s, until he died in 1955 of a heart attack.

THE FUTURE OF BREAKFAST

History has proven that like anything, breakfast is subject to the silly whims and fads borne of society. During the hygiene craze of the late 1800s, food was "scientific" nearly to a fault; cereals were advertised as "predigested" to sound modern and, ultimately, to boost sales. Today, with food media rapidly reaching its zenith (though many will insist that food blogging already peaked years ago; that it has even jumped the proverbial shark, perhaps), breakfast can only reach ridiculous new heights. The enduring bacon mania and pornographic macro-images of runny egg yolks dripping down the side of a flaky buttermilk biscuit will join the ranks of websites devoted entirely to desserts for breakfast, the art and science of vegan sausage patties, or interactive, GPS-enabled bicycle maps to the hottest Portland breakfast carts.

Vintage futurism offers an interesting peek into what was supposed to be. According to a 1927 issue of *Popular Science*, a man could come to expect everything from radio waves.[89] After waking up to his futuristic radio alarm clock, a man could listen to his morning news over a loud speaker, of all things, conjectured the article. Even more Jetsonian, "His breakfast may come from the communal kitchen by tubes."[90]

In the atomic age of the 1950s, breakfast would be brighter than ever. "Breakfast will consist of bacon and eggs that you've kept around the house for weeks (fresh as ever, thanks to atomic sterilization)," promised a 1957 article from *Kiplinger's Personal Finance*.[91] This was the prediction for 1982, but food irradiation had actually already been patented in France in 1930.

According to prolific science fiction author H. G. Wells, the future of breakfast was grim. In his dystopian "A Story of the Days to Come" (1899), the breakfast of the 22nd century would consist of "rude masses of bread needing to be carved and smeared over with animal fat before they could be made palatable, the still recognizable fragments of recently killed animals, hideously charred and hacked."[92]

The real fate of breakfast is not so bleak, one hopes, but plenty of scientists hazard that the human diet will eventually come to rely more heavily on the sea. A 2011 press release from Kellogg's reveals that the future of the Full English will be fully fishy; warm crab porridge with seaweed flakes, sardine fingers, and potted herring will replace muesli and bacon and eggs.[93] More importantly, breakfast will finally become an integral meal not to be hurried or skipped. "According to experts," reads the media packet, "breakfast will also be taken as seriously as dinner is today and become the main meal of the day with people sitting down to up to three courses in the next 10 to 15 years."[94] If this prediction holds any merit, the future looks mighty exciting, indeed.

NOTES

INTRODUCTION

1. Garrick Mallery, "Manners and Meals," *American Anthropologist* 1 (July 1888): 196.

2. Maguelonne Toussaint-Samat, *A History of Food* (Chichester, West Sussex, UK: John Wiley & Sons, 2009), 517.

CHAPTER 1: HISTORY AND SOCIAL CONTEXT

1. *Online Etymology Dictionary*, s.v. "breakfast," by Douglas Harper, accessed October 20, 2011, http://dictionary.reference.com/browse/breakfast; Ken Albala, "Hunting for Breakfast in Medieval and Early Modern Europe," in *The Meal—Proceedings of the Oxford Symposium on Food and Cookery 2001* (Devon, UK: Prospect), 2002.

2. Harold McGee, *On Food and Cooking: The Science and Lore of the Kitchen* (New York: Scribner), 1984.

3. Sophie de Beaune, "The Invention of Technology: Prehistory and Cognition," *Current Anthropology* 45, no. 2 (April 2004): 139–62.

4. Sylvain Glémin and Thomas Bataillon, "A Comparative View of the Evolution of Grasses under Domestication," *New Phytologist* 183 (2009): 273–90.

5. Known in much of food literature as panic, the United States Department of Agriculture's PLANTS database lists *Panicum miliaceum* as broomcorn millet, a separate species from *Sorghum vulgare*. Agricultural schools like the University of Kentucky and Purdue list broomcorn as *Sorghum vulgare*, but the USDA lists this species as "grain sorghum" (with an updated synonymy of *Sorghum bicolor* ssp. *bicolor*). Despite botani-

cal science usage of the nomenclature, common convention deems broomcorn a species of sorghum, not millet.

6. Dorian Fuller, "Contrasting Patterns in Crop Domestication and Domestication Rates: Recent Archaeobotanical Insights from the Old World," *Annals of Botany* 100 (May 2007): 903–24.

7. Amanda J. Landon, "The 'How' of the Three Sisters: The Origins of Agriculture in Mesoamerica and the Human Niche," *Nebraska Anthropologist* 40 (2008).

8. H. S. Corran, *A History of Brewing* (Newton Abbot: David and Charles, 1975), 21–22.

9. John Matson, "The Dawn of Beer Remains Elusive in Archaeological Record," *Scientific American Observations* (blog), March 28, 2011, http://blogs.scientificam erican.com/observations/2011/03/28/the-dawn-of-beer-remains-elusive-in-archaeolog ical-record.

10. Karl-Ernst Behre, "The History of Rye Cultivation in Europe," *Vegetation History and Archaeobotany* 1, no. 3 (1992): 141–56.

11. Jane McIntosh, *Handbook to Life in Prehistoric Europe* (New York: Oxford University Press, 2006), 258–60.

12. Albala, "Hunting for Breakfast," 20.

13. H. T. Riley, *The Comedies of Plautus* (London: Henry G. Bohn, York Street, Covent Garden, 1852), 197.

14. *Dictionary of Greek and Roman Antiquities*, s.v. "jentaculum," by William Smith, William Wayte, and G. E. Marindin, accessed October 2011, http://www.perseus.tufts.edu/hopper/text?doc=Perseus:text:1999.04.0063:entry=cena cn&highlight=jentaculum.

15. W. A. Becker, *Gallus; or, Roman Scenes of the Time of Augustus; With Notes and Excursus Illustrative of the Manners and Customs of the Romans* (London: John W. Parker, West Strand, 1844), 358.

16. Pliny the Elder, *The Natural History*, Book XVIII, Chapter 10, "The Natural History of Grain," ed. John Bostock, http://www.perseus.tufts.edu/hopper/text?doc=Pe rseus:text:1999.02.0137:book=18:chapter=10&highlight=puls, accessed October 2011.

17. Becker, *Gallus*, 358.

18. Becker, *Gallus*, 357.

19. Smith, Wayte, and Marindin, "jentaculum."

20. Homer, *The Odyssey* (London: Macmillan, 2005), 265.

21. Athenaeus, *The Deipnosophists*, ed. and trans. C. B. Gulick, vol. 1 (Cambridge, MA: Harvard University Press), 1927–1941.

22. Melitta Weiss Adamson, *Food in Medieval Times* (Westport, CT: Greenwood Press, 2004), 155–56.

23. P. W. Hammond, *Food and Feast in Medieval England* (Phoenix Mill, UK: Alan Sutton, 1993), 104–5.

24. Garrick Mallery, "Manners and Meals," *American Anthropologist* 1 (July 1888): 193–208.

25. Albala, "Hunting for Breakfast," 21.

26. Mallery, "Manners and Meals," 196.

27. Mallery, "Manners and Meals," 196.

28. Colin Spencer, *British Food: an Extraordinary Thousand Years of History* (New York: Columbia University Press, 2002), 87.

29. Albala, "Hunting for Breakfast," 24.

30. Albala, "Hunting for Breakfast," 21.

31. Albala, "Hunting for Breakfast," 22; L. R. Lind, *Gabriele Zerbi, Gerontocomia: On the Care of the Aged; and Maximianus, Elegies on Old Age and Love* (Philadelphia, American Philosophical Society, 1988), 247.

32. Albala, "Hunting for Breakfast," 25.

33. Albala, "Hunting for Breakfast," 25.

34. Albala, "Hunting for Breakfast," 26.

35. Spencer, *British Food*, 129.

36. Spencer, *British Food*, 99.

37. Frederick William Hackwood, *Good Cheer: The Romance of Food and Feasting* (New York: Sturgis and Walton, 1911), 120.

38. Hackwood, *Good Cheer*, 120; Spencer, *British Food*, 83.

39. Spencer, *British Food*, 145.

40. Albala, "Hunting for Breakfast," 26.

41. Anthony Wild, *Coffee: A Dark History* (New York: Norton, 2005), 31.

42. Bennet Alan Weinberg and Bonnie K. Bealer, *The World of Caffeine: The Science and Culture of the World's Most Popular Drug* (London: Routledge, 2001), 3–4.

43. Mark Pendergrast, *Uncommon Grounds: The History of Coffee and How it Transformed Our World* (New York: Basic Books, 2010), 8.

44. Laura Martin, *Tea: The Drink that Changed the World* (North Clarendon, VT: Tuttle, 2007), 23.

45. Martin, *Tea*, 120–23.

46. Unknown, "History of the English Breakfast Tea: The True Origin of English Breakfast Tea," ΛΟΓΟΙ, http://www.logoi.com/notes/english_breakfast_tea.html, accessed October 2011.

47. Ken Albala, *Food in Early Modern Europe* (Westport, CT: Greenwood Press, 2003): 232.

48. Spencer, *British Food*, 259.

49. Spencer, *British Food*, 158.

50. William Grimes, "At Brunch, the More Bizarre the Better," *The New York Times*, July 8, 1998, http://www.nytimes.com/1998/07/08/dining/at-brunch-the-more-bizarre-the-better.html?sec=travel&pagewanted=1.

51. Andrea Broomfield, *Food and Cooking in Victorian England: A History* (Westport, CT: Greenwood Press, 2007), 25.

52. Pierre Blot, *What to Eat, and How to Cook It* (New York: D. Appleton & Co., 1863), 247.

53. Fannie Merritt Farmer, *The Boston Cooking-School Cookbook* (Boston: Little, Brown and Co., 1869), 36.

54. *Feeding America*, s.v. "Blot, Pierre, (1818–August 29, 1874)," accessed October 2011, http://digital.lib.msu.edu/projects/cookbooks/html/authors/author_blot.html.

55. David Quist and Ignacio H. Chapela, "Transgenic DNA Introgressed into Traditional Maize Landraces in Oaxaca, Mexico," *Nature* 414 (November 2001): 541–43.

56. Linda Murray Berzok, *American Indian Food* (Westport, CT: Greenwood Press, 2005), 133.

57. Raymond A. Sokolov, *Fading Feast: A Compendium of Disappearing American Regional Foods* (Jaffrey, NH: David R. Godine, 1998), 231.

58. Brian A. Nummer, "Historical Origins of Food Preservation," *National Center for Home Food Preservation*, May 2002, http://www.uga.edu/nchfp/publications/nchfp/factsheets/food_pres_hist.html, accessed October 2011.

59. Ruth Clifford Engs, *Clean Living Movements: American Cycles of Health Reform* (Westport, CT: Greenwood Press, 2001): 7–9.

60. Engs, *Clean Living Movements*, 97.

61. Ella Kellogg, *Healthful Cookery: A Collection of Choice Recipes for Preparing Foods, with Special Reference to Health* (Battle Creek, MI: Modern Medicine, 1904), 249.

62. Ironically, Kellogg's is now the manufacturer of several sugary breakfast cereals that are not widely associated with health, including Honey Smacks (formerly known as Sugar Smacks). In a 2008 comparison of the nutritional value of twenty-seven cereals marketed toward children, U.S. magazine *Consumer Reports* found Kellogg's Honey Smacks was one of the top two unhealthy brands, being comprised of more than 50 percent sugar by weight. Three of the top five next-worst cereals (Corn Pops, Froot Loops, and Apple Jacks) are also Kellogg's products. *Consumer Reports* recommended that parents choose cereal brands with better nutrition ratings for their children.

63. Lynne Olver, "FAQs: Popular 20th Century American Foods," *Food Timeline*, http://www.foodtimeline.org/fooddecades.html, accessed October 2011.

64. Olver, *Food Timeline*.

65. Pop Tarts, http://www.foodtimeline.org/foodpies.html#poptarts, accessed October 2011.

66. Jack Mingo and Erin Barrett, "Nothing More Than Fillings: The True History of Pop Tarts," *Whole Pop Magazine Online*, http://www.wholepop.com/973580985/features/toasters/poptarts.htm, accessed October 2011.

67. Benjamin Spock, *Dr. Spock Talks with Mothers: Growth and Guidance* (Boston: Houghton Mifflin, 1961), 73.

68. Andrew F. Smith, *Oxford Encyclopedia of Food and Drink in America*, vol. 1 (New York: Oxford University Press, 2004), 27.

69. Federico Soriguer, Gemma Rojo-Martínez, M. Carmen Dobarganes, José M. García Almeida, Isabel Esteva, Manuela Beltrán, M. Soledad Ruiz De Adana, Francisco Tinahones, Juan M. Gómez-Zumaquero, Eduardo García-Fuentes, and Stella González-

Romero, "Hypertension Is Related to the Degradation of Dietary Frying Oils," *American Journal of Clinical Nutrition* 78 (2003): 1092–97.

70. Eileen Kennedy and Carole Davis, "US Department of Agriculture School Breakfast Program," supplement, *American Journal of Clinical Nutrition* 67 (1998):798S–803S.

71. United States Department of Agriculture, Special Supplemental Food Program for Women, Infants, and Children (U.S.), *Report to Congress on Cereals Containing Fruit in the WIC Supplemental Food Packages* (Alexandria, VA: Food and Nutrition Service, USDA, 1991).

72. Glenn Arthur Corliss et al., "Simulated Bacon Product and Process," U.S. Patent 3930033, filed February 4, 1974, and issued December 30, 1975.

73. Henry Mayhew, *London Labour and the London Poor: A Cyclopaedia of the Condition and Earnings of Those That Will Work, Those That Cannot Work, and Those That Will Not Work*, vol. 1 (London: Charles Griffin & Company, 1851), 39.

74. Bernice Kanner, "Hot Buns," *New York Magazine*, March 30, 1987.

CHAPTER 2: AROUND THE WORLD IN A MEAL

1. Charles Mackay and Allan Ramsay, *A Dictionary of Lowland Scotch* (London: Whittaker and Co., 1888), 35.

2. Marion Nestle, *Food Politics: How the Food Industry Influences Nutrition and Health* (Los Angeles: University of California Press, 2007), 323.

3. From John Capgrave's *Lives of St. Augustine and St. Gilbert of Sempringham and a Sermon* (1422) "[Jacob] supplanted his broþir, bying his fader blessing for a mese of potage."

4. Clifford A. Wright, *A Mediterranean Feast: The Story of the Birth of the Celebrated Cuisines of the Mediterranean, from the Merchants of Venice to the Barbary Corsairs, with More Than 500 Recipes* (New York: HarperCollins, 1999), 496.

5. From Clifford Wright via Paula Wolfert, http://www.cliffordawright.com/caw/recipes/display/bycountry.php/recipe_id/948/id/8, accessed January 2012.

6. Ladies of Toronto and Chief Cities and Towns in Canada, *The Home Cook Book* (Toronto: Musson Book Co., Ltd., 1877), 235.

7. Ella Ervilla Kellogg, *Every-day Dishes and Every-day Work* (Battle Creek, MI: Modern Medicine, 1897), 137.

8. Bob Flaws, *The Book of Jook: Chinese Medicinal Porridges: A Healthy Alternative to the Typical Western Breakfast* (Boulder, CO: Blue Poppy Enterprises, Inc., 1995), 4.

9. John Hoddinott, John A. Maluccio, Jere R. Behrman, Rafael Flores, and Reynaldo Martorell, "Effect of a Nutrition Intervention during Early Childhood on Economic Productivity in Guatemalan Adults," *The Lancet* 371, no. 9610 (February 2008): 411–16.

10. Benjamin Sillman Sr. and Benjamin Sillman Jr., comp., "Contributions to the English Lexicography," *American Journal of Science and Arts* 40 (April 1841): 35.

11. Mary Johnson Lincoln, *Mrs. Lincoln's Boston Cook Book: What To Do and What Not To Do in Cooking* (Boston: Roberts Bros., 1884), 110.

12. Theodore Flood, ed., "The Art of Prolonging Life," *The Chautauquan: A Weekly Newsmagazine* 21 (April–September 1895): 129.

13. John Harvey Kellogg, "Flaked Cereals and Process of Preparing Same," U.S. Patent 558393, filed May 31, 1895, and issued April 14, 1896.

14. Anna Revedin et al., "Thirty Thousand-Year-Old Evidence of Plant Food Processing," *PNAS* 107, no. 44 (2010), http://www.pnas.org/content/107/44/18815.

15. Jacques Le Goff, *Time, Work, and Culture in the Middle Ages* (Chicago: University of Chicago Press, 1982), 94.

16. Though soothing and comforting to plenty, the blandness of milk toast lent itself to the moniker of Caspar Milquetoast, the wimpy character from H. T. Webster's comic strip "The Timid Soul," which ran from 1912 to Webster's death in 1952. The word "milquetoast" is still part of the American vernacular, referring to a person who is unassertive or spineless.

17. Etymology dictionaries consistently name the year 1703 as the first time "muffin" is put into writing in the English language, yet none cite the source; Charles Dickens, "Dainty Bread," *All the Year Round*, vol. 4, September 10, 1870, 344–47.

18. "Lender's Bagels: Celebrating 85 years of Premium Bagels," http://www.lender sbagels.com/about.html, accessed November 27, 2012. Louis Jordan's 1949 jump blues hit "Beans and Cornbread" mentions bagels and lox as two things that go together.

19. Eliza Leslie, *Directions for Cookery, in Its Various Branches* (Philadelphia: Carey & Hart, 1837), 371.

20. Maud C. Cooke, *Breakfast, Dinner and Supper, or What to Eat and How to Prepare It* (Philadelphia: J. H. Moore, 1897), 328. The full title page of *Breakfast, Dinner and Supper, or What to Eat and How to Prepare It* continues: *Containing All the Latest Approved Recipes in Every Department Of Cooking; Instructions For Selecting Meats and Carving; Descriptions of the Best Kitchen Utensils, Etc. Including Hygienic and Scientific Cooking; Rules For Dinner Giving; Use of the Chafing Dish; Menu Cards For All Special Occasions; Cooking For Invalids; Valuable Hints For Economical Housekeeping, Etc. The Whole Forming a Standard Authority on the Culinary Art.*

21. Ken Albala, *Pancake: A Global History* (London: Reaktion, 2008), 22.

22. Albala, *Pancake*, 30.

23. Albala, *Pancake*, 30.

24. Albala, *Pancake*, 29.

25. Hannah Glasse, *The Art of Cookery, Made Plain and Easy: Which Far Exceeds Any Thing of the Kind Yet Published* (London: W. Strahan, J. and F. Rivington, J. Hinton, 1747), 159.

26. Amelia Simmons, *American Cookery, or the Art of Dressing Viands, Fish, Poultry, and Vegetables, and the Best Modes of Making Pastes, Puffs, Pies, Tarts, Puddings, Custards, and Preserves, and All Kinds of Cakes, from the Imperial Plum to Plain Cake: Adapted to this Country, and All Grades of Life.* (Hartford: Simeon Butler, Northamp-

ton, 1798), 34. Available online at http://digital.lib.msu.edu/projects/cookbooks/html/books/book_01.cfm.

27. Sarah Annie Frost, *The Godey's Lady's Book Receipts and Household Hints* (Philadelphia: Evans, Stoddart & Co., 1870), 325.

28. Frost, *Receipts and Household Hints*, 325.

29. Susan Coolidge, *Eyebright: A Story* (Boston: Roberts Brothers, 1894), 156.

30. Maria Parloa, *Miss Parloa's Young Housekeeper: Designed Especially to Aid Beginners: Economical Receipts for Those Who Are Cooking for Two or Three* (Boston: Estes & Lauriat, 1894), 237.

31. Sarah Tyson Heston Rorer, *Mrs. Rorer's Philadelphia Cook Book: A Manual of Home Economics* (Philadelphia: Arnold & Co., 1886), 252; Estelle Woods Wilcox, *The Dixie Cook-Book* (Atlanta, GA: L. A. Clarkson & Co., 1883), 398.

32. Charlotte Mason, *The Lady's Assistant for Regulating and Supplying Her Table* (London: J. Walter, 1777), 372.

33. Sarah Josepha Buell Hale, *The Good Housekeeper, Or, The Way to Live Well and to Be Well While We Live* (Boston: Horace Wentworth, 1839), 101.

34. M. Tarbox Colbrath, *What to Get for Breakfast* (Boston: James H. Earle, 1882), 198.

35. Charles Dickens, "The Cupboard Papers, VIII: The Sweet Art," *All the Year Round*, vol. 9, November 30, 1872, 60–61.

36. "New Pastry to Rival France's Art Confection," *Oakland Tribune*, August 9, 1917, 6, available at http://newspaperarchive.com/oakland-tribune/1917-08-09/page-6.

37. Frost, *Receipts and Household Hints*, 326.

38. Frost, *Receipts and Household Hints*, 343.

39. John Bostock and Henry Thomas Riley, trans., *The Natural History of Pliny*, vol. 3 (London: Bell, 1856–1893), 84.

40. John Harvey Kellogg, *The Home Book of Modern Medicine: A Family Guide in Health and Disease*, Vol. 2 (Battle Creek, MI: Good Health, 1909), 911.

41. Henry Dwight Sedgwick, *In Praise of Gentlemen* (New York: Little, Brown & Co., 1935), 110.

42. Wesley Hospital Bazaar Committee, *The New Century Cook Book: Compiled from Recipes Contributed by Ladies of Chicago and Other Cities and Towns, and Published for the Benefit of Wesley Hospital, Chicago* (Chicago: Wesley Hospital Bazaar Committee, 1899).

43. Robert Maxwell, *Select Transactions of the Honourable the Society of Improvers in the Knowledge of Agriculture in Scotland* (Edinburgh: Sands, Brymer, Murray & Cochran, 1743), 275.

44. "Kraft Foods Corporate Timeline," available at http://www.kraftfoodsgroup.com/SiteCollectionDocuments/pdf/CorporateTimeline_KraftGroceryCo_version.pdf, accessed November 28, 2012.

45. D. Eleanor Scully and Terence Peter Scully, *Early French Cookery: Sources, History, Original Recipes and Modern Adaptations* (Ann Arbor: University of Michigan Press, 2002), 230.

46. Marion Harland, *Breakfast, Luncheon and Tea* (London: Routledge, 1875), 16.

47. Harland, *Breakfast, Luncheon and Tea*, 16.

48. Walter B. Dickson, *Poultry: Their Breeding, Rearing, Diseases and General Management* (London: William Smith, 1838), 133.

49. Sallie Joy White, *Cookery in the Public Schools* (Boston: D. Lothrop Co., 1890), 68.

50. The nom-de-plume of English sports editor Arthur Gay Payne. It is unknown why he wrote cookery books under a female pseudonym.

51. Phillis Browne, *The Dictionary of Dainty Breakfasts* (London: Cassell & Co., LTD, 1899), vi.

52. Scully and Scully, *Early French Cookery*, 231.

53. Horace Annesley Vachell, "The Rich Fool and the Clever Pauper," *Overland Monthly and Out West Magazine* 23, no. 7 (1894): 51. Blue Point oysters are from Blue Point, New York, which may lead some to conclude that the story actually takes place at the University Club in New York, putting the invention of Eggs Benedict back in New York. However, in 1881 Ernest Ingersoll from the U.S. Bureau of Fisheries published an article called "The Oyster Industry," which discussed the great success of seeding oyster beds in the San Francisco Bay with spat from Blue Point. The rest of the article makes other references to San Francisco.

54. Written by New York's Union Club chef Adolphe Meyer, *Eggs and How to Use Them* (1898) lists no fewer than ninety-eight different ways to serve poached eggs, each given a sophisticated French name.

55. William Rubel, "Eggs in the Moonshine with Cream," in *Eggs in Cookery: Proceedings of the Oxford Symposium on Food and Cookery 2006* (Devon, UK: Prospect Books, 2007), 214.

56. Adolphe Meyer, *Eggs, and How to Use Them* (New York: self-published, 1898), 12.

57. Anna Barrows, ed., *Eggs: Facts and Fancies About Them* (Boston: D. Lothrop & Co., 1890), 117.

58. Ange Denis M'Quin, *Tabella Cibaria* (London: Sherwood, Neely & Jones, 1820), 86.

59. Ude instructs the cook to bake the eggs in well-buttered China cups "in red ashes, and then use the salamander (broiler) till the eggs are done soft." Today, eggs en cocotte are usually distinguished from shirred eggs by the use of a bain marie, or ramekins immersed in a hot water bath in the oven.

60. An omelet made of parsley, mint, savory, sage, tansy (probably *Tanacetum balsamita*, or costmary), vervain, clary sage, rue, dittany (*Origanum dictamnus*, a species of oregano), fennel, southernwood (*Artemisia abrotanum*, a type of mugwort or wormwood); the herbs are minced and mixed with beaten eggs and baked in a buttered dish. With the tansy, clary sage, and southernwood, this would have been a very strongly flavored, aromatic dish that verged on medicinal.

61. Margaret Dods, *The Cook and Housewife's Manual: A Practical System of Modern Domestic Cookery and Family Management* (Edinburgh: Oliver & Boyd, 1862), 340.

62. Dods, *The Cook and Housewife's Manual*, 340.

63. Browne, *Dictionary of Dainty Breakfasts*, iv. Vaseline was used to coat eggs for preservation in the 19th century.

64. Martha McCulloch-Williams, *Dishes & Beverages of the Old South* (New York: McBride, Nast & Company, 1913), 184.

65. William Langland, *Piers Plowman* (Whitefish, MT: Kessinger Publishing, 2004), 94.

66. Other names include, but are not limited to: one-eyed jack, Rocky Mountain toast, Alabama toast, toad-in-the-hole (not to be confused with the British dish of sausage roasted in a Yorkshire pudding), Guy Kibbee eggs, gas house eggs, and eggs in a blanket.

67. Fanny Lemira Gillette, *Mrs. Gillette's Cook Book: Fifty Years of Practical Housekeeping* (Akron, OH: Saalfield Publishing Company, 1908), 148.

68. Samuel Pepys, *Diary, 1662* (Berkeley: University of California Press, 2001), 10. "I went to breakfast in my chamber, upon a Coller of brawne." He was then chastised for eating meat on a fast day.

69. Isaac Burney Yeo, *Food in Health and Disease* (London: Cassell & Co., Ltd., 1896), 465.

70. John Pinkerton, *A General Collection of the Best and Most Interesting Voyages and Travels in All Parts of the World*, vol. 13 (London: Longman, 1812), 718.

71. Numerous recipes for sausages, forcemeats, meat puddings, and meat loaves appear in *Apicius*.

72. Thomas Low Nichols, *Forty Years of American Life* (London: Longmans, Green and Co., 1874), 246.

73. Nichols, *Forty Years*, 246.

74. Colbrath, *What to Get for Breakfast*, 115.

75. Thomas Murrey, *Breakfast Dainties* (Bedford, MA: Applewood Books, 2008), 43.

76. Mary Hooper, *Handbook for the Breakfast Table: Varied and Economical Dishes* (London: Griffith & Farran, 1873), 45.

77. Marion Harland, *Common Sense in the Household: A Manual of Practical Housewifery* (New York: Scribner & Sons, 1871), 87.

78. Asa W. Bartlett, *History of the Twelfth Regiment, New Hampshire Volunteers in the War of the Rebellion* (Concord, NH: I. C. Evans, printer, 1897), 398.

79. Joel Stein, "Chicken for Breakfast," *Time*, June 26, 2008, http://www.time.com/time/magazine/article/0,9171,1818200,00.html#ixzz1xp1AUHL7.

80. John 21:12.

81. Georgiana Hill, *The Breakfast Book* (London: Richard Bentley, 1865), 117.

82. Colbrath, *What to Get for Breakfast*, 167.

83. Lydia Maria Francis Child, *The American Frugal Housewife: Dedicated to Those Who Are Not Ashamed of Economy* (New York: Samuel S. and William Wood, 1841), 60.

84. Browne, *Dictionary of Dainty Breakfasts*, 10.

85. Browne, *Dictionary of Dainty Breakfasts*, 10.

86. Browne, *Dictionary of Dainty Breakfasts*, 11.

87. Estelle Woods Wilcox, *Buckeye Cookery, and Practical Housekeeping: Compiled from Original Recipes* (Minneapolis, MN: Buckeye Pub. Co., 1877), 324.

88. Molly O'Neill, "What's for Breakfast?; Hanoi," *The New York Times*, May 10, 1998, http://www.nytimes.com/1998/05/10/magazine/what-s-for-breakfast-hanoi.html.

89. Jezreel Jones, "An Account of the Moorish Way of Dressing their Meat (with Other Remarks) in West Barbary, from Cape Spartel to Cape de Geer," *Philosophical Transactions of the Royal Society of London*, vol. 21 (London: S. Smith and B. Walford, 1700), 248–59.

90. Jones, "An Account of the Moorish Way," 248.

91. Arthur Robert Kenney-Herbert, "Culinary Jottings for Madras," in *Culinary Jottings, a Treatise for Anglo-Indian Exiles* (Madras, India: Higginbottom & Co., 1885), 1.

92. Gideon Hiram Hollister, *The History of Connecticut, from the First Settlement of the Colony to the Adoption of the Present Constitution* (New Haven, CT: Durrie & Peck, 1855), 431.

93. Lincoln, *Mrs. Lincoln's Boston Cook Book*, 288.

94. Hill, *The Breakfast Book*, 33.

95. Hill, *The Breakfast Book*, 33.

96. Sir George Webbe Dasent, "Lady Sweetapple; Or, Three to One," *Appletons' Journal of Literature, Science and Art* 145–70 (New York: D. Appleton & Co., 1872), 682.

97. Harland, *Breakfast, Lunch and Tea*, 46.

98. Spencer, *British Food*, 189.

99. William Andrus Alcott, *The Young House-keeper, Or, Thoughts on Food and Cookery* (Boston: G. W. Light, 1838), 225.

100. Harland, *Breakfast, Lunch and Tea*, 191.

101. John Harvey Kellogg, *The Household Monitor of Health* (Battle Creek, MI: Good Health, 1891), 87.

102. Alcott, *Young House-keeper*, 198.

103. Emma Pike Ewing, *Cooking and Castle-Building* (Boston: J. R. Osgood and Co., 1890), 154.

104. Edward Johnson, *The Hydropathic Treatment of Diseases Peculiar to Women: And of Women in Childbed; With Some Observations on the Management of Infants* (London: Simpkin, Marshall, 1850), ix, 51, 57.

105. "Letters from Mr. Toulmin of Kentucky, " *Monthly Magazine and British Register*, vol. 9 (April 1, 1800), 223.

106. Harland, *Breakfast, Luncheon and Tea*, 191.

107. Sidney Ringer, *A Handbook of Therapeutics* (New York: William Wood & Co., 1876), 147.

108. *Woman's Home Companion* 78, no. 9–12 (1951): 98.

109. Jessup Whitehead, *The Steward's Handbook and Guide to Party Catering* (Chicago: J. Anderson & Co., 1889), 245.

110. C. Anne Wilson, *The Book of Marmalade: Its Antecedents, Its History and Its Role in the World Today, Together With a Collection of Recipes for Marmalades and Marmalade Cookery* (Philadelphia: University of Pennsylvania Press, 1985), 54.

111. William Mackintosh, "An Essay on Ways and Means for Inclosing, Fallowing, Planting, &C. Scotland: And That in Sixteen Years at Farthest," 1729, http://books .google.com/books?id=YH9ZAAAAYAAJ&source=gbs_navlinks_s.

112. Samuel Johnson, *The Works of Samuel Johnson, LL.D.: With an Essay on His Life and Genius*, vol. 8 (London: Luke Hensard & Sons, for J. Nichols & Son, 1810), 271.

113. Samuel Pepys, *The Shorter Pepys*, ed. Robert A. Latham (Berkeley: University of California Press, 1985), 38.

114. Lettice Bryan, *The Kentucky Housewife: Containing Nearly Thirteen Hundred Full Receipts* (Cincinnati, OH: Shepard & Stearns, 1839), 217.

115. Andrew F. Smith, *Pure Ketchup: A History of America's National Condiment with Recipes* (Columbia: University of South Carolina Press, 1996), 19.

116. Parloa, *Miss Parloa's Kitchen Companion*, 501.

117. Knight et al., "Apparatus for Producing Prepared Hash Brown Potato Product," U.S. Patent 3854393, filed January 22, 1973, issued December 17, 1974.

118. Hooper, *Handbook for the Breakfast Table*, 43.

119. Brigid Allen, *Food: An Oxford Anthology* (Oxford: Oxford University Press, 1995), 164.

120. Charles Henry Cook, John Greville Fennell, and J. M. Dixon, *The Curiosities of Ale & Beer: An Entertaining History* (London: Swan Sonnenschein & Company, 1889), 275.

121. Myra Jehlen, *The English Literatures of America: 1500–1800* (London: Routledge, 1997), 753.

122. Henry William Lewer, ed., *A Book of Simples* (London: S. Low, Marston, 1908), 153.

123. Reprinted in *Curye on Inglysch* in 1985.

124. Andrew Picken, *The Black Watch* (Philadelphia: E. L. Carey & A. Hart, 1835), 40.

125. Maguelonne Toussaint-Samat, *A History of Food* (Chichester, West Sussex, UK: John Wiley & Sons, 2009), 517.

126. Anthony Florian Madinger Willich and James Mease, *The Domestic Encyclopaedia: Or, a Dictionary of Facts and Useful Knowledge, Comprehending a Concise View of the Latest Discoveries, Inventions, and Improvements, Chiefly Applicable to Rural and Domestic Economy* (Philadelphia: W. Y. Birch and A. Small, 1803), 126.

127. Bennett Alan Weinberg and Bonnie K. Bealer, *The World of Caffeine: The Science and Culture of the World's Most Popular Drug* (New York: Routledge, 2001), 173.

128. Sir John Sinclair, *The Code of Health and Longevity: Or, a General View of the Rules and Principles Calculated for the Preservation of Health, and the Attainment of Long Life* (London: Sherwood, Gilbert & Piper, 1844), 69.

129. Jim Chevallier, "Breakfast in the Eighteenth Century: The Unexamined Meal," http://chezjim.com/18c/breakfast-18th.htm, accessed June 2012.

130. Arthur Hill Hassall, Lancet Analytical Sanitary Commission, *Food and Its Adulterations* (London: Longman, Brown, Green, and Longmans, 1855), 113.

131. Eleanor O. Curtiss, *For Young Souls* (London: Order of Christian Mystics, 1941), 17.

CHAPTER 3: BREAKFAST AT HOME

1. Mark Girouard, *Life in the English Country House: A Social and Architectural History* (New Haven: Yale University Press, 1978), 99.

2. William Moore, *Elements of Midwifery* (London: Printed for J. Johnson, 1777), 41.

3. Henry Mayhew, ed., *The Greatest Plague of Life, Or, The Adventures of a Lady in Search of a Good Servant* (London: Routledge, Warne & Routledge, 1864), 248.

4. Harriet E. Clark, "A Dainty Breakfast Room," *The Decorator and Furnisher* 22, no. 1 (April 1893): 28–29.

5. Catharine Esther Beecher and Harriet Beecher Stowe, *The American Woman's Home: Or, Principles of Domestic Science; Being a Guide to the Formation and Maintenance of Economical, Healthful, Beautiful, and Christian Homes* (New York: J. B. Ford, 1872), 32.

6. Christine Terhune Herrick, *What to Eat, How to Serve It* (New York: Harper & Bros., 1891), 17. Herrick was the daughter of cookbook author Mary Terhune, better known as Marion Harland.

7. Herrick, *What to Eat, How to Serve It*, 19.

8. Herrick, *What to Eat, How to Serve It*, 23.

9. Finchley Manuals of Industry, *Household Work, or the Duties of Female Servants* (London: Joseph Masters, 1850), 9.

10. Mary Foote Henderson, *Practical Cooking and Dinner Giving: A Treatise Containing Practical Instructions in Cooking; in the Combination and Serving of Dishes; and in the Fashionable Modes of Entertaining at Breakfast, Lunch, and Dinner* (New York: Harper & Brothers, 1876), 33.

11. Henderson, *Practical Cooking and Dinner Giving*, 34.

12. Andrea Broomfield, *Food and Cooking in Victorian England: A History* (Westport, CT: Greenwood Publishing Group, 2007), 35.

13. Broomfield, *Food and Cooking in Victorian England*, 36. The stress on perfecting toast was more evident in the American (1891) version of Soyer's *Modern Housewife*.

14. *Mrs. Beeton's Every-day Cookery and Household Guide*, 1872, quoted in Andrea Broomfield, *Food and Cooking in Victorian England: A History* (Westport, CT: Praeger, 2007), 39.

15. Herrick, *What to Eat, How to Serve It*, 17.

16. "On Newspapers," *The Scots Magazine*, October–November 1797, 731.

17. Theodore Sedgwick Fay and Joseph Dewey Fay, "Newspapers," in *Dreams and Reveries of a Quiet Man: Consisting of the Little Genius, and Other Essays* (New York: J. & J. Harper, 1832), 20.

18. Herrick, *What to Eat, How to Serve It*, 29.

19. Harriet Beecher Stowe, *Sunny Memories of Foreign Lands*, vol. 2 (Boston: Phillips, Sampson, 1854), 6–7.

20. Herrick, *What to Eat, How to Serve It*, 40.

21. Henderson, *Practical Cooking and Dinner Giving*, 35.

22. Thomas Maurice, "Memoirs," *The Monthly Review, or Literary Journal Enlarged*, September–December 1822, 96.

23. Stowe, *Sunny Memories of Foreign Lands*, 7.

24. Girouard, *Life in the English Country House*, 34.

25. Between 1890 and 1940, the average American household was reduced from 4.9 to 3.8 persons, according to United States Census Bureau data.

26. William Draper Brinckloe, "The Home I'd Like to Have," *Ladies' Home Journal*, April 1922, 26.

27. H. C. Crocker, "The Breakfast Nook," *Popular Mechanics* 36, no. 5 (November 1921): 783.

28. Edwin James Houston and Arthur Edwin Kennelly, *Electric Heating* (New York: W. J. Johnston Co., 1895), iv.

29. Maud Lucas Lancaster, *Electric Cooking, Heating, Cleaning, Etc: Being a Manual of Electricity in the Service of the Home* (London: Constable & Company, Ltd., 1914).

30. Elizabeth Atwood, "Electricity in the House," *American Homes and Gardens*, March 1913, 107.

31. Atwood, "Electricity in the House," 107.

32. New York Edison Company, "Table Cookery," *The Edison Monthly*, July 1919, 271.

33. Quoted in Sherrie A. Inness, *Dinner Roles: American Women and Culinary Culture* (Iowa City, IA: University of Iowa Press, 2001), 85.

34. The patent for the automatic pop-up toaster was filed by Charles Strite in 1919, but the Model 1-A-1 Toastmaster, based on a redesign of Strite's model, was not introduced by the Waters-Genter Company until 1926.

35. Arthur Asa Berger, "The Crux of Toast," *Harper's Magazine*, December 1990; also available at http://www.geocities.ws/danhiggins3/toastcontent/crux.html.

36. According to data provided to the International Housewares Association by the NPD Group in 2002: http://www.housewares.org/pdf/mw/MW_vol3no1.pdf.

N O T E S

37. Breakfast breads like waffles may have been in Steckbeck's blood; the name Steckbeck comes from the German meaning "baker who lives by a path or bridge."

38. Lancaster, *Electric Cooking*, 89.

39. Robert Hewitt, *Coffee: Its History, Cultivation and Uses* (New York: D. Appleton & Co., 1872), 77.

40. Hewitt, *Coffee*, 78.

41. Hewitt, *Coffee*, 79.

42. Charlie Sorrel, "Automatic Breakfast Machine Fails to Awake Interest," *Wired*, March 16, 2009, http://www.wired.com/gadgetlab/2009/03/automatic-break, accessed September 20, 2012.

43. Andrew Liszewski, "Toaster Griddle Is the Perfect Appliance for Lonely Breakfasts," *Gizmodo*, http://gizmodo.com/5855645/toaster-griddle-is-the-perfect-appliance-for-lonely breakfasts, accessed September 20, 2012.

44. Helen Lefferts Roberts, *Putnam's Handbook of Etiquette: A Cyclopaedia of Social Usage, Giving Manners and Customs of the Twentieth Century* (New York: G. P. Putnam's Sons, 1913), 215.

45. Herrick, *What to Eat, How to Serve It*, 24.

46. Betty Friedan, *The Feminine Mystique* (New York: Norton, 1997), 469.

47. The original name of the cereal when it was released in 1951 was Sugar Frosted Flakes, but the word "sugar" was dropped in the 1980s, when most cereal companies were attempting to give their products a healthier facelift. The sugar content of the cereal has never been altered.

48. The Kellogg Company ran numerous advertisements for their Variety Pack cereal in 1956, primarily in *Life* magazine: http://tinyurl.com/codrzeh and http://tinyurl.com/bss9km7.

49. Flora Haines Loughead, *Quick Cooking: A Book of Culinary Heresies for the Busy Wives and Mothers of the Land* (New York: G. P. Putnam, 1887), 6. Loughead, ahead of her time, had plenty more pressing cares than cooking. On his website *Lives of the Dead—Mountain View Cemetery in Oakland*, Michael Colbruno writes, "She was a journalist, married three times, had five children by two husbands, worked her own mining claims, farmed thirty-five acres, wrote many articles, short stories and more than a dozen books. Today, she is probably best remembered as the 'Mother of Lockheed Corporation.'"

50. Loughead, *Quick Cooking*, 6.

51. International Food Information Council, "How Children Are Making Food Choices." *IFIC Review*, 1992.

52. "For the Girls," *The Railwayan* 32, no. 9 (October 1948): 96.

53. Mary Ellen Schoonmaker, "Guess Who Does the Housework," *Working Mother*, February 1988, 74.

54. Bob Davis, "Come into the Kitchen, Boys." *The Delineator*, July 1936, 20-21.

55. Ladd Plumley, "Boys and Cookery," *American Cookery*, October 1917, 177-79.

56. "Lightening the Burdens of a Bachelor," *Popular Science Monthly* 96 (June 1920): 57.

57. Bozeman Bulger, "What to Cook When the Wife Is Away," *Ladies' Home Journal*, July 1921, 75.

58. Brick Gordon, *The Groom Boils and Stews: A Man's Cook Book for Men* (San Antonio, TX: Naylor Company, 1947).

59. Frank Sullivan, "A Bachelor Looks At Breakfast," in *Frank Sullivan at His Best* (Toronto: Dover, 1996), 4–7.

60. Robert Capon, *Supper of the Lamb: A Culinary Reflection* (New York: Macmillan, 1989).

61. Thomas Adler, "Making Pancakes on Sunday: The Male Cook in Family Tradition," *Western Folklore* 40 (1981): 45–54.

62. James Beard, *James Beard Delights and Prejudices* (Philadelphia: Running Press, 1992), 4–5.

63. "What My Dad Cooked," *Esquire*, June 2012, http://www.esquire.com/features/food-drink/dad-cooked-0612#slide-1.

64. It is possible that when Riley's character recalled his mother cracking eggs into the boiling water that he was referring to the method of using egg whites to filter the coffee—a technique employed by some people in those days.

65. Ida Bailey Allen, *Solving the High Cost of Eating: A Cook Book to Live By* (New York: Farrar, Straus and Company, 1952), 44–45.

66. Also known as "mother's little helper," amphetamines were freely prescribed by family doctors in the 1950s and 1960s to help housewives overcome boredom and ennui or to maintain their girlish figures. Amphetamines are now Schedule II drugs under the United States Controlled Substances Act of 1971.

67. M. Tarbox Colbrath, *What to Get for Breakfast* (Boston: James H. Earle, 1882), 259.

68. Colbrath, *What to Get for Breakfast*, 259.

69. "Aunt Babette," *"Aunt Babette's" Cook Book* (Cincinnati: Block Pub. and Print Co. 1889), 179.

70. Mary Wood-Allen, "A Christmas Breakfast," *American Motherhood* 23 (1906): 459–62. As a pediatrician, most of Dr. Wood-Allen's work was on the dangers of precocious puberty; she wrote numerous books warning parents against letting their adolescents grow up too fast.

71. Wood-Allen, "A Christmas Breakfast," 459–62.

72. Eliot Wigginton, *Foxfire Christmas: Appalachian Memories and Traditions* (Chapel Hill: University of North Carolina Press, 1996), 91.

73. Edith M. Thomas, *Mary at the Farm and Book of Recipes Compiled During Her Visit Among the "Pennsylvania Germans"* (Norristown, PA: John Hartenstine, 1915), 194, http://digital.lib.msu.edu/projects/cookbooks/html/books/book_69.cfm.

74. Thomas, *Mary at the Farm*, 194.

75. John Brand and Henry Bourne, *Observations on Popular Antiquities* (London: T. Saint, 1777), 332.

76. Christine Terhune Herrick, *New Idea Home and Cook Book* (New York: I.H. Blanchard, 1900), 145.

77. Mrs. M. E. Parmelee, "The Easter Breakfast," *Table Talk* 19 (April 1904): 174.

78. Stephanie Coontz, *The Way We Never Were: American Families and the Nostalgia Trap* (New York: Basic Books, 1992), 151–54.

79. Herman Lee Meader, *Reflections of the Morning After* (Boston: H. M. Caldwell Co., 1903), 17.

80. M. F. K. Fisher, "An Alphabet for Gourmets: A–B." *Gourmet Magazine*, December 1948, http://www.gourmet.com/magazine/1940s/1948/12/mfkfisheranalphabetforgourmets?currentPage=, accessed November 18, 2012.

81. Jessamyn Neuhaus, e-mail message to author, September 12, 2012.

82. Rocky Fino, *Will Cook for Sex: A Guy's Guide to Cooking* (Las Vegas, NV: Stephens Press, LLC, 2005), 64.

CHAPTER 4: BREAKFAST OUT

1. William Cobbett, *The Emigrant's Guide: In Ten Letters, Addressed to the Tax-Payers of England* (London: Mills, Jowett & Mills, 1829), 68.

2. Shamrock Society, *Emigration to America: Hints to Emigrants from Europe, Who Intend to Make a Permanent Residence in the United States* (New York: W. Hone, 1817), 8.

3. Shamrock Society, *Emigration to America*, 8.

4. James Loucky, Jeanne Armstrong, and Lawrence J. Estrada, *Immigration in America Today: An Encyclopedia* (Westport, CT: Greenwood Publishing Group, 2006), 123.

5. Lafcadio Hearn, *La Cuisine Creole: A Collection of Culinary Recipes from Leading Chefs and Noted Creole Housewives* (Bedford, MA: Applewood Books, 2008), 237.

6. Cathy Luchetti, *Home on the Range: A Culinary History of the American West* (New York: Villard Books, 1993), 6.

7. Luchetti, *Home on the Range*, xxv.

8. Laura Ingalls Wilder, *Little House on the Prairie* (New York: Harper Collins, 2010), 39.

9. Wilder, *Little House on the Prairie*, 52.

10. Frances Milton Trollope, *Domestic Manners of the Americans* (London: Whittaker, Treacher, & Co., 1832), 281.

11. Mark Twain, *Roughing It* (New York: Harper & Bros., 1913), 26.

12. Twain, *Roughing It*, 26.

13. Twain, *Roughing It*, 26.

14. John Camden Hotten, *The Slang Dictionary: Etymological, Historical, and Anecdotal* (London: Chatto and Windus, 1874), 297.

15. Twain, *Roughing It*, 27.

16. Orsamus Turner, *History of the Pioneer Settlement of Phelps and Gorham's Purchase, and Morris' Reserve* (Rochester, NY: William Alling, 1851), 417.

17. John Bakeless, *Daniel Boone: Master of the Wilderness* (Lincoln: University of Nebraska Press, 1939), 60.

18. Samuel Bowles, *Across the Continent: A Summer's Journey to the Rocky Mountains, the Mormons, and the Pacific States, with Speaker Colfax* (New York: Hurd & Houghton, 1865), 21, 25, 78.

19. Richard F. Burton, *The City of the Saints* (New York: Harper & Bros., 1862), 60.

20. Burton, *City of the Saints*, 62.

21. Burton, *City of the Saints,* 84.

22. Samuel Bowles, *Our New West* (Hartford, CT: Hartford Publishing Co., 1869), 135.

23. James D. Porterfield, *Dining By Rail: The History and Recipes of America's Golden Age of Railroad Cuisine* (New York: Macmillan, 1998), 20.

24. Lynda West, *Half Hours in the Wide West* (London: Daldy, Isbister, & Co., 1877), 87–88.

25. West, *Half Hours*, 87–88.

26. West, *Half Hours*, 87–88.

27. "Adjustable Dining Table for Motor Cars," *Popular Mechanics*, October 1914, 500.

28. Paul W. Kearney, "So You'll Drive," *The Rotarian*, April 1939, 36–38.

29. Jack in the Box, "Our Story," http://www.jackinthebox.com.

30. Kevin Cain, "The McDonald's Coffee Lawsuit," *Journal of Consumer & Commercial Law* 11, no. 1 (2007): 14–18.

31. United States Census Bureau Fact Finder, "Commuting Characteristics by Sex: 2011," http://factfinder2.census.gov/faces/tableservices/jsf/pages/productview .xhtml?pid=ACS_11_1YR_S0801&prodType=table, accessed October 2, 2012.

32. Bruce Horovitz, "Bike-Riding Mom Denied at Drive-Through Turns to Twitter," *USA Today*, August 20, 2009, http://usatoday30.usatoday.com/money/industries/ food/2009-08-19-twitter-bicycle-drive-through-bike-tweet_N.htm.

33. A. K. Sandoval-Strausz, *Hotel: An American History* (New Haven, CT: Yale University Press, 2008), 12.

34. George Washington, *The Diary of George Washington, from 1789 to 1791* (New York: C. B. Richardson & Co., 1860), 50.

35. "Letters from Mr. Toulmin of Kentucky," *Monthly Magazine and British Register*, vol. 9, July 1, 1800, 548.

36. John Bristed, *America and Her Resources; Or a View of the Agricultural, Commercial, Manufacturing, Financial, Political, Literary, Moral, and Religious Capacity and Character of the American People* (London: Henry Colburn, 1818), 448.

37. Lately Thomas, *Delmonico's: A Century of Splendor* (Boston: Houghton Mifflin, 1967), 260.

38. Thomas Sheraton, *The Cabinet Dictionary. To Which is Added a Supplementary Treatise on Geometrical Lines, Perspective, and Painting in General* (London: W. Smith, 1803), 103.

39. Trollope, *Domestic Manners of the Americans*, 108.

40. Charles Eyre Pascoe, *London of To-Day: An Illustrated Handbook* (London: Simpkin, Marshall, Hamilton, Kent, & Co., Ltd., 1890), 57.

41. "Young America in Old England," *Lippincott's Magazine*, October 1881, 411.

42. Lizzie Borden was acquitted of the murders, and there have been no other suspects charged.

43. Lizzie Borden Bed & Breakfast Museum, http://www.lizzie-borden.com.

44. Caroline Reed Wadhams, *Simple Directions for the Waitress or Parlor Maid* (New York: Longmans, Green and Co., 1917), 29.

45. Lou Martin, "Look People in the Eye, Be the First to Say Hello, & Never Buy a Beige Car . . . and Other Words of Advice From 'Life's Little Instruction Book,'" *Weekly World News*, August 8, 1995, 35.

46. N.S. Richardson, D.D., "Church Work and Party Work: (2.) Reports of the Meetings of the Church Missionary and Evangelical Knowledge Societies," *The American Quarterly Church Review and Ecclesiastical Register, Volume 18* (New York: N.S. Richardson, 1867), 597.

47. George Alfred Townsend, *The New World Compared with the Old: A Description of the American Government, Institutions, and Enterprises, and of Those of Our Great Rivals at the Present Time, Particularly England and France* (Hartford, CT: S. M. Betts & Company, 1869), 406.

48. John Melish, *Travels in the United States of America in the Years 1806 & 1807, and 1809, 1810 & 1811* (Philadelphia: T. & G. Palmer, 1812), 247–48.

49. "On the Night Shift," *Popular Mechanics*, November 1942, 57–60.

50. Chris Onstad, *The Achewood Cookbook: Recipes for a Lady or a Man* (self-published, 2003), 21.

51. Henry Mayhew, *London Labour and the London Poor: A Cyclopaedia of the Condition and Earnings of Those That Will Work, Those That Cannot Work, and Those That Will Not Work*, vol. 1 (London: Charles Griffin & Company, 1851), 39.

52. McDonald's, "The Birth of the Egg McMuffin," http://www.aboutmcdonalds.com/mcd/our_company/amazing_stories/food/the_birth_of_the_egg_mcmuffin.html.

53. William Grime, *Appetite City: A Culinary History of New York* (New York: North Point Press, 2010), 193.

54. Charles Reznikoff, *By the Waters of Manhattan* (New York: Charles Boni, 1930), 123.

55. Richard W. Slatta, *The Cowboy Encyclopedia* (New York: Norton, 1996), 351.

56. Jo Jeffers, *Ranch Wife* (Tucson: University of Arizona Press, 1993), 39.

57. Inez McFee, *The Young People's Cookbook; Or, How the Daytons Cooked at Home and in Camp* (New York: Thomas Y. Crowell, 1925).

58. Tourist, "The Experience of Three Weavers in a Logging Camp in Maine," *Fibre & Fabric: A Record of American Textile Industries in the Cotton and Woolen Trade* 13, no. 343 (September 26, 1891): 256–57.

59. Michael J. Varhola, *Life in Civil War America* (New York: F+W Media, 1989), 166.

60. George Browne, *An American Soldier in World War I* (Lincoln: University of Nebraska Press, 2006), 12–13.

61. John T. Edge, *Donuts: An American Passion* (New York: G. P. Putnam's Sons, 2006), 62.

62. John Fisher and Carol Fisher, *Food in the American Military: A History* (Jefferson, NC: MacFarland, 2010), 243.

63. Harold Howland, *Theodore Roosevelt and his Times: A Chronicle of the Progressive Movement* (New Haven, CT: Yale University Press, 1921), 52–72.

64. Howland, *Theodore Roosevelt*, 52–72.

65. Theodore Roosevelt, *Theodore Roosevelt: An Autobiography* (New York: Charles Scribner's Sons, 1913), 288.

66. Charles T. Bourland and Gregory L. Vogt, *The Astronaut's Cookbook* (New York: Springer, 2010), 29–32.

67. Amy Shira Teitel, "Steak, Beans and Vests: NASA's Weird Traditions," *Discovery News*, http://news.discovery.com/space/steak-beans-and-vests-a-look-at-nasa-traditions-120820.html.

68. Albert Shaw, "Food-Aided Education: Experiments in Paris, London and Birmingham," *The Review of Reviews* (New York: Review of Reviews Corporation, 1891), 618–21.

69. Shaw, "Food-Aided Education," 618–21.

70. Thomas Fosbroke, *An Original History of the City of Gloucester* (London: John Nichols and Son, 1819), 300–1; quoted in *Journal of American Folklore* 5 (1892): 147.

71. Harvey A. Levenstein, *Paradox of Plenty: A Social History of Eating in Modern America*, Part 12 (Berkeley: University of California Press, 2003), 55.

72. USDA, "School Breakfast Program," February 21, 2012, http://www.fns.usda.gov/cnd/breakfast/AboutBFast/ProgHistory.htm.

73. Huey P. Newton, "Hoover and the F.B.I.," Public Broadcasting Station, Luna Ray Films, LLC, 2002, http://www.pbs.org/hueypnewton/people/people_hoover.html.

74. Newton, "Hoover and the FBI."

75. Nik Heynen, "Bending the Bars of Empire from Every Ghetto for Survival: The Black Panther Party's Radical Antihunger Politics of Social Reproduction and Scale," *Annals of the Association of American Geographers*, April 2009, http://nheynen.myweb.uga.edu/pdf/Annals.

76. Cuthbert Bede, *The Adventures of Mr. Verdant Green: An Oxford Freshman* (Boston: Little, Brown & Co., 1893), 273.

77. Bede, *Adventures of Mr. Verdant Green*, 273. A "barn-door fowl" is a hen that has stopped laying.

78. Thomas De Witt Talmage, *Around the Tea-Table* (Philadelphia: Cowperthwait & Company, 1875), 74.

79. Talmage, *Around the Tea-Table*, 74.

80. Charles Franklin Thwing, *If I Were a College Student* (New York: T. Y. Crowell & Co., 1902), 7.

81. Charles Franklin Thwing, *Letters From a Father to His Son Entering College* (New York: Platt & Peck Co., 1912), 27.

82. William Lyon Phelps, "Eating Breakfast," in *Essays on Things* (London: Macmillan, 1930), 151–55.

83. Phelps, "Eating Breakfast, 151–55.

84. James W. Clarke, *Defining Danger: American Assassins and the New Domestic Terrorists* (New Brunswick, NJ: Transaction, 2012), 236.

85. Amy E. Houlihan, "Stress and Self-control: A Test of Contrasting Pathways to Health Risk Behavior" (PhD dissertation, Iowa State University, 2008).

86. Matthew T. Gailliot, "The Physiology of Willpower: Linking Blood Glucose to Self-Control." *Personal and Social Psychology Review* 11, no. 4 (November 2007): 303–27.

87. *Famous Last Meals*, http://www.famouslastmeals.com/search/label/Charles%20Peace.

88. Jonathan Goodman, *Bloody Versicles: The Rhymes of Crime* (Kent, OH: Kent State University Press, 1993), 172–73.

89. Stephen G. Michaud and Hugh Aynesworth, *The Only Living Witness: The True Story of Serial Sex Killer Ted Bundy* (Irving, TX: Authorlink, 1999), 343.

90. Paul Dickson, "battle breakfast," *War Slang: American Fighting Words & Phrases since the Civil War* (Mineola, NY: Courier Dover Publications, 2011).

91. "The League's Big Pancake Day," *McClure's Magazine*, vol. 51, March 1919, 55.

92. "The League's Big Pancake Day," 55.

93. Cora Linn Daniels and C. M. Stevans, eds., *Encyclopaedia of Superstitions, Folklore, and the Occult Sciences of the World* (Honolulu, HI: University Press of the Pacific, 2003), 132.

94. Daniels and Stevans, *Encyclopaedia of Superstitions*, 132.

95. Isabella Beeton, *Book of Household Management* (London: Ward, Lock, & Company, 1888), 1320.

96. Beeton, *Book of Household Management*, 1319.

97. Marion Harland and Virginia Terhune Van de Water, *Everyday Etiquette: A Practical Manual of Social Usages* (Indianapolis: Bobbs-Merrill Company, 1905), 75.

98. Edward L. Queen, Stephen R. Prothero, and Gardiner H. Shattuck, *Encyclopedia of American Religious History*, vol. 1 (New York: Facts on File, 2009), 685.

99. Omer Call Stewart, *Peyote Religion: A History* (Norman: University of Oklahoma Press, 1987), 209.

100. Stewart, *Peyote Religion*, 369.

CHAPTER 5: BREAKFAST IN THE ARTS AND MEDIA

1. "*The Breakfast Club* (1985): Did You Know?" *Internet Movie Database*, http://www.imdb.com/title/tt0088847/trivia.

2. Homer, *The Odyssey* (London: Macmillan, 2005), 265: "while the men prepared their breakfast in the thin light, paying little heed to the barnyard din."

3. Anthony Trollope, *An Autobiography* (Newcastle upon Tyne: Cambridge Scholars Publishing, 2008).

4. Sir Walter Scott, *Waverley Novels*, vol. 1 (London: John C. Nimmo, 1898), 96.

5. Thomas Love Peacock, *Crotchet Castle* (London: T. Hookham, 1831), 21–23.

6. Peacock, *Crotchet Castle*, 21–23.

7. Herman Melville, *Moby-Dick; or, the White Whale* (Boston: St. Botolph Society, 1892), 33–35.

8. Nathaniel Hawthorne, *The Best Known Works of Nathaniel Hawthorne* (Whitefish, MT: Kessinger, 2003), 180.

9. Hawthorne, *Best Known Works*, 180.

10. Hawthorne, *Best Known Works*, 180.

11. Hawthorne, *Best Known Works*, 180.

12. Mark McWilliams, *Food and the Novel in Nineteenth-Century America* (Lanham, MD: AltaMira, 2012), 101.

13. Hawthorne, *Best Known Works*, 183.

14. Marion Harland, *At Last: A Novel* (New York: Carleton, 1870), 11.

15. Louise Bennett Weaver and Helen Cowles Le Cron, *A Thousand Ways to Please a Husband with Bettina's Best Recipes* (New York: Britton, 1917).

16. Mary Wood-Allen, *What a Young Woman Ought to Know* (Philadelphia: Vir Publishing, 1913), 124.

17. Saki, "Filboid Studge, The Story of a Mouse that Helped," in *The Chronicles of Clovis* (Middlesex: Echo Library, 2006), 52–53.

18. Saki, "Filboid Studge," 52–53.

19. Saki, "Filboid Studge," 52–53.

20. Saki, "Filboid Studge," 52–53.

21. Saki, "Filboid Studge," 52–53.

22. Saki, "Filboid Studge," 52–53.

23. J. R. R. Tolkien, *The Hobbit; Or, There and Back Again* (*The Enchanting Prelude to The Lord of the Rings*) (New York: Random House, 1997), 29.

24. Tolkien, *The Hobbit*, 129.

25. Thomas Mann, *The Magic Mountain* (New York: Random House Digital, 2005), 35.

26. A. A. Milne, *Winnie the Pooh* (New York: Dutton Juvenile; Deluxe Edition 2009), 147.

27. A. A. Milne, *House at Pooh Corner* (New York: Dutton Juvenile; Deluxe Edition 2009), 5.

28. Michael Bond, *A Bear Called Paddington* (London: HarperCollins UK, 2012), 83.

29. Thomas Pynchon, *Gravity's Rainbow* (New York: Penguin, 1995), 10.

30. Art Hermitage, *Breakfast of a Young Man*, http://www.arthermitage.org/Pieter -Cornelisz-van-Slingeland/Breakfast-of-a-Young-Man.html, accessed November 10, 2012.

31. Box Vox, "Bobby Grossman's Corn Flakes, Die Originalen," http://www.beach packagingdesign.com/wp/2011/03/bobby-grossmans-corn-flakes-die-orinalen.html, accessed November 20, 2012.

32. The Strut, "See Bobby Grossman's 'Cornflake' Photos," June 11, 2012, http://www.thestrut.com/2012/06/11/see-bobby-grossmans-cornflake-photos, accessed November 10, 2012.

33. Mr. Breakfast, "Rock Stars Eating Breakfast," October 4, 2012, http://mrbreak fast.com/breakfast/?p=1385, accessed November 7, 2012.

34. Marilyn Monroe, "How I Stay in Shape," *Pageant Magazine*, September 1952, 120–27, http://glamournet.com/legends/Marilyn/monthly/shape1.html, accessed November 29, 2012.

35. Jon Huck, "Breakfast," February 20, 2007, http://jonhuck.com/breakfast, accessed November 29, 2012.

36. *Five Easy Pieces*, directed by Bob Rafelson (1970; Culver City, CA: Sony Pictures Home Entertainment, 1999), DVD.

37. *Falling Down*, directed by Joel Schumacher (1993; Burbank, CA: Warner Home Video, 1999), DVD.

38. *Reservoir Dogs*, directed by Quentin Tarantino (1992; Santa Monica, CA: Artisan Entertainment, 1997), DVD.

39. *Reservoir Dogs*.

40. *Pulp Fiction*, directed by Quentin Tarantino (1994; Santa Monica, CA: Miramax Lionsgate Films, 2011), DVD.

41. Some of Tarantino's other films pay homage to the morning meal as well. In *From Dusk till Dawn* (1996; written by Tarantino, directed by Robert Rodriguez), the protagonist family plans their border crossing to Mexico—where the film takes place—while seated at the breakfast table. In *Kill Bill Volume 1* (2003), a gun is hidden inside a box of General Mills Kaboom cereal.

42. *The Public Enemy*, directed by William Wellman (1931; Burbank, CA: Warner Home Video, 2005), DVD.

43. Richard Schickel, *The Men Who Made the Movies: William A. Wellman*, 1973, http://www.imdb.com/title/tt0070922.

44. Steve Zimmerman, *Food in the Movies*, 2nd ed. (Jefferson, NC: McFarland, 2010), 207–11.

45. *Gone with the Wind*, directed by George Cukor (1939; Burbank, CA: Warner Home Video, 2000), DVD.

46. *The Clock*, directed by Vincente Minnelli (1945; Burbank, CA: Warner Home Video, 2007), DVD.

47. *Winter Meeting*, directed by Bretaigne Windust (1948; Beverly Hills, CA: MGM, 1998), VHS.

48. "Episode #001," *Twin Peaks*, written and directed by David Lynch and Mark Frost (Los Angeles: Spelling Television, April 8, 1990), TV.

49. "Episode #001," *Twin Peaks*.

50. "Parks and Recreation: Ron and Tammy (#2.8)," *Parks and Recreation*, written by Greg Daniels and Michael Schur, directed by Troy Miller (Universal City, CA: Universal Television, November 5, 2009), TV.

51. John Dunning, *On the Air: The Encyclopedia of Old-Time Radio* (Oxford: Oxford University Press, 1998), 114–17.

52. Dunning, *On the Air*, 114–17.

53. Dunning, *On the Air*, 657–58.

54. The Ultimate Ramblin' Rod Page, http://www.platypuscomix.net/fpo/history/ramblinrod.html, accessed November 29, 2012.

55. Tim Hollis, *Hi There, Boys and Girls!: America's Local Children's TV Shows* (Jackson: University Press of Mississippi, 2001), 49.

56. "'Clark Kent' for Sugar Frosted Flakes w/Tony the Tiger," YouTube video clip, http://www.youtube.com/watch?v=h60gmICXVJM, accessed November 29, 2012.

57. "Ghostbuster Cereal," YouTube video clip, http://www.youtube.com/watch?v=NUhdXB_-k4A, accessed November 29, 2012; "C3PO's Star Wars cereal commercial," YouTube video clip, http://www.youtube.com/watch?v=Fe3TWZ_3qRg, accessed November 29, 2012.

58. Jon Wahlgren, "Nintendo Cereal System Sells For $200," Nintendo Life, February 22, 2010, http://www.nintendolife.com/news/2010/02/nintendo_cereal_sys tem_sells_for_usd200, accessed November 29, 2012.

59. Rod Taylor, "The Good Old Days," Promo, September 1, 2003, http://chief marketer.com/campaigns/marketing_good_old_days, accessed November 29, 2012.

60. Stew Miller, "20 Wacky Cereal Box Prizes," Gunaxin, July 5, 2010, http://humor.gunaxin.com/20-wacky-cereal-box-prizes/64050, accessed November 29, 2012.

61. Susan Linn, *Consuming Kids: Protecting Our Children from the Onslaught of Marketing & Advertising* (New York: Random House Digital, 2005), 100.

62. Howard L. Taras, "Advertised Foods on Children's Television," *Archives of Pediatrics and Adolescent Medicine* 149, no. 6 (1995): 649–52.

63. J. L. Harris et al., "Cereal FACTS (Food Advertising to Children and Teens Score): Limited Progress in the Nutrition Quality and Marketing of Children's Cereals," http://www.rwjf.org/en/research-publications/find-rwjf-research/2012/06/cereal-facts -report-20121.html, accessed November 13, 2012.

64. Ameena Batada et al., "Nine Out of 10 Food Advertisements Shown During Saturday Morning Children's Television Programming Are for Foods High in Fat, Sodium, or Added Sugars, or Low in Nutrients." *Journal of the American Dietetic Association* 108 (2008):673–78.

65. General Mills, Inc., "A Rather Humble Beginning," *Wheaties History*, 2010, http://www.wheaties.com/pdf/wheaties_history.pdf, accessed November 18, 2012.

66. Fanny Brice, performance of "Cooking Breakfast for the One I Love," by Billy Rose and Henry Tobias (Camden, NJ: Victor, 1930).

67. Brice, "Cooking Breakfast."

68. Dusty Springfield, performance of "Breakfast in Bed," by Eddie Hinton and Donnie Fritts, on *Dusty in Memphis* (New York: Warner Music Group, 1969).

69. Supertramp, "Breakfast in America," by Roger Hodgson and Rick Davies, on *Breakfast in America* (Santa Monica, CA: A&M, 1979).

70. Pink Floyd, performance of "Alan's Psychedelic Breakfast," written by David Gilmour, Roger Waters, Nick Mason, and Richard Wright, on *Atom Heart Mother* (London: Harvest Records/EMI, 1970).

71. Pink Floyd, "Alan's Psychedelic Breakfast."

72. Pink Floyd, "Alan's Psychedelic Breakfast."

73. Tom Waits, performance of "Intro to Eggs & Sausage," by Tom Waits, on *Nighthawks at the Diner* (New York: Asylum Records, 1976).

74. Tom Waits, performance of "Eggs & Sausage," by Tom Waits, on *Nighthawks at the Diner* (New York: Asylum Records, 1976).

75. Charles Dickens, "Dainty Bread," *All the Year Round*, September 10, 1870, 344–47.

76. Dickens, "Dainty Bread," 344–47.

77. "Breakfast. From the Pall Mall Gazette." *New York Times*, September 24, 1876, http://query.nytimes.com/mem/archive-free/pdf?res=F40D12F93D54107A93C6AB1 782D85F428784F9, accessed November 19, 2012.

78. Samuel Butler, "Bacon for Breakfast," in *The Note-Books of Samuel Butler* (New York: E. P. Dutton, 1917), 33.

79. Biddy Bye, "Breakfast May Be Substantial, Though Eggless and Meatless," *The Pittsburgh Press* (Pittsburgh, PA), November 29, 1918.

80. *The Lewiston Daily Sun* (Lewiston, ME), October 8, 1947.

81. *The Evening Independent* (St. Petersburg, FL), October 9, 1947, 1; *Prescott Evening Courier* (Prescott, AZ), October 10, 1947, 1.

82. Katherine Louise Smith, "Hygienic Honeymoon," *Boston Cooking School Magazine* 3, no. 4 (1898):171–74.

83. M. F .K. Fisher, "An Alphabet for Gourmets: A–B," *Gourmet*, December, 1948, http://www.gourmet.com/magazine/1940s/1948/12/mfkfisheranalphabetforgourmets?c urrentPage=2, accessed November 15, 2012.

84. M. F. K. Fisher, "Consider the End," *Gourmet*, October 1958, http://www .gourmet.com/magazine/1950s/1958/10/fisherconsidertheend, accessed November 15, 2012.

85. Fisher, "Consider the End."

86. Robert P. Tristram Coffin, "British Breakfast," *Gourmet*, October, 1948, http:// www.gourmet.com/magazine/1940s/1948/10/coffinbritishbreakfast, accessed November 15, 2012.

87. Coffin, "British Breakfast."

88. Coffin, "British Breakfast."

89. Robert E. Martin, "An Amazing Vision of the Future: Scientist Foresees a World Run by Radio," *Popular Science*, June 1927, 29.

90. Martin, "An Amazing Vision," 29.

91. W. M. Kiplinger, "Changing Times," *Kiplinger's Personal Finance*, June 1957, 27.

92. H. G. Wells, "A Story of the Days to Come," *The Pall Mall Magazine*, June–October 1899.

93. Kellogg's UK, "The Great British Breakfast of the Future," 2011, http://www.kelloggs.co.uk/whatson/pressoffice/News/kelloggs-corporate-news/the-great-british-breakfast-of-the-future, accessed November 19, 2012.

94. Kellogg's UK, "Great British Breakfast."

SELECTED
BIBLIOGRAPHY

Adamson, Melitta Weiss. *Food in Medieval Times*. Westport CT: Greenwood Press, 2004.

Albala, Ken. *Eating Right in the Renaissance*. Berkeley: University of California Press, 2002.

——. *Food in Early Modern Europe*. Westport, CT: Greenwood Press, 2003.

Allen, Gary, and Ken Albala. *The Business of Food: Encyclopedia of the Food and Drink Industries*. Westport, CT: Greenwood Press, 2007.

Belasco, Warren, and Philip Scranton. *Food Nations*. New York: Routledge, 2002.

Berzok, Linda Murray. *American Indian Food*. Westport, CT: Greenwood Press, 2005.

Bianchi, Suzanne M., John P. Robinson, and Melissa A. Milkie. *Changing Rhythms of American Family Life*. New York: Russell Sage Foundation, 2006.

Bower, Anne, ed. *African American Foodways*. Urbana: University of Illinois Press, 2007.

Broomfield, Andrea. *Food and Cooking in Victorian England: A History*. Westport, CT: Praeger, 2007.

Colbrath, M. Tarbox. *What to Get for Breakfast*. Boston: James H. Earle, 1882.

Corran, H. S. *A History of Brewing*. Newton Abbot: David and Charles, 1975.

Deutsch, Jonathan, and Anne Hauck-Lawson. *Gastropolis*. New York: Columbia University Press, 2009.

Donahue, Jonathan. *Man with a Pan*. New York: Algonquin, 2011.

Engs, Ruth Clifford. *Clean Living Movements: American Cycles of Health Reform*. Westport, CT: Greenwood Press, 2001.

Hackwood, Frederick William. *Good Cheer—The Romance of Food and Feasting*. New York: Sturgis and Walton, 1911.

Hale, Sarah Josepha Buell. *The Good Housekeeper, Or, The Way to Live Well and to Be Well While We Live*. Boston: Horace Wentworth, 1839.

Hammon, P. W. *Food and Feast in Medieval England*. Phoenix Mill: Sutton Publishing, 1993.

Harland, Marion. *Breakfast, Luncheon, and Tea*. London: Routledge, 1875.

Harris, Jessica. *High on the Hog*. New York: Bloomsbury USA, 2011.

Herrick, Christine Terhune. *What to Eat, How to Serve It*. New York: Harper & Bros., 1891.

Jakle, John A., and Keith A. Sculle. *Fast Food*. Baltimore: Johns Hopkins University Press, 1999.

Kellogg, Harvey. *The Home Book of Modern Medicine: A Family Guide in Health and Disease*. Vol. 2. Battle Creek, MI: Good Health Publishing Company, 1909.

Leslie, Eliza. *Directions for Cookery, in Its Various Branches*. Philadelphia: Carey & Hart, 1837.

Levenstein, Harvey. *A Revolution at the Table*. Berkeley: University of California Press, 2003.

Levine, Susan. *School Lunch Politics*. Princeton, NJ: Princeton University Press, 2010.

McIntosh, Jane. *Handbook to Life in Prehistoric Europe*. New York: Oxford University Press, 2006.

Neuhaus, Jessamyn. *Manly Meals and Mom's Home Cooking*. Baltimore: Johns Hopkins University Press, 2003.

Pendergrast, Mark. *Uncommon Grounds: The History of Coffee and How It Transformed Our World*. New York: Basic Books, 2010.

Pollan, Michael. *In Defense of Food: An Eater's Manifesto*. New York: Penguin, 2008.

Poppendiek, Janet. *Free for All: Fixing School Food in America*. Berkeley: University of California Press, 2011.

Ray, Krishnendu. *The Migrant's Table*. Philadelphia: Temple University Press, 2004.

Root, Waverly, and Richard de Rochemont. *Eating in America*. New York: Ecco Press, 1981.

Schlosser, Eric. *Fast Food Nation*. New York: Houghton Mifflin, 2001.

Simmons, Amelia. *American Cookery*. Hartford: Simeon Butler, Northampton, 1798.

Smith, Andrew, ed. *Oxford Encyclopedia of Food and Drink in America*. New York: Oxford University Press, 2004.

Spencer, Colin. *British Food: An Extraordinary Thousand Years of History*. New York: Columbia University Press, 2002.

Tannahill, Reay. *Food in History*. New York: Crown Publishers, 1989.

Toussaint-Samat, Maguelonne. *A History of Food*. Cambridge, MA: Blackwell Reference, 1993.

Wagne, Tamara, and Narin Hassan. *Consuming Culture in the Long Nineteenth Century: Narratives of Consumption, 1700–1900*. Lanham, MD: Lexington Books, 2007.

Weinberg, Bennet Alan. *The World of Caffeine: The Science and Culture of the World's Most Popular Drug*. London: Routledge, 2001.

Wild, Anthony. *Coffee: A Dark History*. New York: Norton, 2005.

INDEX

INDEX

INDEX

Toulmin, Harry, 81, 135

INDEX

Toulmin, Harry, 81, 135
trains, 2, 132–134, 136, 141, 142; dining cars, 132–134, *133*
Transcontinental Railroad, 132
trappers, 130–131
traveling, breakfast while, 126–135
Trollope, Francis Milton, 130, 137
truck stop, 144
Tunis, 33
Twain, Mark, 100, 130
Twin Peaks, 179

Ude, Louis Eustach, 196n59
United States Department of Agriculture (USDA) School Breakfast Program, 26, 127, 155

vegetables, 83–85
vegetarianism, 20–22, 26, 36–37, 40, 57, 69, 84, 166
Venner, Tobias, 14
vermin, 125, 136, 149–151
Victorian era, 16, 34, 60, 69, 71, 72, 78, 79, 94, 98–99, 133, 137, 144, 160, 185
video games, 181
Vietnam, 34, 76, 77
Vonnegut, Kurt, 151, 163

waffle iron, 104–105, 107
waffles, 50, 75, 104–105, 122, 142, 171, 179, 202n37; chicken and, 50, 73, 142; frolics, 50; frozen, 24, 107; restaurants specializing in, 142–143, *143*
wagon trail, 126, 129
waitress, 138–139, 163, 176–177, 179, 184
Waits, Tom, 184
Warhol, Andy, 174
Washington, George, 49, 135

wealthy class, 17, 94
wedding breakfast, 160
Wellman, William, 177
What to Get for Breakfast, 51, 71, 74, 119, 120
wheat, 6; einkhorn (*Triticum boeoticum*), 6, 8; emmer (*Triticum dicoccum*), 6, 8, 29; faro, 8; porridge, 8, 29; spelt, 8
Wheaties, 163, 182. *See also* General Mills
whiskey, 80, 83, 87
WIC. *See* Special Supplemental Nutrition Program for Women, Infants and Children
Wilcox, Estelle Woods, 50, 73
Wilder, Laura Ingalls, 18, 129
Williams, Roger, 36
wine, 11, 13, 86, 87, 100, 150, 170; akratos, 10, 86; mulsum, 8, 10
Wingfield, Thomas, 12
Winnie the Pooh 168–169
women, 23, 24, 26, 81, 94, 99, 108–110, 114, 116–117, *117*, 126, 166, 173, 177; in the workforce, 38, 93, 106–108, 111, 133. *See also* housewives; mothers
working class (poor), 11–12, 15–17, 20, 35, 71, 127, 133, 140, 141, 146, 155–156, 158, 170, 171, 173
World War I, 41, 60, 150; rationing during, 3, 111, 185; women in the workforce during, 106–108
World War II, 44, 72, 91, 114, 142–143, 150–152; rationing during, 3, 23, 38, 89, 145, 146, 185; women in the workforce during, 38, 93, 108

yogurt, 22, 23, 30, 46, 54–56, *55*, 58, 91, 108, 125; cheese made from (labneh), 46, 56
youtiao 34, 53

ABOUT THE AUTHOR

Heather Arndt Anderson is a Portland, Oregon–based food writer. Her recipes have been published in the cookbook *One Big Table: 600 Recipes from the Nation's Best Home Cooks, Farmers, Fishermen, Pit-Masters, and Chefs*, and she is a contributing writer to the magazines *The Farmer General* and *Remedy Quarterly*. In her food blog Voodoo & Sauce, the most popular posts are about breakfast.